# Cousins
# Maine
# Lobster

## How One Food Truck Became
## a Multimillion-Dollar Business

### Jim Tselikis and Sabin Lomac

with Blake D. Dvorak

Foreword by Barbara Corcoran

ST. MARTIN'S PRESS 〽 NEW YORK

www.stmartins.com

Library of Congress Cataloging-in-Publication Data

Names: Tselikis, Jim, author. | Lomac, Sabin, author. | Dvorak,
    Blake D., author.
Title: Cousins Maine Lobster: how one food truck became a
    multimillion-dollar business / Jim Tselikis and Sabin Lomac;
    with Blake D. Dvorak; foreword by Barbara Corcoran.
Description: First edition. | New York: St. Martin's Press, [2018] |
    Includes bibliographical references.
Identifiers: LCCN 2017045750| ISBN 9781250122179 (hardcover)
    | ISBN 9781250122193 (ebook)
Subjects: LCSH: Cousins Maine Lobster (Food franchise)—History.
    | Chain restaurants—United States. | Food trucks—Maine. |
    Entrepreneurship.
Classification: LCC TX945.5.C678 T57 2018 | DDC
    647.95741—dc23
LC record available at https://lccn.loc.gov/2017045750

Our books may be purchased in bulk for promotional,
educational, or business use. Please contact your local bookseller
or the Macmillan Corporate and Premium Sales Department
at 1-800-221-7945, extension 5442, or by email at
MacmillanSpecialMarkets@macmillan.com.

First Edition: April 2018

10  9  8  7  6  5  4  3  2  1

*To Enzo—*
*You're my biggest and best accomplishment.*
*I will always be here to guide and support you.*
*Dream big, the world is yours, anything is possible.*
*I love you.*
*—SL*


*To Maggie—*
*For supporting me with endless love, laughter, and loyalty.*
*Thank you for reminding me to always be silly and enjoy life,*
*and for allowing me the opportunity to chase my number one goal,*
*each and every day, of making you the happiest woman alive.*
*To a life full of health, smiles and love.*
*—JT*

# CONTENTS

## PART THREE | TWO COUSINS AND A BRAND

# ACKNOWLEDGMENTS

To our parents: Jeannie Lomac, Julie and Steve Tselikis . . . we love you and thank you for your love, support, and consistent reassurance that we can accomplish anything we want in life. You have always taught us to follow our dreams, to be good people, to support our family, have fun, and smile. We are forever grateful for your love and for putting up with us!

To our grandparents: Mina and Joe Lomac, Mary and John Lomac, Julia Tselikis: Words could never describe our love and bond with each of you. You created the values that we have today—the values we built a business around and the values we carry with our friends and family. Our hearts will always be filled with the sweetest and purist memories of us together.

Erika Hartounian and Maggie Tselikis: You are our rocks, through good and bad, high and low. You feel our stress, anxiety, pain, and you take it in stride. You are kind, beautiful, and caring. We love you and thank you for all that you do.

Shaun Higgins: Forever our brother. We are so thankful you are on this ride with us. You bleed Cousins Maine Lobster. Your passion and dedication has allowed us to continue to take huge steps and reach unforeseen gains. Let's get to the top of the hill.

Annie Tselikis: We are beyond thankful for all that you have done and continue to do for us and Cousins Maine Lobster.

We are excited for the future and know you and Oliver will always be by our side every step of the way. We love you!

Barbara Corcoran: Your fearless mentality has allowed us to take risks and reach for heights we never knew existed. We are family, forever.

To the entire CML Family: We all are a part of this magical journey. Each of us is writing history. We thank you for all of your dedication, care, passion, and vision.

Yun Linger, Clay Newbill, Sami Aziz, and the *Shark Tank* family: To say "we couldn't have done it without you" would be the understatement of our lifetime. Wow! Thank you so much. You literally made our dreams come true.

Jason Allison: You're a legend, a handsome legend at that. Thank you for years of loyalty, trust, and generosity.

Kat Cole: Your guidance, mentorship, and friendship go beyond words. Thank you so much.

Diane Perez: Extra love for you, always. Let's get that brownstone!

Blake Dvorak and Kirsten Neuhaus: Thank you all for working so hard on this project and making our dream a reality.

Taj Lomac, Tristan Lomac, Orion Melvin, and Sky Melvin: You guys can do anything you want in this world! Work hard, be good men, and have as much fun as possible.

Our team in LA: You are the best in the business. Smart, dedicated, focused, and always willing to go the extra mile. We are lucky to have such a foundation. Thank you.

To our true friends, our brothers, you support us and keep us laughing always, we appreciate you and love you.

We couldn't forget you: The Lomac and Lomac MacNair family, Bobby and Betsy Fino, Steve and Shannon Lacovara, the Higgins family, Morey Highbarger, John Norton and the Cozy family, Jonathan Norton, Shawn McEwen, Vinny and Char Maietta, Pistol and Christine Cloutier, Peggy Stitham,

Geoff Hassan, Mark Cuban, Daymond John, Jack Canfield, Nick Loukes, the BCH family, Big Brothers Big Sisters of Los Angeles, Lawrence Pittman, Jacob Marroquin, Pam Dipietro Hale, the HC boys. To everyone who has helped us and supported us along the way, we could never thank you enough. Love to you all!

# FOREWORD

"Barbara, welcome to the family."

With those words, Jim and Sabin embraced me in a great big Maine hug. I wasn't about to complain. When these guys walked into the Tank, I saw what everyone at home would see—two handsome studs whom I wish I was young enough to date. Alas, I was old enough to be their mother, but I had just agreed to be their new business partner. I didn't know it at the time, but I had made one of the best business deals of my career. Readers are about to learn why I can say that without fear of exaggeration. But let me offer a few thoughts before I let the cousins take over (which they do a lot).

Jim and Sabin don't lack confidence. It emanated from them that day in the Tank and remains one of their primary strengths as businessmen. Confidence is an attractive quality, especially in a young entrepreneur, and I spotted it immediately. So did the other sharks, some of whom could barely contain their laughter when Jim and Sabin valued their one-truck company (yes, just one) at over a million dollars. That's confidence.

The result was a scene I had witnessed countless times on *Shark Tank*: a young, idealistic entrepreneur (or two) standing helplessly before the bright studio lights as the sharks gobble up big chunks of their dreams. Most contestants don't handle it very well. Sweating and exhausted, many lose focus and stumble over simple questions and start to fall apart. One by one the sharks bow out.

Jim and Sabin? They never missed a beat. They took the worst the sharks dished out and still had the confidence to negotiate with me over equity. I was impressed.

You don't see that type of composure from two untested, wet-behind-the-ears entrepreneurs. I decided these guys were different. Sure, they were in love with their product, but so are most of the contestants we see on the show. The difference was that Jim and Sabin were in love with their product for all the right reasons. They had a vision for Cousins Maine Lobster that went way beyond more trucks or bigger sales. Their vision was more personal and intimate. For them, Maine wasn't a catchy marketing gimmick. Maine was their home, and that mattered to them more than anything else; it was a gift they wanted to share with the world.

Since joining their family, I've watched Jim and Sabin grow from a couple of young studs to confident hotshots and mature business partners. Along the way, they've also become excellent parents to their growing family of franchisees—now in twenty cities. That one truck has become the flagship of a fleet of sleek black Cousins Maine Lobster trucks that deliver the best lobster rolls anywhere this side of the Gulf of Maine— to say nothing of their restaurant or online businesses. That sort of success doesn't just happen.

How *does* it happen? I've learned to look for the same characteristics in all my future partners. They must have energy and hustle, work really hard, both physically and mentally, and they need to be fast on their feet. One reason I look for these characteristics today is because of Jim and Sabin. They have grown Cousins Maine Lobster into a hugely successful business precisely because they have a rule that they will never be outworked by anyone else. Although they have turned into ace businessmen, they are still the same hungry, passionate, and incredibly driven guys that I saw walk into the Tank all those years ago.

Even more special is their ability to weather the tribulations of entrepreneurship. I've watched Jim and Sabin overcome obstacles that would put most young entrepreneurs out of business—from higher prices to a weakened supply chain to disgruntled franchisees and disappointing sales. In the pages that follow, readers are going to see how a couple of pros move on from disappointment and failure. Jim and Sabin always round the corner with smiles on their faces and an uncanny optimism that makes a hit of every bad turn.

But perhaps the quality I most admire in Jim and Sabin is this: they don't listen to me. I'm serious. During any given Skype call, I'll make a least a dozen rock-solid suggestions, based on years of building successful businesses, to solve a myriad of problems. I leave the conversation convinced that they'll each name one of their children, boy or girl, Barbara Ann, as a token of their appreciation. But on the very next call I learn that they didn't do a single thing I told them. They did exactly what they wanted to do!

That's the mark of a true entrepreneur. Jim and Sabin are the captains of their own ship. They lead their own troops and to hell with anyone that thinks differently. Don't mistake this for arrogance. They have no problem asking questions—hundreds and hundreds of questions. And I'm happy to give them hundreds and hundreds of answers. But once armed with the right information, they forge ahead, guided by a vision and a confidence that have carried them forward since the day they set out in their very first truck.

They make no apologies, and neither should you. If you learn one thing from Jim and Sabin's story, learn this: no one can build your company for you.

—BARBARA CORCORAN

# INTRODUCTION

# It Almost Didn't Happen

The news wasn't good.

It was the night before we were scheduled to tape our segment on ABC's *Shark Tank*, and a producer for the show had called to tell us that Barbara Corcoran wouldn't be there. It was probably the worst news we could've received at that moment. Sabin held the phone to his ear, looking at Jim for a sign of what to say. Jim shrugged.

"Well, let us know if anything changes," Sabin said to the producer, then hung up.

We found ourselves in a terrible bind. Every day for the last month or so, we had practiced for our appearance on the show. We had quizzed each other with note cards and pretended to be specific sharks. You think you've done television marathons? Please. We watched fifty episodes in a row to study the sharks as closely as we could. We learned which shark bit on which company and why. We learned why otherwise successful entrepreneurs left the show empty-handed. And we learned why some with barely a dollar in sales had the privilege of watching the sharks outbid each other for a chance to invest.

Having only been in business for less than three months, we knew we couldn't fall back on our sales history too heavily. Sales were good, but they were new and untested. Every dime we had made came from one food truck in one city. There were a lot of dimes for so small an operation, but it wasn't exactly the kind of enterprise that led the sharks to see millions of dollars in potential sales.

It was during this planning period that we homed in on Barbara Corcoran. For reasons we'll explain later, we saw that Barbara had the experience, connections, and outlook that we would want to have in an investor and partner. We made the decision to tailor our entire pitch to Barbara. It was a gamble, to be sure. By targeting Barbara, we might inevitably alienate the other four sharks in the studio. Perhaps we would get lucky and entice one of the other Sharks. The one thing we knew for sure was that we wanted Barbara in our corner as we grew this business.

But we knew that getting any offer was going to be hard, if not impossible. Our other option was to deliver a more generalized pitch that could appeal to the most sharks, in the hope that one would bite. Perhaps if we had been in business for a year or longer; perhaps if we had tried our business model in cities other than Los Angeles; perhaps if we had quit our day jobs . . . If these things had been true when we entered the Tank, then maybe, just maybe, we could have pursued this option.

But none of those things were true the night before we were scheduled to appear on *Shark Tank*. We had one truck operating in one city, and only one of us lived in that city at the time. No, it was going to be Barbara or no one at all.

And now, we were just told, Barbara wasn't going to be there. Our plan was in shambles.

"Well . . . ?" asked Jim.

Sabin shrugged. "They're calling us back to let us know."

Then we waited.

———

Cousins Maine Lobster had opened for business only a few months earlier. April 27, 2012, was not what those in the restaurant world would call a "soft opening." It was more like jumping from a perfectly good airplane, ten thousand feet in the air, without a parachute. The night before, we still didn't have the truck or the lobster meat. We picked up both the next morning and cruised to our first stop that day—only to learn that we had forgotten the register. Just to make things even more interesting, none of our eight employees had ever stepped foot on a food truck or knew how to make a lobster roll. We weren't even sure how the grill worked.

When we finally arrived at the location—thirty minutes late—we saw a large crowd. What a lucky break! We were going to set up shop right next to all these people. It was only when we parked and jumped out of the truck that we learned this wasn't just some random mob. They were our customers. Once we realized this our spirits instantly sank. We had already committed one of the cardinal sins in the food world: we had kept our customers waiting.

In a situation like that there's only one thing you can do: make it up. While our truck employees read the manual for turning on the grill, the two of us grabbed some fresh lobster meat and mingled with the crowd. We hadn't planned on giving out free samples that day, but we also knew that many of those waiting had never had genuine Maine lobster. It'd be like giving out free flutes of Dom Pérignon. Californians appreciate quality product and they certainly know their seafood. But Maine lobster is in a class all its own. Even those in line who had tasted it before had probably had it at a fancy restaurant where they paid fifty bucks for a one-and-a-half-pound lobster. Here we were, giving the stuff out for free—and you better believe they ponied up a few bucks for little bit more.

We had planned on hitting another stop that day but never made it. When our lobster meat ran out at the first stop, we had to call it a day—an exhausting, frustrating, yet rewarding day.

———

Looking back, we had done a thousand things wrong. Add them all up and there's no reason why we should ever have made it to day two. But as naïve as we might have been about the rigors of the food truck business, we have never been wrong about our product. And the thing is, we don't produce it, we don't grow it, and we don't even fish it out of the ocean ourselves.

But we respect it. More than that, we respect what it represents and what it means to others, because we know what it means to us. If you want to know the secret to our success, you can stop reading now. Respect for Maine lobster is our secret. But Maine lobster is so much more than a seafloor crustacean. That delicious animal might be what we sell, but it's more than what's on the plate—which is damn good!

We didn't have all of this figured out that first day as clearly as we do now. Back then, we were just two cousins from Maine who thought that Southern Californians might like a taste of home—a lobster roll. (They do.) Since then, we've come to learn and appreciate just what it is we sell. We've always known it was special, but now we know why. We think you should know why, too, either because you love our product as much as we do, or because you want to achieve your entrepreneurial dreams yourself. We wrote this book for both types of reader.

Before we get ahead of ourselves, we have a more pressing question to answer: What on earth were all those people doing there waiting for us?

———

The night before our opening day, the LA branch of the life-style site UrbanDaddy.com had come across a picture we posted on Twitter announcing the new Cousins Maine Lobster. The picture showed the two of us as little kids with our grandfather on a rocky Maine beach. It might seem strange that we announced our company to the world with a family picture that didn't show a truck, a lobster roll, or even a lobster. It just showed us, with our grandfather, having a uniquely Maine moment. But *that's* what we wanted to sell: a uniquely Maine moment. Our chosen medium—the channel through which our customers would experience this moment—happened to be the lobster roll. At its heart, however, we wanted people to experience, if only briefly, a bit of our cherished memories growing up as Mainers.

That was the idea, anyway. We had no idea if anyone would get it. But UrbanDaddy reposted the picture, along with our planned location the next day, and something happened. It struck a chord with those who saw it. We were lucky that Urban-Daddy gave us the best free publicity we could've asked for, but we wonder now if the response would've been the same if we had posted a lobster or some other generic picture. Those who saw it saw something authentic. Or maybe they just wanted lobster rolls . . .

In any case, it did the trick and we had our first sold-out day. Not long after that, we got a call from *Shark Tank*. We never got an official confirmation, but we have always assumed that the producers had seen the UrbanDaddy post as well and put us on their radar. Those were crazy days for us. We were certainly making money, but not enough to quit our day jobs. Jim, who still lived in Boston at the time, spent most of those days on an air mattress on the floor of Sabin's LA apartment. We knew we had *something*—what it was, we couldn't say.

Was it just the amazing lobster roll? (Probably.) Was it the way we loved chatting up our customers? (Didn't hurt.) Was it our devilish good looks? (Absolutely not.)

Whatever it was, we now had an opportunity us to go on national television and sell it to America. Or such was our impression at the time. Being typical sports guys, we had never seen the show. And we couldn't say why they were interested in a pair of cousins who ran a food truck. The producers were patient with us and explained how the show worked—an entrepreneur pitches five "sharks," who then choose whether to invest in the company.

Once we figured this out we just stared at each other, both having the same thought: "Why the hell would anyone want to invest in a food truck?"

We couldn't find a satisfactory answer. Sure, we figured that America would be interested in the food truck craze, which we were certainly riding. And yes, we knew we had a good story to tell: two cousins from Maine selling their state's signature dish to Southern Californians. We sold that story every day and were doing pretty well—for a single food truck. And, of course, we recognized the short-term publicity wave we would catch just by being on the show.

Then what? We were proud of our success but also terribly conscious that we were two untried entrepreneurs. What business did we have going on a popular, nationally televised show where we stood zero chance of landing a deal? More likely, we would make fools out of ourselves.

It wasn't right for us. Not yet. We just weren't ready for *Shark Tank*.

---

For the next month or so, the popularity of Cousins Maine Lobster became sky high, as did our profits. We continued to speak with the producers of *Shark Tank* and gradually felt better about this amazing opportunity and our chances of actually securing a deal. By this point, we could answer the question that had stumped us the first time around: "Why the hell would anyone want to invest in a food truck?" Because a food truck makes money.

Now that we were regular viewers of the show, we saw what enticed the sharks and what didn't. More importantly, it was much clearer to us what we had and what we didn't. If we were ever going to do the show it would be to make the best deal we could with the right shark. The short-term publicity jolt wasn't tempting anymore. To go on the show just for that felt cheap to us. Inauthentic. And because we knew our business better we also knew that we didn't have what the sharks most want to see—a strong sales history, a plan for growth, and complete and total commitment from the entrepreneur.

Our sales were good, but not strong enough for long enough. Our plan for growth? Here we had vague notions in our heads. More trucks certainly, but then what? How many? Where would they go? Would we franchise? At which point, Sabin asked what "franchise" meant . . .

Finally, we both still had our day jobs. When the sharks hear that they hear "hobby." A lucrative, time-consuming, and stressful hobby, but a hobby nonetheless.

No, we weren't ready. Not quite yet.

Over the next two weeks, we probably asked everyone we knew their advice, so much so that our friends stopped answering our calls. Anyone would be lucky to have the chance to pitch to the "Sharks," so what was holding us back? Maybe we were scared of the spotlight that national television provides? Maybe this was just a passing fad that didn't have true business longevity? Maybe the indecision was centered around us being scared to take that ultimate leap into running our own business and risking it all? Whatever it was, it was eating us alive. In early June, we had one fateful call with a producer at *Shark*

*Tank*, which was likely more of a therapy session than anything. We hung up and knew we would be idiots if we didn't take this chance. By this point, we had grossed more than $100,000 off our single truck. Things had started to move very quickly, and we had reached a decision point with our little business: either we expand or we keep just the one truck. We had to decide quickly— for reasons we'll explain later—and *Shark Tank* helped us make the decision. We would expand and get a second truck, but we didn't have the capital to do so. That was our growth plan for *Shark Tank*. We were both finally ready to turn Cousins Maine Lobster into a full-time job.

Sales—check.

Growth plan—check.

Commitment—check.

Yes, we were ready to go on *Shark Tank*.

———

Over the next several weeks we watched around fifty episodes of the show. We wanted to know everything we could about the sharks: the questions they asked; the answers they liked, as well as the ones they hated. We studied each shark, both on and off the show. We knew their backgrounds, their areas of interest and expertise (not always the same), and the kind of answers that sparked their excitement and curiosity. Then we made flashcards, with real questions the sharks had asked on the show, and quizzed each other. We became a bit obsessive about it. We'd take turns pretending to be sharks and asking rude questions. We're both very competitive and loved stumping or embarrassing each other. We also made sure to practice our poise and self-control. As we watched episode after episode, we saw several contestants buckle under the pressure. Sometimes it was a question that put them off their game; other times it was just harsh criticism. We wanted to make sure we were ready for both. We set ourselves a goal: whether we made a deal or not, we would be the best-prepared contestants the show had ever seen. We wouldn't wilt under the bright lights of the studio (they're really freaking bright) nor would we let America see us unable to answer a simple question. It was the old parenting adage most of us heard when we were kids: it doesn't matter if you fail if you did your best.

And while we studied, we began to focus our pitch and tailor it to a single shark: Barbara Corcoran. For starters, Barbara had invested in a few food companies, namely Pork Barrel BBQ and Daisy Cakes, and we had heard great things about these two young companies. Barbara also had the type of temperament we needed to have in our shark. Now, it is true that all the sharks put on a television persona for the cameras. Some like to be the good cop, others the bad cop. But the truth is that all of them care deeply about their investments. All of them are brilliant. But we focused on Barbara because, well, frankly, she reminded us of our mothers. She seemed to appreciate the reasons behind a business, aside from the purpose of making money.

Why lobster? Why Maine? The answers to these questions get to the heart of our company. We wanted a shark who would want to know the answers, just as our mothers wanted to know the answers.

So, that was our plan: we were going to go on the show with a specific shark in mind. We would tailor our pitch directly to her. We needed Barbara to bite.

And then, the night before the taping, we were told Barbara wasn't going to be there.

Damn.

———

Those were some agonizing minutes in the hotel room, waiting for the producer to call back. We spoke little to each other, as our brains scrambled for a solution. Had we made a mistake putting all our eggs in the Barbara Corcoran basket? Should we scrap our pitch and start over? Shouldn't we just be happy with the opportunity? This wasn't the first time we had to confront serious questions about our company and about ourselves, but it certainly felt like the most consequential. We imagine that most businesses go through a moment like this early on. They are presented with a great opportunity, but one also fraught with dangers if not handled properly. The challenge is to see through the opportunity—look beyond the immediate benefit. Does this get you to where you want to be? If the details of the opportunity change, what does that do to the opportunity overall? In our case, the detail that changed was the presence of Barbara Corcoran. For some contestants that might have been a minor detail, easily overlooked in favor of the bigger opportunity; but for us, Barbara *was* the opportunity. We were going on *Shark Tank* to do a deal with her. The publicity, the exposure—those were wonderful but secondary considerations. We had to strip the opportunity of all that Hollywood glitz and look at *Shark Tank* for what it is: a chance to take your company to another level. Everything depended on Barbara.

The phone rang and Sabin answered. Sabin's smile told Jim all he needed to know. Barbara would be there.

The next day, we found ourselves standing outside the big doors that open into the Tank. The previous eighteen hours hadn't passed without incident. We had hoped to get in front of the sharks before lunchtime, for obvious reasons. But never count on a television show sticking to its schedule. Lunch blew past, and still we waited. Finally, at around three or four o'clock in the afternoon, we were called from the green room and told to get ready. We were next. Jim felt himself recalling his college hockey days, mentally preparing himself before the game starts. Sabin went over the pitch in his head, again and again.

And before us those big doors loomed, the same ones we had watched open to dozens of dreaming entrepreneurs just like us. Barbara and four other sharks sat on the other side. In seconds, we would walk in, just two cousins with a food truck. Who would walk out?

Then the doors opened . . .

# PART ONE

# Two Cousins and a Truck

# Where Our Story Begins

The day we entered the Tank, Cousins Maine Lobster had a single food truck that earned around $100,000 a month in sales. Four years later, our company consists of twenty-one food trucks in thirteen cities, a restaurant in West Hollywood, and an online retail business, all of which has earned over $20 million in sales. We expect to get ten new trucks on the street this year, plan to open more restaurants, and are ready to expand internationally.

Since our initial episode aired on October 19, 2012, we've been featured in four follow-up *Shark Tank* episodes (more than any other contestants), have made the rounds on *The Chew, The Today Show,* and *The Queen Latifah Show,* and have been featured in *Entrepreneur Magazine, Food & Wine Magazine,* and *Saveur Magazine.* We've also had the number one lobster roll as voted by *Tasting Table* for three years in a row—a streak we have every intention of continuing. More important, in 2013, our success allowed us to create Cousins for a Cause, a nonprofit organization that has partnered with Big Brothers Big Sisters of Greater Los Angeles to help build awareness and raise money for that amazing foundation.

Not bad for a couple of guys with no formal business training.

So what did we have? Two things: we had passion and we had a story. We wrote this book to tell you about both, because we want you to know that it's all possible. Your dreams. Your idea. Your business. You don't need all that much to make these things happen—but you do need passion and a story. Imagine yourself as one of the sharks in the Tank that day, and in walk two guys who ask you to invest in a food truck. A food truck! Yes, those jalopy diesel monsters that hang out outside corporate offices and clog traffic. What a wonderful business opportunity!

You would ask if we had any start-up experience. Our answer: no.

You would ask if we had any franchising experience. Our answer: no.

You would ask if we had any food or restaurant experience. Our answer: no.

Now, give us your money!

Yet that's exactly what we did. We asked for someone to give us money so that we could buy another food truck, because one wasn't enough. Someone did, because she understood, as you must understand, that when it comes to starting a successful business only a couple things matter: passion and story. (Having crazy-delicious lobster rolls helps . . . ) We're living proof that it doesn't matter what industry you're in, or how nutty your idea is: if you approach your business with passion—a meaningful connection to a great idea—then you will learn what you need to know. We certainly did. Passion isn't about waking up one day and deciding to open a business or make some quick cash by throwing something against the wall to see if it sticks. You become an entrepreneur because you see how your passion or connection to something could make you able to offer a truly great product or unique service.

Money? Yes, money is important for all the obvious reasons. We each invested about $25,000 of our own money before making a dime. But we didn't start Cousins Maine Lobster to make money—or, put another way, we didn't start it to *only make money*. So, why did we start it? We'll get to that later. For now, you need to decide what kind of entrepreneur you want to be. There are several different types of entrepreneur, but we'll stick with just two. One type, the type we are, has a passion for that one thing—that one idea, that one product, that one service. To achieve that one thing, they pour their heart and soul into it. Maybe it works and maybe it doesn't. But for this type of entrepreneur, the passion is the product and there is no endgame. We don't have an exit strategy for Cousins Maine Lobster. We have found the one job that we each want to do for the rest of our lives. Doing this one thing makes us happy and that's what we value: doing something that makes us happy.

For another type of entrepreneur, money is the passion. They build businesses to sell them and make money. Maybe it's a one-off, get-rich-quick scheme. Or maybe they just enjoy starting something new. We tip our Bruins caps to those who have a seemingly endless reservoir of great ideas that attract investment money. And while we've expanded Cousins Maine Lobster beyond the food truck, we're not get-rich-quick guys. We have no intention of selling our business or moving on to another business. Cousins Maine Lobster *is* our business. Now, entrepreneurs in this category aren't any better or worse than the type we are, but this book isn't for them.

We're not here to tell you how to make a billion dollars by selling your app idea—because we have no idea how to do that. We hope you earn the type of money that makes you happy, but we don't guarantee it. We're not here to show you how to retire at thirty or forty or fifty—because for us, work is the juice. We love what we do: we don't want to retire. And we're certainly not here to show you how to make more money by working less—in fact, just the opposite. If you follow what we say here, you'll work harder than you ever have in your life. As the cliché goes, if you're following your passion, it won't feel like work at all. (This is mostly true, but damn, some days are very long.)

We're here to tell you how we turned our passion—our story—into something greater than ourselves. It doesn't get any simpler than this: if we could do it, then so can you. There's nothing all that unique about us. We're not geniuses. We did pretty well at our old day jobs, but it's not like we were in the C-suite. We're not marketing gurus, sales ninjas, or Six Sigma black belts. We're just two guys who decided to serve lobster rolls from a food truck.

It may not sound like much, but there's passion there. There's a story, too. We hope ours will inspire yours.

## OUR STORY IS MAINE

Our story begins in America's first frontier. In many ways, Maine remains a frontier. While all the river valleys have been mapped, many remain untamed, in the same condition that the Native Americans found them when they called this land home. Mainers continue to hug the coast, the source of all community and wealth in a state short on both. To understand our story, you must first understand this unique place. Or, perhaps a better way of putting it: you must understand it better than you do now. You will probably never truly understand it. We don't. We both grew up in Maine and yet we are considered relative newcomers. If you packed your things and moved there tomorrow, don't expect to be welcomed as a Mainer. It takes more than a driver's license. In fact, it takes more than a generation or two to be considered a native. Try six or seven generations. There are families in Maine who can trace their ancestors to the original Scotch-Irish settlers of the late seventeenth and early eighteenth centuries—long before the United States, and just barely after the very idea of New England as a geographic region, with its own culture and sense of self.

The fact is that Maine has never been an easy place to call home. But that's what makes it so damn unique—and extremely frustrating to those who come here to do business. And it's always been that way. Which isn't to say that Maine is all that much different from where you're from. It has its unique history and place in Americana, just like your hometown. But there's a twist with Maine. Whether it's the geography, climate, or people, those who come to Maine unprepared are in for a big surprise.

The first company in Maine, known as the Plymouth Company, had no clue what it was doing. We suppose a lot of companies start like that: a bit overwhelmed, a bit unsure, and all too prone to making mistakes. Forget thriving: the best a start-up can do in those first few days is survive. It was certainly that way for us, as it was for the 124 colonists aboard the two ships of the Plymouth Company of England, which arrived on the Maine coast in 1607. Before them stretched a beautiful but mostly unexplored frontier of opportunity and danger. They thought they were ready. We did, too, when we entered a different—and yes, far less dangerous—frontier. We were both wrong. Fortunately, that's where the similarities end.

This wasn't the first time the English shareholding company had tried to establish a permanent presence in Maine. The previous year, the company captain got lost on the voyage over. Like, really lost. He ended up in the Caribbean, where he and his crew were captured by pirates. The interesting thing about that expedition is that, had they landed anywhere from Florida to Nova Scotia and built a settlement, then it would have been the first English settlement in America. But the Jamestown, Virginia, settlers beat them to it.

Undeterred, the head of the Plymouth Company, one Sir Ferdinando Gorges, somehow convinced his investors to throw good money after bad and quickly organized a second voyage. This time the ships made it to Maine, which must have been a moral victory for all involved. But they probably would've been better off had they just turned around. Apparently, the colonists only had a vague sense of Maine's geography and climate, because they built their trading fort at the head of the Kennebec River. We're only slightly exaggerating when we say that any other spot on the Maine coast would've been preferable. The tides turned the colonists' harbor into a mudflat for half the day, while the winter winds pummeled the little community without mercy. Welcome to Maine. Mistake number one.

Mistake number two was the newcomers' mistreatment of the local Native American tribes, particularly the Mawooshen Wabanakis. This was problematic for two reasons. First, the company's entire business model depended on making a profit through trade with the locals. So, pissing them off was the same as pissing off their customers. Second, when you find yourself in a strange land, far from home, facing your first Maine winter, making friends with those who've lived there for thousands of years would be a pretty good idea. At least, don't kidnap or kill any of them. Guess what the colonists did? You have to wonder if they regretted that mistake when they were chewing bark in the middle of January . . .

The third and final mistake was the colonists' ignorance of the true potential of Maine, which wasn't what could be mined, farmed, or hunted on land. The colonists had just come from Europe, where famines were frequent and meat was rare and expensive. You could say that there was a pretty decent business opportunity for the company that discovered a limitless supply of easily procured protein. And it's not like the colonists were unaware of the swarms of lobster and groundfish just off the

Maine coast. According to historian Colin Woodard, a good fisherman in those days could pull up 350 to 400 cod *a day*.

Although just as plentiful, lobster wasn't a viable option back then, because there was no way to transport it without refrigeration. As we've discovered, lobster spoils extremely fast even under the best conditions, which the seventeenth-century colonists certainly didn't have. Lobster would have its day, but not yet. Which left cod, as Woodard writes:

> Cod . . . was nearly perfect. Properly dried and salted, codfish would keep for many months. It was relatively light and easy to transport and, since salt cod was a cheap source of animal protein, there was an insatiable demand for it in the markets of Europe.

But the little settlement at the mouth of the Kennebec wasn't there to fish. They were there to build a trading empire for the Plymouth Company, one fur and one beaver pelt at a time. The empire didn't last a year. Starving, freezing, and wholly wretched, the colonists decided that their first winter in Maine would be their last and sailed back to England in the spring of 1608.[1]

We can sympathize. Maine is a gorgeous, almost idyllic location . . . in the summer. By the winter, we're not unhappy that we've chosen sunny Southern California as our home away from home. We get back, every few months, to see family and do some business. Maine's place in our hearts has never been in doubt. But when we embarked on this journey together, we didn't realize how intimately our childhood home would haunt our every decision. When we look at any business opportunity, we ask ourselves two questions. First, does the opportunity get us to where we want to be long-term? Second, does the opportunity reflect well on Maine? In other words, by pursuing this opportunity are we doing right by those in Maine whose values, ethics, hard work, and support have allowed us to be successful?

We must answer yes to both questions before moving ahead. We respect Maine as much as we respect our lobster and our customers. It is part of our story. Heck, we even put it in our name! Which is why we wanted to tell the story of the Plymouth Company, because for us, the fate of that first company in Maine is a cautionary tale for all businesses that seek to capitalize on what our home has to offer.

Those first settlers to Maine weren't necessarily bad people, but they didn't respect the land or its inhabitants. They brought their own ideas about how things should work to a place where things had been working quite well for thousands of years. Is it any surprise that life proved unbearable to them? Likewise, we aren't the first guys who have had the bright idea of bringing Maine lobster to the masses, taking it out of the fancy restaurants and serving it up the way we ate it as kids, the way all Mainers eat it—on a paper plate, fresh from the pot, with a sprinkle of lemon and butter.

But those other guys brought their own ideas to how things should be done, rather than adapting their methods to Maine. And when things got rough, they chose to split and leave their suppliers—the fishermen and the communities who rely on what's pulled up from the sea—behind. Now, the Wabanaki Indians were probably happy to see the Plymouth Company settlers hightail it back to England. But when outsiders bolt from their Maine suppliers today, it's the suppliers and all who rely on them who get hurt.

For this reason, the Maine lobster industry is very cautious about who it does business with. They've been burned one too many times. Other Americans look at Maine's skepticism of outsiders as an eccentric, perhaps slightly arrogant trait. But this skepticism has been born from hundreds of years of dealing with greedy, exploitative outsiders whose only interest in Maine, its people, and its waters has been what they can take. It was that way between the first English settlers and the Wabanaki and other Indian tribes who called the Maine coast home thousands of years before Columbus. It was that way when the first Scotch-Irish settlers were lured to Maine with promises of free plots of land only to be told later that they owed rent to some Massachusetts land baron who had bought a piece of paper. And it was that way when the groundfish industry collapsed in the mid-twentieth century and thousands of Maine fishermen, their families, and their communities watched helplessly as the great fish companies closed or moved away.

Maine today isn't what the English settlers found when they built that first fort at the head of the Kennebec River. And yet it's remarkable how little has changed. These days, there aren't any settlers, there are only natives, the ones whose connection to Maine, its people and its land, go back generations. Maine's economy has grown beyond what swims or scurries along the floor of the ocean, and yet it's amazing how dependent every coastal community is on lobster.

And it's this one product, the lobster, which has come to symbolize all that is great, unique, and precious about our home. We are now part of that story. When our trucks pull up at stops in Los Angeles, Nashville, Phoenix, Raleigh, or Houston, we don't want our customers to just see Cousins Maine Lobster; we want them to see Maine. We want them to see the story of a state whose history has been lived out along a rocky, inhospitable, but stunningly beautiful coast. We want them to see the generations of Mainers who have lived and died by what they pulled from the ocean floor. We want them to see a way of life that, with minor differences, has remained more or less the same since before America's founding.

That's how we see ourselves. Arrogant? No, aspirational. Cousins Maine Lobster is but one very small piece of Maine's story, but we cherish even that little bit. This connection with something larger than ourselves—larger than a fleet of trucks or a restaurant or a television show—reminds us that our passion continues to drive this business. It reminds us of where we came from, how far we've come, and where we want to go.

That's how our story begins. How does yours begin?

## THE PRINCIPLES BEHIND YOUR STORY

Finding your story is an essential element of any successful business, but we recognize that not everyone has a great story to tell—yet. We didn't have ours right away. All we had was a vague notion that we wanted to capture a feeling from our childhood: the feeling of being with family and friends eating lobster. The memory was strong enough in both of us that we believed it was the basis for a business, but memories don't sustain businesses. When you're working nonstop and there are a thousand little details, how do you hang on to the story that sparked the idea for your business in the first place? It's especially intense when the business that was once just a bunch of notes and numbers on a spreadsheet becomes an actual concrete thing that is your (sometimes sole) source of income.

Unfortunately, a lot of start-ups that move beyond those first crazy days lose their story: they forget their passion. They let the details and the demands of the day take precedence over the needs of the business. It's a common-enough problem, but it also signals the beginning of the end. So, how do you balance the practical concerns while still staying true to that original vision? How do you grow and maintain the same level of enthusiasm you had grinding out your business plan at Starbucks after a long day at your "real" job? We wanted to write this book because we remember what it was like to be wondering "What's next?"

We know what it's like to have built something from scratch and have an emotional attachment to a business. We understand what it's like to be both excited and maybe even scared to move up to the next level. It's perfectly normal to feel some apprehension. How you go about taking those next steps can have a big impact on the future of your company. You've built something that works, but now you must scale up to sustain what you've built. It's a different ball game. There's the obvious issue of financing, but once that's tackled you need to be ready to handle everything from changes in leadership and infrastructure to marketing initiatives and reaching a bigger customer base. The nuts and bolts of what it will take for you is specific to whatever it is you do, but we believe the lessons we learned while scaling up authentically can apply to *any* business. We hope that the stories and principles we're going to share in this book will help you tackle "What's next?" with the same determination and passion you tackled those first days as a business. We want you to feel excited about what's next and all the possibilities that come along with it, not worried about selling out or totally losing control of the company that's like a child to you.

And we can start right now. Each chapter in this book will end with a lesson—a distillation of what the previous stories, episodes, and moments we related mean for the way we run our business. But another way to look at these lessons is as principles. We started Cousins Maine Lobster with some of these principles already in mind. Over time, some of those original principles have changed, while we learned others as we grew. Our principles have changed because of the decisions, the mistakes, and the successes we've had along the way. But there's also no reason to hide these principles from you until the end of each chapter. In fact, it's never too soon to start to list the principles that will help guide your business. Like ours, your principles will change over time—if they don't, then something is wrong. They will evolve, adapt, shrink, and grow with your company and your story. Let them. Don't be a slave to your principles. They exist to help you keep sight of what's important.

Here are our principles, in the order you will come across them in the chapters that follow.

1. **Pursue your dreams with the best of intentions**. If your entrepreneurial dreams amount to "I want to make money," then you will likely fail. Aim higher. Start something because it's your passion. The money follows passion.

2. **Ask a million questions**. You are never in greater danger than when you think you know what you're doing. You're not going to know everything, or much at all, when you start. Don't pretend you do; instead, ask questions.

3. **Know who you are**. Finding your identity is one of the challenges of a new business. But you need to find your identity if you hope to weather the pressure of the tough times ahead. Knowing who you are will serve like an anchor, keeping you and your business grounded while you venture into the unknown.

4. **Play the long game**. Your new business will be presented with chances for quick sales that might seem right at the time but won't get you to where you want to be. These opportunities are tantalizing because they seem to offer easy money, but there's no foundation. If you play the long game, and know where you're headed, you'll know when to say no.

5. **Know why you do it**. The purpose of your company will change over time. We started with a simple idea, and that

idea hasn't changed—but why we do it has. Make your business about more than you or what you sell.

6. **Surround yourself with greatness**. In the beginning, you're going to do everything. But as you grow, you'll have to let others help you. This isn't as easy as it sounds; what makes it easier is finding the best people possible to trust with your business. This not only includes employees, but also consultants and advisors.

7. **Not every opportunity is the right opportunity**. Finding what's right for your business takes up a lot of your time running it. Particularly after you've achieved a measure of success, you'll be inundated with too-good-to-pass-up opportunities, yet most of them are garbage. You must be able to sniff out the garbage.

8. **Know what brings you back to your center**. Running a business changes you. You will be burned, your trust will be abused, and you will make mistakes. Your challenge is holding on to that part of you that should never change—that part that made you start a business in the first place. You need to know what brings out that part of you, what makes that part shine, and what makes that part unchangeable.

9. **Build something that lasts**. As a business owner, you never stop building. But there comes a moment when you realize you have to protect what you've already built. The company, the employees, the customers—these are all part of your brand, your culture. And your culture exists to protect and promote what you've built.

10. **Give something back**. Money and fame can happen when you've built something successful. But they aren't the purpose of success. You become successful so you can

use your success in the pursuit of something greater. Find something that is greater than you or your company and pour your heart into it.

Can you list your principles right now? Even if your company is no more than a crazy idea in your head, write down the principles by which you would build this company. Go ahead and steal some of ours, if you like them. Just be forewarned that these are principles we have learned in the crucible of experience. They won't mean the same thing to you as they do to us. But that's what ideals are for, right? Something to aspire to?

And that is the great lesson we wish to impart to you. When you set out to live your passion, you are doing more than building a business. You are creating something greater than you. It won't feel like that at first—shoving ten guys on a food truck when no one knows how to use a grill isn't exactly the great beginning we had in mind. But eventually, and especially in those dark hours, you will be hit with a profound sense of fulfillment. And it will leave you just as quickly as the weight of the business crashes down around your head. But for that one moment, you will know the feeling that you've built something that *matters*.

At least, that's our hope. Now, let's get on with the rest of the story.

# A Memory of Jim's Backyard

The year 2011 found us on opposite sides of the country. Jim lived in Boston and worked in sales for a medical device company while Sabin was a real estate agent in Los Angeles. We hadn't talked to each other in years. Maybe we weren't in our dream jobs, but we made decent money and life was good. We rarely thought about each other, except during our infrequent trips home to visit family.

And life very well might have gone on like that, each of us as far away from the other as possible, the memory of our shared childhood growing up on the Maine coast fading away. Neither of us had any plans to rock the boat.

But that's when Jim got in touch with his ex-girlfriend, who just happened to live in LA. A few conversations later and Jim found himself considering her invitation to visit. She didn't have to sell him very hard. A chance to escape the Boston winter was just the sort of vacation an overworked sales representative needed.

Then Jim remembered that Sabin lived in LA. Aha! Two birds, one stone. Jim would just say he wanted to visit his long-lost cousin, whom he loved and missed dearly. He loved and missed Sabin so much that Jim had to send him a message on Facebook just to get his number. Of course Sabin was overjoyed to hear from Jim, and couldn't wait to show him around town. It felt good for both of us to catch up over the phone, all those years apart just passing under the bridge. But Jim's motives for going to LA hadn't changed; he just had a better excuse.

Get out of dreary Boston, enjoy the California sunshine, see the ex, and, oh, catch up with Sabin—this was Jim's plan. It would've worked beautifully, but thank God it didn't.

## A MAINE CHILDHOOD

There are those entrepreneurs who show a knack for the art of creating and growing businesses from a very early age. Some start selling lemonade on the sidewalk and move on to Internet retail by the time they're in high school. Others challenge themselves with a new technology or platform, and start their entrepreneurial careers by doing something that's never been done.

We weren't either kind. In fact, there's no reason to expect that we'd grow up to become entrepreneurs. It's probably the myth of the prodigy that keeps so many would-be entrepreneurs on the sidelines. One of the main reasons we wrote this book was to prove that childhood precociousness or technical brilliance aren't required to start and build a company. You won't find any signs of our future business acumen by digging through our school report cards. You'll be equally hard-pressed to see the younger versions of us as anything other than normal boys, certainly not prodigies or budding capitalists.

In short, we were just kids growing up in Maine. And that's all we needed.

Let's start with Jim. Jim and his older sister Annie (whom

you'll meet later) grew up in Cape Elizabeth, Maine, the children of Steve and Julie Tselikis. Cape Elizabeth is your typical coastal Maine town, small, middle class, and chock-full of history. Named after the sister of King Charles I, the land was first owned by the same Ferdinando Gorges who did such a bang-up job funding several expeditions to the Maine coast. Quick side note on Gorges: although the guy spent most of his life trying to become the effective emperor of Maine, he never visited once. It set a pattern for the next hundred-or-so years where the legal owners of Maine land couldn't be bothered to live in, or even visit, their vast holdings. Of course, that didn't stop them from "protecting" their property at the point of a sword to drive off or even kill those who actually lived there and worked the land and sea.

The seventeenth and early eighteenth centuries were some hard years for the early Maine settlers. Like most of Maine's coastal towns, Cape Elizabeth was destroyed during one of the many Native American wars that ravaged the region in this period. As historian Colin Woodard tells us:

> For a quarter of a century, Maine was the scene of Balkan-like desolation, warfare, lawlessness, and ethnic slaughter. In 1689, all of Maine's settlers north of Wells—up to four thousand people—fled for their lives. Many of those who got away found themselves in the streets and poorhouses of Boston. Many of those who did not came to slow and gruesome ends. From 1689 to 1713, not a single English home stood in all of Maine north of Wells, which lies twenty-five miles south of what is now Portland.[2]

Cape Elizabeth was caught in the middle of this terrible slaughter. It was eventually rebuilt, just like many of its neighbors, and officially incorporated on November 1, 1765. Growing up amid such history is mostly lost on a child, particularly

since there aren't all that many landmarks or monuments me-
morializing the town's four-hundred-years-long story. Again,
this makes Cape Elizabeth fairly ordinary among Maine's
coastal towns, where history isn't remembered so much as it is
still lived.

Jim's parents, Steve and Julie, were Maine natives who both
grew up in the same area, not far from Portland. Although he
started out studying psychology, Steve would turn to accounting and earn his CPA. And while accounting suited Steve, it
wasn't his passion, a sentiment that we share. But it was fortuitous that we had someone so close to us who understood the
complex, confusing stuff—things like addition, subtraction, and
long division. Even then, Steve spent most of his career working in real estate development, which he enjoyed far more than
accounting, and picked up a lifetime of useful knowledge and
wisdom about putting together business deals.

Jim's mother, Julie, was the nurse at her son's middle school.
For a kid, it's a blessing and a curse having your mom on staff
at school: Sometimes you can get away with shenanigans, but
often the maternal presence keeps you in line. However, it set
a pattern between Jim and Julie that endures to this very day:
you go to the school nurse when there's something wrong, and
Jim *still* goes to his mother when something's wrong.

More importantly, Jim witnessed Mainers' infamous work
ethic in his parents. Even on the weekends, Steve often would
put in a half day at the office, while Julie's mother did most of
the caretaking of Jim and Annie during the week. In fact, when
Jim was about ten, Steve noticed that his son took an interest
in the nicer things some friends of the family, mostly lawyers
and doctors, had in their homes. Rather than criticize those
who owned expensive things, Steve asked his church if they
could use an extra hand to help clean up on the weekends.
Wouldn't you know it, but Steve knew someone who could use
some work. It wasn't a really labor-intensive job, but it taught

Jim the value of a dollar. While most of his friends spent their weekends playing sports, Jim helped clean the church. And when we say "clean," we're not talking about sweeping floors and emptying the garbage. We're talking about scrubbing toilets and urinals that had just been used. We're talking about being on hands and knees washing the floors. To this day, Steve looks back on Jim's first job as "one of the best things" he did for his son.

Jim eventually discovered sports, too. In a big way. Jim was always a driven, determined boy, but when he started playing hockey, he discovered an outlet for his competitive side. Jim hates to lose. Hates it. And he threw himself into hockey like he did everything else: with single-minded determination. It wasn't long before Jim's coaches saw the raw talent and the makings of a genuine athlete. In Maine, hockey is a big deal, but most of Jim's friends treated it more like a hobby than a passion. The level of competition wasn't equal to Jim's talents, so Steve began to take him to Minnesota to play in hockey tournaments. By high school, Jim was ready to leave Cape Elizabeth—and the public school system—behind to hone his talents at a private school. Money was an issue, but Jim handled that by getting a scholarship to play hockey at Phillips Exeter Academy in New Hampshire—not so far as Los Angeles but far enough for Julie to cry when her boy went off on his first great adventure.

Then there was Sabin. It's not that his childhood was all that different from Jim's, but it *was* different. Raised by a single mother, Sabin grew up about fifteen minutes from Jim in Scarborough. Unlike Jim, Sabin wasn't born in Maine, but in California. His mother, Jeannie, however, felt that her native Maine would be a more suitable place to raise her son, and they would also be next to family. So, Jeannie packed up everything she and her little four-year-old owned and drove the three thousand miles to Scarborough, Maine.

Nearly a hundred years older than Cape Elizabeth, Scarborough is a place boiling in history. Scarborough was destroyed in King Philip's War, one of the many English-Indian conflagrations that was fought between 1675 and 1678 up and down the New England coast. "Though it is largely forgotten today, a larger proportion of America's population died in King Philip's War than in any other war in our nation's history," writes Woodard.[3] The Indian wars eventually subsided, as the natives were overwhelmed by disease and simple numbers. They retreated to the Maine woods, bidding farewell to the coast they had called home for thousands of years.

And just like Cape Elizabeth, Scarborough rose from the ashes—only to barely survive its next catastrophe, Sabin Lomac. We kid, but only just. The truth is that Sabin was a great kid who turned into a slightly rambunctious adolescent. It wasn't anything too illegal—mostly pranks, like graffiti. And, yes, there was one time that Sabin was arrested for scalping tickets to a concert in Worcester, Massachusetts. He also got into trouble a few times for fighting and playing hooky. Even if Sabin limited his shenanigans to the PG-13 variety, he was clearly headed in the wrong direction, which helps explain why Jeannie signed him up for Big Brothers Big Sisters of America. It was an experience that thoroughly transformed Sabin's life.

Sabin's Big Brother's name was Stephen, a Coast Guard member from New Jersey who provided the fatherless Sabin with the support and stability he so desperately lacked. He helped Sabin channel his energy into more productive arenas, like sports. Where Jim found hockey, Sabin excelled on the basketball court. He also found more creative outlets for his wilder side, and eventually the troubled kid turned into a leader on his team and among his friends. Well, except when he decided to perm his hair in high school—no one wanted to follow him down that path.

Like Jim, Sabin started working at a young age. He learned

quickly that if he wanted something he had to pay for it himself. Being in a single-parent household meant that there simply wasn't enough money for the sorts of things kids love—sports equipment, video games, and, later, clothes. So, Sabin earned his own. At thirteen, he began bussing tables at a seafood restaurant in town. Before Sabin left for college, he had had more than thirty jobs, which included working at the Clambake, Best Buy, Chili's, Marshview Restaurant, Anjon's, Lois' Natural, B-Fit, Dunstan School Restaurant, Black Point Inn, Pizza Time, Dimitri's, Sand Dollar Inn, and Salty Bay Seafood.

Of course, when you're a kid, you rarely realize when you're in the middle of a life lesson. Jim certainly didn't see his father's motive behind making him clean the church every weekend, nor did Sabin understand how he was forging a work ethic that would one day surpass that of most of his peers. We were both hard workers and we both thank our parents for making us work for the things we wanted. We debated whether to include some variation of "work hard" as one of our principles, but in the end we decided that hard work isn't a unique entrepreneurial trait. It's like breathing—it's the bare minimum one must accomplish to get anywhere in life. Still, if you don't have a good work ethic, then you won't be much of an entrepreneur. That's just how it is.

In any case, Sabin also began to pursue his first passion, acting, more seriously. As a kid, he had done some commercials and other small parts, clearly influenced by Jeannie, who worked as a theater director. By his teenage years, Sabin had decided he wanted to try acting as a profession and began to look beyond Maine for opportunities.

So where did our lives intersect? It was mostly during family gatherings—birthdays, holidays, the usual moments when all our nutty relatives got together. We weren't the only cousins in the bunch, but we formed a friendship as kids that we now realize went deeper than most cousin friendships. We certainly liked the same things, and established a bond playing *NHL '94*—a very popular hockey video game at the time. But it would be the family gatherings at Jim's house in Cape Elizabeth that would create the intimate bond that would one day build a company.

In Maine, the summer lobster bake is so normal and common that it's part of the rhythm of life there. It's just what families do when they get together in those few precious months when the weather is perfect—and Maine summers *are* perfect. The scene is simple but beautiful: The family would gather at the Tselikis's, a total of five cousins, several aunts and uncles, and grandparents. Steve would get the water boiling, which isn't just for lobster, but also clams and corn. The aroma would permeate the backyard, while the sound of kids playing and laughing was a steady drum in the background. The adults would sip their beer, wine, and cocktails, and we kids roughhoused until we were sweaty and dirty. Then the food would be brought out onto large picnic tables, spread out over old newspapers, and that's when we'd dive in. Of course, there would be leftovers, which is where the lobster roll comes in. Much like that the old standby, the turkey sandwich, which is the perfect leftover meal after Thanksgiving, the lobster roll is the best way to enjoy lobster after a bake.

As we said, this scene isn't at all unique to our family. It's a scene that plays out every summer day in Maine—and any Mainer would recognize that gathering in Jim's backyard. Like a lot of childhood memories, the lobster bakes are ingrained in our hearts as pristine, almost idyllic. And as we grew older and took on our own struggles, challenges, and worries, the ghosts of Jim's backyard seemed to call to us, reminding us of the way life should be. We still gather there when we can, but, of course, it's different. Those same grandparents who would chase us, hug us, and teach us how to pick a lobster clean are now gone. The parents, aunts, and uncles who used to haul the bags of live lobster, the cases of beer, and the ice now prefer to rest with a drink while the younger generation does the heavy lifting. The laughter and squeals of us kids have become the mature banter of grown adults—well, maybe "mature" is too strong a word. We appreciate those precious hours all the more now, all of us together again, even as we mourn the passing of those carefree summer days of our childhood, when nothing mattered more than showing our grandfather how fast, strong, or tough we were.

The college years found Jim at the College of the Holy Cross in Worcester, Massachusetts, where he played Division I hockey, while Sabin let his acting bug take him to Hofstra University on Long Island to study drama. After graduation, Jim stayed in the Boston area and eventually got into medical sales for Stryker Corporation. Meanwhile, Sabin hung around New York City, landing the occasional acting role, but also earned his real estate license to make ends meet. It wasn't long before acting took Sabin to Los Angeles, as it usually does for actors. Jim vaguely remembers hearing that Sabin had "moved away"—which means away from New England—but he wasn't there to see his cousin off. We had gone our separate ways.

Our jobs after college certainly taught us some necessary skills for starting and growing our own business, but we'll get to those lessons later. What's important is at this stage in our lives is that after we left college—well, Jim graduated a couple years before Sabin—we slowly lost contact with each other. The gatherings in Jim's backyard became less frequent, our connection to Maine more tenuous. That seemed normal to us, as it must for most. You grow up to leave home behind and build your own future. The absolute last thought in either of our heads was to take what we had known as children and re-create it.

And then, years later, out of nowhere Jim called Sabin.

# AN EX, A VIDEO GAME, AND BOOZE—LOTS OF IT

The plan was for Jim to see Sabin for a day or so, catch up, see how life had been treating him, but then reconnect with Amanda. The exact opposite happened. Yes, Jim saw Amanda, but seeing Sabin again brought all those old childhood memories surging forth—for both of us. Jim didn't realize how excited Sabin would be to show him around LA. He couldn't have left Sabin even if he had wanted to. We visited famous Venice Beach, saw the sights, but mostly we talked. We talked about our families, our grandfather, with whom we were both very close, and how much we missed Maine and all it meant to us.

In the evening, Sabin took Jim to a sushi place on Sunset Boulevard, and the talk continued—only this time, we added copious amounts of beer, cocktails, and sake. Damn, but it felt good to catch up. We were old friends, but we were also family. We didn't realize how rare that was when we were kids, but now we understood that special bond. After all, you don't get to choose your family; but you get to choose your friends. We were both, and we couldn't help but slightly regret the years that had passed in silence between us.

The talk ranged from childhood to college to work, and back again. We remembered how different our childhoods had been. We probably had some vague notion of it when we were young—Jim was a bit more clean-cut while Sabin had always been more rebellious—but that was as far as it had gone. We saw that the old spark we had as kids was still there—a sort of yin and yang, if that makes sense. If we didn't quite finish each other's sentences, we were close.

But the more surprising thing to us was that we remembered (and cherished) the same things from back home—family, tradition, and lobster. Now, we didn't come up with Cousins

Maine Lobster right there over sake bombs, but we did talk around it. We talked about Jim's backyard and the great times we had there. Compared to our current lives, we missed how simple and peaceful life had been back then. We certainly couldn't have articulated it at the time—we were both pretty blasted by this point in the evening—but the idea came to us that, even if our childhood was gone, we could still recapture some small part of it by working together.

Now, we had no idea what we would do. Although we both worked for companies, we acted like independent contractors. We were accustomed to operating on our own and loved that freedom, even if we were answerable to a boss and all that at the end of the day. As we talked, we both realized we saw that our "perfect jobs" had the same element: working for ourselves, doing what we wanted to do. We realize a lot of people have that dream, so don't think that this was any great flash of insight. But we had made our first step as entrepreneurs. We wanted to work for ourselves and we wanted to work together. Not bad for a night neither one of us can recall in any great detail.

That might have been that. Talking about big dreams is what drinking is for—then the next morning rolls around, bringing with it a wicked headache, and those big dreams die in the sober light of day. Only, this was different. When we awoke the next morning, we discovered that we were ready to delve deeper into our crazy idea to work together. We cracked open a large bag of Cool Ranch Doritos—*the* best hangover cure—and picked up where we left off.

What *could* we do together? That was the big question, but we had no answer for it then. With mouths full of Doritos, we fired up *NHL '94* again, just like the old days, and brainstormed as we played. The next day, Jim flew back to Boston, but it wasn't goodbye. At the very least, we were determined to stay in touch, even if our crazy idea of working together fell apart. But it didn't. Over the next several weeks, we talked often. It wasn't anything too substantial, but it kept the conversation alive and our brains working on a possible solution.

Then one day, Sabin asked the question again: "What do you think we could do together?" For whatever reason, Jim mentioned lobster, as in: "What about lobster?"

## YES, WHAT ABOUT LOBSTER?

It wasn't very inspiring or clear-sighted. It was just a word—an image really. An image of what lobster represented to both of us: Maine, family, home . . . We mulled it over, wondering what in the world we could do with lobster. Open a lobster shack in Maine? That didn't seem like the sort of thing either one of us would have been good at.

But it did get us talking about food. There was a moment when Sabin tossed out the idea of sandwiches, just like the ones we remembered scarfing down in Maine at Amato's. We quickly scratched that. If we didn't know anything about food, we knew less about making Italian-style hoagies. But there we were again, our minds back in Maine. Why?

Neither one of us could've articulated it very well then, but it's clear to us now that what we wanted to *do* was re-create our childhoods. The first half of that was just working together; the second, tougher part was creating a product or service that we could sell. Lobster seemed like the obvious choice, but how would we sell lobster? Mainers have always been a bit tickled by lobster's fancy, elite status outside of our state. Don't get us wrong: we believe lobster is a delicacy, but it's a democratic delicacy. It's a delicacy that is—and should be—enjoyed by all. Yet was there even a market for the sort of lobster fare we had in mind—the lobster we ate in Jim's backyard—outside Maine? Would Californians, for example, want to buy lobster that wasn't served in an expensive restaurant at fifty dollars a pound? We weren't sure yet. But at least we knew that that wasn't the sort of lobster experience we had in mind. The goal wasn't simply to sell lobster—it was to sell *Maine* lobster in the *Maine* way.

The more we talked the clearer the idea became in our minds. We wanted to sell the kind of lobster we ate—and still eat—in Jim's backyard: simple, clean, and delicious. Nothing fussy. We knew we couldn't do this anywhere near New England, because the sort of lobster meal we had in mind was fairly ordinary around there. We had to get far away, and Los Angeles was about as far away from Maine as one could get. So, then we whittled it down to two options. Option number one was to open a restaurant in Los Angeles. But Sabin knew the restaurant business—he had worked in more than a dozen, after all—and opening his own sounded like a bridge too far. Our overhead would be terrible, we would need huge up-front investment, and, finally, Jim couldn't see how he could open a restaurant three thousand miles away from where he lived and worked. Which brought us to option number two: a food truck. This being 2011, food trucks were sort of the hot new thing in the culinary world. We knew about them, particularly Sabin, who saw them all the time scooting around LA. But that was about it.

What was their overhead?

How much did a truck cost?

What was considered a good day in sales?

We didn't know the answers to any of these questions. The idea of the food truck, the two of us palling around LA selling lobster out of a window to Californians who had never tasted Maine lobster before, appealed to us. We would be working together, selling a sample of our childhood that we knew very well. Sure, we knew *nothing* about everything else that goes into a successful food truck, but that didn't bother us. That's an important point for all of you budding entrepreneurs out there:

had we known the complexities of a food truck, we might not
have gotten into the business at all. You'd be surprised how far
ignorance will get you.

Regardless, Sabin promised Jim he would get the answers
to most of these questions. But we should also pause here to mention that Sabin had some misgivings about the whole thing.
While Jim seemed ready to move on from his life in Boston,
Sabin had found enormous success in the real estate industry.
His bosses, Rob and Lio, were Sabin's role models in many
ways. Both immigrants who came to the US to pursue their
own dreams, Rob and Lio defined hard work, commitment,
and, most of all, optimism for Sabin. Rob was from Iran and
had moved to the US to escape the revolution that gripped his
country in the late 1970s, while Lio was from Morocco. They
came together to build a real estate business and started to make
a lot of money doing short sales on foreclosures during the housing downturn. Sabin was one of the first agents they hired—and
it was a great job for the budding actor. His hours were his own,
which allowed him to pursue auditions and other acting gigs
during the day and at night. Before long, Sabin was closing ten
deals a month and managing over fifty listings. He was killing it.

The point is, Sabin wasn't looking for an escape hatch when
Jim landed at LAX that day. Even if he wasn't busy doing the
thing he came to LA to do—act—he knew how lucky he had
gotten meeting up with Rob and Lio. So, when talk with Jim
turned toward starting a venture, Sabin took it all with a grain
of salt. He was very excited to work with his cousin again, but
if things didn't work out, such is life. Sabin also wasn't convinced that opening any food business was a great idea. The
idea for a food truck was more appealing than a restaurant, but
Sabin still kept a cool head about the whole thing.

We had discussed it over the phone a few times and run
some numbers. We figured that to make a food truck worth-
while and not lose money—never mind making money—we

would need to sell fifty to sixty customers (or tickets) a day. It seemed like a lot, but doable. Despite his misgivings, Sabin said he would find out if they were in the ballpark with their sales figures.

How? By talking to the people who operate food trucks. It was a simple enough plan, and so Sabin went to work. As a real estate agent, Sabin was in his car all day anyway, so doing quick stops on the way to and from his properties wasn't a big ordeal. Plus, Sabin loves to schmooze. Had he just starting yammering questions at the guys inside the trucks, he probably would've been told to shove it. At least, we certainly would have done that to some nosy guy bugging us while we're working. But Sabin was a bit subtler, and if Cousins Maine Lobster ever closes, he probably would become a good reporter. He knows how to make people talk.

The number that caused Sabin to reconsider his misgivings about starting a food truck business was 120. As in, he learned from a kid working on a food truck—and not a particularly unique or successful truck—that they sold 120 tickets a day— or twice what we had initially projected needing. If we could pull that off, then we would have a moneymaker on our hands. Sabin's misgiving began to slip away.

But what really brought Sabin on board was Jim's signature determination. He was relentless, using every moment to push Sabin into believing in our crazy idea. Sabin had seen Jim pursue something with single-minded focus before—usually during our *NHL '94* games as kids—but now he was on the receiving end. It was like trying to stand upright in a hurricane. Eventually, Sabin said yes, if only to make Jim shut up. We kid . . . but only a little.

But now Sabin had a vision of selling 120 tickets a day. He was on board, and it was time to tell Jim. Several weeks after Jim's trip to LA, he got a call from Sabin while standing outside a Boston hospital.

"Well?" said Jim.

"We're doing a food truck," said Sabin.

## LESSON
## PURSUE YOUR DREAM WITH THE BEST OF INTENTIONS

The first thing one learns as an entrepreneur is that there is no science to starting a business. After all, science is the pursuit of knowledge through the use of reason. There is very little reason behind starting a business. The urge that makes one want to start something on his or her own is pure passion—or at least it should be. What moves you? What inspires you? What do you do when you aren't working? These are the simple ways you discover your passion. And whatever your answer to those questions, that's what you should be doing as an entrepreneur.

Now, we said at the start of this that there are those entrepreneurs who have excelled at building businesses from the very beginning. For them, the creation of something new is the juice. We aren't like this, and we doubt you are either. Maybe after you build your first company, you'll want to build another, and we wish you luck. This type of entrepreneur has to look at starting a new business *dispassionately*. They aren't so much looking to turn their passion into a day job as they are looking to fill a void in a particular market—and make gobs of money doing it. They study industries, markets, tech trends, and read the *The Wall Street Journal* front to back, searching for that opportunity. Folks like this are very good at starting businesses this way. Like we said, they have a knack for it and they approach it very scientifically.

We were all passion, with very little reason. The amount of reason we put into our little idea was just enough to believe that it could work. Everything else was about turning our passion into something that we could market. In a word, we're talking about money here. We wanted to make sure that we stood a reasonable chance of making a buck or two, but we had no intention of becoming rich from it. Yes, we all need money, but that wasn't what drove us. What pushed us to start this crazy adventure was the passion we both shared for our childhood memories—the way life should be, eating lobster with family and friends, on a gorgeous summer day off the coast of Maine. *That's* what we wanted to sell. *That* was our passion. And you should notice something more in that: we basically did this for ourselves. If there was a selfish motive in our thinking at the time, that was it. We wanted to re-create Jim's backyard for *us*.

We had both been in the real working world long enough to know what we loved—and what we missed. Seeing each other again in LA was more than a reunion of old cousins; it was a brief but powerful step backward in time. We were kids again, if only for a moment. But that moment lasted long enough that we were greedy for it to come again. The food truck was simply a way for us to get back to that time. It would be our DeLorean. And that was the origin of Cousins Maine Lobster— two regular guys who missed being kids.

So, this is our first lesson to you, because it's a lesson we never want to forget: make sure your dreams are worth pursuing and then go after them with the best of intentions. Family, happiness, service, joy—these were the things that went into our absurd dream of working together selling lobster out of a truck. But we know they were the right things because they are still what get us out of bed every morning. Five years later, we're still trying to get back to Jim's backyard.

# Questions and Answers

"Holy shit, that's ours!"

This is what Sabin said while we were in his car driving down Interstate 405 in Los Angeles on the afternoon of April 27, 2012. He was pointing to the big black food truck ahead of us, with our logo of a red lobster inside an outline of the state of Maine and the words COUSINS MAINE LOBSTER emblazoned on the side. It was a beautiful sight and Sabin was right: it was ours.

What a feeling.

We were on our way to our very first location. It was launch day, the culmination of nearly six months of planning, preparation, hard work, and endless worry. And for a brief moment on the 405, we were able to appreciate how far we had come— but only for a moment. In just a few minutes we would arrive at our first location, late and totally unprepared.

For now, we felt more alive and fulfilled than we had ever been in our lives. What had started as a slightly inebriated conversation between two long-lost cousins was now a real business. We owned that beautiful black truck; we had raised the money to purchase it and stock it. There were employees on that truck, our employees. There was real Maine lobster on that truck, the very lobster we ate as kids.

Like anything that is created, the final product often hides much of what went into its creation. Our customers are only supposed to see a streamlined, flawless operation that delivers them delicious lobster with a touch of Maine on the side. That's the final product. But the making of it—the sausage making, so to speak—that's the ugly part. Customers don't care about that, unless you're reading this, in which case we assume you do. And like any creation, the final product is so much more than what your customers, your readers, or members of your audience see.

Our dreams were on that truck. Even though neither of us was ready at that moment to make Cousins Maine Lobster our full-time job, we were both thinking about it. We had come this far, and we had had fun doing it, certainly more fun than we had anticipated. Well, maybe "fun" isn't the right word. Is training fun? Is practice fun? Not usually, although there are fun moments. Rather, you train and you practice so that when it's game time, you can win. The training makes the victory *worth it*. And that's how we felt driving down the highway. The sight of our truck, filled with our dreams, our work, our sweat (more of which would be spilled in the hours ahead)—this was like our big victory. We had done it. Jim's backyard, once just a childhood memory of the good ol' days, had come alive; it was rolling down the 405 with cupboards full of buns, whoopie pies, and a refrigerator full of butter and Maine's own delicacy.

How did that happen? How the hell did we get here from a booze-filled night eating sushi reminiscing about the old days?

# LET'S START A BUSINESS!

Looking back, it was a mess. We were two guys without a clue in the world about what we were doing. It was also fun, but in that living-on-the-edge kind of way. Starting a business from nothing is probably the best experience you'll never want to have again. The memories are great, we can laugh now, but good Lord, it was nuts.

How does one start a business? This isn't some philosophical question. It was real for us. We had no idea. What do we do first? Do we register as an LLC? Do we buy a truck? Do we learn how to make lobster rolls? Do we build a web site? The questions seemed endless. At first, we just had a dozen to answer. Before long, we had hundreds. We couldn't seem to answer one without raising two or three more. It was like whack-a-mole.

The moment Sabin called Jim to tell him that we were doing a food truck, our lives changed completely. We didn't realize it then. It was like our lives were altered ever so slightly, so slightly that we hardly noticed at the time. But the farther we traveled down our new path, the larger the divergence became. And each question we answered, the farther away from our old lives we went. Each problem was like a rung in the ladder. To solve it, we had to keep climbing.

We're going to try to break this down simply for our readers, but realize that it was anything but simple at the time. We approached everything haphazardly, without much direction or forethought. Eventually, we were able to streamline things into something resembling a coherent start-up strategy, but in the beginning, there was darkness. We wouldn't see the light for many, many months.

## THE TRUCK

If you're going to have a food truck business, the first thing you need is a food truck. Don't laugh. This was seriously how our thinking went at the time. This was our "strategy." But so what? We had a tangible problem we had to solve. This rather elementary notion gave us our first task. How much does a food truck cost and where can we buy one? Jim did some research online and started calling truck manufacturers all over the country, from California to Florida. The difference in quotes was pretty large, but it all came down to how tricked out we wanted our truck to be. New or used? The best equipment, "good enough" equipment, or bare bones? Cheap and practical—these were our watchwords. Jim could hear his father in his head looking at all the options, saying over and over again, "cheap and practical, cheap and practical." Even then, we learned that a used truck with no equipment from a respected manufacturer would cost between $75,000 and $80,000. You could say this was our first "Oh, fuck" moment.

We were each prepared to put down $25,000 of our own money toward the business, but that was all we could afford. The rest would have to come from a bank loan, which presented us with our second "Oh, fuck" moment: we had to put together a business plan that would convince someone to finance a food truck. You should understand that none of this was apparent to us at the time. We didn't have a plan. Instead, we had a series of problems for which we had to find solutions. It went something like this:

Problem one: buy a food truck. Solution: get financing. Problem two: find someone who will finance us. Solution: create a business plan.

This is how we operated at the time. Problem, solution;

problem, solution. And we almost gave up on this very first problem. After putting in twelve-to-fourteen-hour days at his sales job, Jim spent his evenings at a Starbucks across the street and worked on a business plan that he hoped would entice some investors. It didn't. (Jim blames the lattes.) Over the period of a month or so, Jim reached out to some thirty investors, and none of them were interested. No investor was willing to take a risk on two guys without food experience or business credit, who, by the way, wanted a three-year lending deal. Eventually, Jim did find a group of investors, but the process was demoralizing. It exposed us to all the things that we hadn't considered when deciding to start a company. It was like we thought we had to climb a simple hill, only to watch the clouds roll away and reveal Mount Everest.

Financing done, we made a deal with an LA truck builder, who would have our first truck ready in three months. We didn't know that the truck would be several weeks late, but there was one bit of fortuitous news. We learned that the truck we had bought was an old Cape Cod Potato Chips truck. Sure, it was Massachusetts, but close enough.

## THE FOOD

The next part of the food truck business is, of course, *food*. We'll get to how we obtained our lobster supply in a moment. Before we could even think about that, however, we needed to know that we could make our signature dish, the lobster roll. We should add that we weren't that concerned about getting it wrong. Our goal wasn't anything fancy; in fact, we just wanted to serve the lobster rolls we ate as kids. As we mentioned previously, the lobster roll holds the same place in the lobster bake as does the turkey sandwich after Thanksgiving. It's what you make out of leftovers—and in some cases, it's better than the original meal.

Well, why the lobster roll and not the whole lobster? Fair question, but with a good answer. First, buying whole Maine lobster would be prohibitively expensive. The biggest problem with lobsters is that you need to ship them while they're still alive, then you need to keep them alive until you drop them in the boiling pot of water right before serving. The whole process, from the shipping to the storing to the serving, just doesn't work with a food truck. Or, perhaps it's more accurate to say that it was beyond our means at the time. Moreover, the numbers just didn't work for us then. For example, a two-pound lobster only yields about half a pound of meat; a one-and-a-quarter pound lobster yields a quarter pound of meat. But you don't pay for the meat; you pay for the weight of the live lobster, or gross weight, as it's called. As much as we would have loved to re-create the Maine lobster bake, it wasn't feasible.

So, that left us buying fresh lobster meat wholesale. The choice of the lobster roll as the signature dish—and an award-winning dish, it would turn out—was relatively simple: a lobster roll is quick and easy to make, requiring few extra ingredients—a bun, butter, and lemon. We could churn this delicious little sandwich out by the dozens, and not need an experienced chef on the truck either. Easy, simple, yet we still had no real experience making them.

But our mothers did.

In what would turn out to be our preferred R&D method, we decided to go home to the Tselikis and Lomac families and turn Jim's kitchen into a lab. With pounds of lobster meat, buns, and butter at our disposal, we learned the art of the lobster roll from the best, Julie Tselikis and Jeannie Lomac. In fact, the whole family got in on the R&D. The beauty of the lobster roll is that less is more; the lobster meat is the star and you need to let it do its thing. So, our job was to make sure we used just the right amount of butter and the right bun. Everything else should fall into place.

Now, of course there is a *little* bit more to it than that. But we can't give away all the secrets to our award-winning lobster roll, now can we? The point is that it depends on the quality of our lobster—and we knew one thing above everything else. Our lobster, its quality, *would be the best in the business.*

## The Personnel

This was a tough problem to solve. We knew that the two of us couldn't run a food truck without help. We also knew that we couldn't be on the truck all the time. After all, we both had day jobs and Jim's was three thousand miles away. But how does one go about hiring employees for a food truck? We discussed multiple approaches to this issue and decided, essentially, to let someone else do it. Specifically, we put an ad up on Craigslist asking for a food truck manager, listing some of the skills we thought applicable. Once hired, this manager would oversee hiring the right employees for the truck.

And that's basically what happened—and we learned a ton because of it. Slowly, the employees were added and we took them through our rigorous training process. Just kidding: there wasn't a training process at all. We trusted that our manager had hired the right people—and we left it at that. We shouldn't have. We've learned since that the most important piece of your business is your workforce. This might seem obvious, but we use the word "important" very literally here. *So much depends on the quality of your team.* It's as simple as that. Yet putting together the right team is anything but simple. There is an entire field of psychology devoted to personnel management. Large companies have human resources departments for a reason. It's all because finding and managing a team is really freaking hard.

And this is an important lesson that every would-be entrepreneur should know before diving in. You are only one person (or maybe two). In the beginning, you will have to do everything, wear every hat. But you won't do that forever and there will come a point, assuming you're successful, when you stop doing what you love and start managing people to do it for you. This isn't an easy transition, and we'll explore it more in the next chapter. But understand that being a boss of a team—being responsible for their performance—is probably the hardest thing you will do as an entrepreneur. You might discover that you hate it or that you aren't good at it. That's not a failure at all. Not everyone should be a manager.

When we started hiring our first employees, we didn't know what we needed. We do now. But our knowledge wasn't gained without a lot of pain. Now, we can talk with someone for a few minutes and know immediately if they have what it takes to work for Cousins Maine Lobster. No one can teach you that. You certainly can't learn that in a book. You will only learn that through experience, through mistakes, through failures.

But you need to start somewhere. We did. And we managed to have eight employees on launch day. We had neglected to teach them anything they needed to know about making lobster rolls—or using the grill, if you remember. Given all that, they did an awesome job.

## THE SUPPLY

Next problem: How do we buy a lot of Maine lobster? Seriously, that was our question. We had no idea how to go about it, a fact made painfully clear when Jim decided to drive up to Maine one day to find the answer. All either of us knew about lobster was that you could walk up to any lobster shack on a Maine pier and usually find your fill—whether it was one or several dozen. That's how Jim's parents bought lobster for the bakes in the backyard. We never even wondered where restaurants buy their lobster meat. It all comes from the same place, right? So, Jim's plan to visit a local lobster shack seemed like an obvious solution.

Now, Jim knows that the look on Derek the Shack Owner's face, when he saw this young punk asking about sourcing hundreds of pounds of lobster, was bewilderment. But at the time, Jim thought Derek was just interested in a pretty sweet business deal—perhaps overwhelmed that such a great deal had landed in his lap. Right. What was probably going through Derek's mind was, "This kid has no fucking idea what he's doing."

Tough but fair. Jim didn't.

Still, Derek offered to ship about thirty pounds of lobster to LA every day. Not bad for a single truck—except his price was ridiculous. As it should be. Derek didn't have the margins to ship so much lobster across the country. That wasn't his business. He would certainly try it, if this crazy kid could pony up the cash. Fortunately, Jim balked at the price and decided to try another way.

And as usual with these things, the solution was staring Jim in the face. Almost literally. The solution was Annie, Jim's sister. It's a bit absurd that it took us so long to go ask Annie for help. Why? Oh, because Annie has worked in the lobster industry in one way or another for nearly a decade, that's why. We know: we're morons. In any case, at the time Annie was working for the Maine Lobstermen's Association, which advocates for a sustainable lobster resource and for the fishermen and communities that depend on it. It stands to reason that Annie would know a thing or two about where to buy wholesale lobster.

She did. She encouraged Jim to come with her to the Seafood Expo North America in Boston. The convention, held every March, is the largest seafood exposition in North America, where thousands of suppliers and buyers from around the world gather. That we had to be told that such a thing existed—by Annie no less—just goes to show that, again, we had no idea what we were doing.

In fact, that's exactly what Annie told Jim. She didn't admonish us for the business idea, which she thought was pretty good. But she was pretty sure that we were in over our heads. She even said to Jim one day, "I think you have no idea what you're doing." That's verbatim.

Tough but fair. We didn't.

The first thing Jim learned at the Expo was that the seafood world was far larger than he had ever imagined. To be honest, we didn't even know there was a lobster industry outside of Maine. Jim spent a half day just talking to other suppliers, learning as much as he could about how the supply chain worked, whether it was lobster, crab, or fish. Eventually, Annie led Jim to the Maine Lobster Pavilion, where a lot of the state's wholesalers had gathered. It was here that Jim first met our suppliers—our first and only suppliers. It was just a quick introduction at first, but Jim continued the conversation later at a happy hour on the wharf.

A deal wasn't struck then. Deals are never struck on first meetings in the lobster world. Jim barely talked about our business model at all. Instead, the suppliers asked him where we were from, our parents, what schools we attended—the usual small talk, but there was a catch. Jim was being judged. Family, home, background—these things mean something to Mainers. They say a lot about a person who otherwise is unknown. Those things don't mean much anymore in the modern world, for better or worse. But in Maine, very few outsiders are accepted into such a native industry as lobstering.

We didn't know it at the time, but a company's relationship with its Maine lobster supplier is special, almost sacred. And like any relationship worth having, it takes time to develop.

Annie said as much to Jim, who finally began to understand the world he had only just entered. It was a world far larger and more complex than anything either of us had considered. The more we learned, the more we understood our own ignorance. We were from Maine and we thought that was enough—enough for us, for our customers, and for our suppliers.

It wasn't enough. Lobstermen, from the fishermen to the wholesalers, don't mess around with hacks. It doesn't matter if you're from Cape Elizabeth or Scarborough. It doesn't matter if you're a millionaire or a world-renowned chef or the president of the United States. They've heard it all before and they've been burned by it all before. If you want to do business with these guys, you need to bring more to the table than cash. A lot of people have cash. Few people have integrity, and even fewer have the interests of Maine and its communities at heart.

During our *Shark Tank* episode, Kevin O'Leary— "Mr. Wonderful" himself—asked us a tough but reasonable question: "What's to keep me from doing what you're doing?" In other words, what couldn't a rich guy like O'Leary buy a bunch of trucks and sell Maine lobster just like us? What makes us so special?

Answer: our suppliers. Kevin O'Leary—or anyone for that matter—couldn't do what we do because they don't have the suppliers. More to the point, they wouldn't get the suppliers, no matter how much money they threw at them. This is the one eternal truth about the Maine lobster industry: suppliers only work with those they can trust. It's about whether their buyer will stick with them through the lean years as much as the good years. Too many of them have been taken by flashy, money-obsessed suits who promise them the world only to bolt the moment the price of lobster rises a buck or more. The suppliers are then left with a surplus of product which they can't just off-load. They must eat the cost.

Jim would spend the next several weeks traveling back and forth to Maine to grow the relationship with our supplier. Eventually a deal was struck, and it wasn't just because of our irresistible charm. As Annie explained to us, the lobster industry was looking for a business like ours. When the housing bubble burst in 2008, it took a lot of industries down with it. Lobster, as a luxury food item, was no exception. In tough economic times, the last things people want to buy are lobsters at forty bucks a pound. People aren't going to the nice restaurants anymore, and those nice restaurants aren't buying as much Maine lobster. The industry took a huge hit.

It became apparent to nearly everyone involved in the industry that Maine lobster had an image problem. It had become the Rolex of fancy food. People outside of New England only bought lobster on those special nights out. It was a bit ironic, because in Maine lobster is more like a Casio—dependable, uncomplicated, and versatile—lobster is food for any occasion, not just the big ones. The challenge was to maintain lobster's status as a delicacy, but one that is available to anyone. There isn't much that the lobstermen could do about the price—the fancy restaurants do give it a markup, but lobster is just plain expensive—but perhaps they could do something about how it's served.

Then along come two guys who have a plan to serve lobster out of a truck.

Any successful business has had its fair share of good luck along the way. This was our first big break. We just happened to come along when the industry was eager to diversify lobster's eating audience. This allowed us to obtain suppliers who maybe otherwise wouldn't have taken a risk on us. It also meant we were welcomed by the industry, accepted almost. It was like these hard-boiled lobstermen said to us, "Good, now go do what you say you'll do. Make us proud."

It was another great moment for us. We had made our first

strides in an industry we have come to embrace as our part of our mission.

Now we just had to deliver.

Which is a long way of saying: thank you, Annie.

# COMING TOGETHER

One day you don't have a business, the next day you do. At what point that happens is a bit of a mystery. Was it when we decided to work together on a food truck? Did it happen when Sabin registered our LLC or put together our first web site? Or how about when Jim, struggling to think of what to put on a PowerPoint presentation he was developing, wrote "Cousins Maine Lobster" at the top of the first slide? It was supposed to be a placeholder until we thought of something better. Or maybe you don't have a business until you make your first buck. At whatever stage it happens, the way you get there is one big convoluted mess.

It's kind of the same way Maine became a state. After the turbulent colonization period, Maine found itself on the outbreak of the Revolutionary War essentially under the authority of Massachusetts. Unlike how other colonies became states, Maine never had a single governing identity. It was a collection of tough folks living on a beautiful, if at times inhospitable, coast scraping together a living farming a few feet of fertile land and fishing the sea for everything else. The families who lived there thought they owned it. But through the vagaries of two centuries of English rule, the real owners of Maine were wealthy businessmen congregated around Boston. These so-called proprietors laid claim to vast stretches of Maine land, to the point that the government in Boston essentially decided to annex the whole damn thing. No one asked the Mainers.

Not even independence from Britain brought Maine any real freedom. The landowners in Boston only pressed their property claims that much harder. Meanwhile, when America and Britain were at it again in the War of 1812, Maine's Boston masters didn't lift a finger to defend their province from British invasion. Not even a British occupation could rouse Boston legislators from going to the aid of their countrymen. As one historian later wrote, "No event in the previous history of the union of Massachusetts and Maine so blatantly revealed the extent to which the interests of Maine could be sacrificed to those of Massachusetts proper."[4]

If New England now is fairly united in its identity—particularly around its sports teams—it's probably only because everyone wants to forget the past. Massachusetts' treatment of Maine in the generation after the Revolution was pretty despicable. The British would eventually leave (again) and Mainers would rebuild (again). This time, however, Massachusetts discovered their backwoods brethren weren't as easy to govern as before. A fever of statehood had taken hold among a populace that had had enough of being the pawns of more powerful interests. New politicians in the Massachusetts legislature also helped Maine's statehood cause. But in the end, it was Mainers themselves who took their futures into their own hands and voted to go their own way, entirely free of any outside influence beyond the new federal government in Washington, D.C.

On March 15, 1820, Maine became the twenty-third state in the new nation. Forty years after the rest of the Union, Maine had achieved its independence. But Mainers would soon discover, as all entrepreneurs do, that creating something new is one thing, while sustaining it, growing it, is something entirely different.

## LESSON
# A MILLION LITTLE QUESTIONS

It was late on the night of April 27, 2012, and we were in Sabin's car on our way home from our first location. We stunk like lobster and sweat. The whirlwind that had been our launch day had yet to fully dissipate. It echoed in our heads like after you leave a loud rock concert. We were dazed, but also strangely content. Jim smiled as he remembered how Sabin, moving frantically in the food truck, just kept asking him, "Dude, when are you moving out here? When are you moving out here?" Sabin knew he would never forget how Jim told one of our brand-new employees—who, let's remember, hadn't been trained at all—to "fuck the scales, just eyeball it," in reference to putting the right amount of lobster meat on the bun.

It could have been the motto for our first day. We just went with it. Nothing seemed to have gone right when we arrived, yet everything worked out. We had been a success. Our customers had loved us. When we look back at how we arrived at the end of our first day, knowing that there would certainly be a second day, we asked ourselves what we did right—especially since it felt like we had done so much wrong.

We've since discovered that our greatest asset in those early, start-up days was our own ignorance. More precisely, we knew we didn't know what we were doing. This provided us a with a good dose of humility. We weren't afraid to start simply. It doesn't get any simpler than asking, "How do we buy a food truck?" Humility also allowed us to accept mistakes and failures. After all, *we didn't know what we were doing.* Of course we fucked up! Of course Jim walked up to a lobster shack asking if he could buy hundreds of pounds of lobster. Of course we drove to our first location without having trained any of our employees on making lobster rolls.

Most of all, humility gave us the freedom to ask questions. We asked them all the time. Simple, stupid, insightful. It didn't matter. We saw no reason to fake expertise in front of others, and especially to ourselves. When Jim spoke with our suppliers at the seafood convention in Boston, the best thing he did was be completely honest. The experts didn't care that he knew nothing about how to procure lobster; they wanted to know if this guy was sincere, if he cared about what he wanted to do. Everything else can be learned, except authenticity and honesty.

So, when you're starting out, don't make the mistake of thinking you need to know everything. It's OK to know nothing, just so long as that pushes you to ask questions. Ask anyone you think knows more than you—and in the beginning, that will be everyone. You'll learn, just as we did.

# 4

# The Maine Way

September 14, 2012

Gary and Lee,

It is with a heavy heart that I email this two-week notice of my resignation. I have worked for you guys since the summer of 2008 and I can honestly say it has been everything I could have asked for and much more. When you interviewed me in your corner office in Waltham you stared me in the eyes and said, "This is where most guys end up, not where they start out of college." And while I firmly believed in myself, you guys gave me the opportunity of a lifetime that most college graduates never get.

It is an understatement to say that I have learned an enormous amount from Surgi [Stryker Corporation] and the two of you. From sales to relationship building, product knowledge, and ultimately how to have fun with what you do for a living, I cannot thank you enough.

I hope you both feel the same way about me,

and how I have produced for the company. Just as you guys presented me with an opportunity in 2008, I now have before me another opportunity that I cannot turn down. I invested in a company with my cousin. At the time, it was nothing more than that—a chance to earn another stream of revenue with no direct involvement on my part and one that did not distract me or take from my productivity at Surgi. Things have changed since then and an opportunity has arisen that I need to try for myself. It may end up being something I regret, but while I am young and do not have family obligations just yet, I think it is important to take a shot at it, just as you both did many years ago with Surgi. I can tell you this—I hope that someday I am as successful at what I create as you two have been.

You have provided me with many tools, lessons, and attributes that I believe will make me successful wherever I go. I never like to burn bridges, especially not with those who have been so good to me. You two fit that mold. Maybe someday our paths will cross again but until then I know I need to try this new venture.

There are no words to thank you for all that you have done for me, opportunities you have presented me, and skills you have taught me. Thank you for 3.5 phenomenal years. I will always be a member of team Surgi and wish you and the group continued success, prosperity, and good health.

Best,
Jimmy/Z

Meanwhile, three thousand miles away, Sabin's bosses, Rob and Lio, wondered why the hell Sabin was still coming into the office. Not that he was coming in all that much those days after we had taped *Shark Tank* but before it had aired. Always our greatest cheerleaders, Rob and Lio were constantly pushing us—well, mostly Sabin—to grow the company faster than we would have ever dared. If it sounds odd that Sabin's bosses wanted Sabin to spend less time doing the job they paid him to do, well, just keep reading.

When it came, Sabin's departure from real estate was less dramatic than Jim's resignation, but no less significant. By September 2012, we had committed ourselves to Cousins Maine Lobster. It was no longer a hobby. We had taken the final step of the entrepreneur; we had gone all in. The last vestiges of our old lives, the ones we had lived when we met over sushi almost a year earlier, were gone.

Well, that isn't quite true. Rather, we should say that we had come home, we had returned to Maine, to our roots—even if we were still three thousand miles away.

## THE FIRST CALL

On our first day of business, we made $6,500. It was a tidy sum, and looked especially good spread out all over the floor of Sabin's apartment that night. We stared at it, trying to take it all in—the money and the moment. It's not that we had never had that much money; it's that we had never seen that much money in bills and coins (although we also had used the mobile payment app, Square). Who does anymore? It's all digits on your bank statement these days. Which is just one reason we were in such a giddy mood that night.

We had made our first money selling authentic Maine lobster

just being ourselves. Or, more accurately, we had succeeded our first day out by doing it the Maine Way.

What is the Maine way? It's a commitment to the people and values that make Maine more than a state. The previous six months or so would have been for nothing if we had rolled onto our first location having compromised the values of our home and its people. If, for example, we had sold anything other than 100 percent Maine lobster, we would have failed, no matter how much of that lobster we might have sold. If we had been anything less than 100 percent honest with our suppliers, then we would have been no better than all those who had sought to exploit Maine and its resources over the centuries.

Staring at all that money, we felt like we were two guys who owned a lobster shack on the coast. This was our day's haul. This would change quite soon, but we're happy now that everything from the moment we rolled up on-site to the way we spilled the money onto Sabin's floor had been raw and real that first day. It provided us with a goal, or, rather, an aspiration: that no matter what happened, we would always do it the Maine way.

The feeling was only momentary, but the commitment was supposed to last as long as Cousins Maine Lobster. How could we know that our pledge would be put to the test only days later? But that's when *Shark Tank* called.

Food truck owners who haven't been in business a week aren't supposed to appear on national television. So, when the call came, we were at a loss for words. The producer explained that going on the show would be a great opportunity for us, regardless of whether we partnered with one of the sharks. We didn't disagree. It seemed like we had been offered a golden ticket that would lead to instant business success. Why wouldn't we immediately jump at this opportunity?

Now, we could say the right thing here: how we weren't prepared to give up a percentage of our business; how we were committed to growing naturally before being guided by some corporate suit. Those things aren't necessarily wrong, but they aren't the real reasons either. This business, this hobby, this food truck—what was it?

We didn't know. Not only that, but we didn't know what we *wanted it to be*. Yes, we had some semblance of a company now, if we understand a company to be anything that sells a product or service. That box was checked. But that was about it. And if we couldn't answer this simple question—"What do we want Cousins Maine Lobster to be?"—then how in the world did we expect to go on television and sell it to America?

However, we knew what we didn't want to be. We didn't want to be a joke or a flash in the pan. We didn't want to over-extend ourselves too soon and jeopardize what we had built. We understood that we had started something that was extremely fragile. Not only were we—its creators and owners—new to everything, but so was this idea of providing a delicacy like Maine lobster to the people. Our first few locations had proved successful. So? Did that mean that there was a taste for lobster rolls all over America? Absolutely not.

At least, this was the voice of reason in our heads, telling us to take it easy, to go slow. Our emotions were all over the place, fueled in no small part by our apparent runaway success and no sleep. Those first few weeks were a bit of a blur, but we were selling out at a lot of our locations. Early customer reviews on sites like Yelp drove the curious to check out this new truck selling lobster rolls. Our conversations with customers told us that the whole notion of Maine lobster was almost foreign to Southern Californians, who otherwise consider themselves quite the gourmands. Heck, even Maine was strange to them, as our first logo revealed. It showed a lobster inside an outline of the state's borders. We stopped counting how many customers asked why the lobster was inside a misshapen box.

"Is that a lobster trap?"

"No, um, it's Maine."

"Oh."

This was quite funny, particularly for Sabin, who had had a foot in both worlds, California and Maine, since he was a boy. But Jim was a stranger in a strange land. He is a Yankee through and through, with Yankee values and attitudes. The Californians loved it and ate up our Maine sensibilities just as heartily as our lobster. Being the novelty in a place like LA can pay off quite well, but not forever. Eventually, the novel becomes the ordinary. So, you better have something more to offer than your New England charm (which is a bit of an oxymoron). We wanted to believe we did, but couldn't be certain. In any case, *Shark Tank* seemed like an early test for us.

In fact, it's because *Shark Tank* had been so wildly successful that we were hesitant when the opportunity first arose. We weren't ready for that limelight. We weren't ready to answer the sharks' questions. And we didn't know what we would do even if, by some miracle, we inked a deal. But we were tempted. Who wouldn't be? Looking back, were our initial concerns correct? Absolutely, even more than we realized at the time.

The night after our very first food truck service we sat there staring at the pile of money and we thought we had made it. Sure, there was a lot left to do, but most of the real hard stuff—the truck, the suppliers, the employees—those things had been done (or so we thought). Now it was all about finding the time between our busy jobs to get the truck out a few days a week.

Once again, we knew nothing.

# OH, RIGHT, MONEY MATTERS

Let's start first with that pile of money on Sabin's floor. Even though we hadn't paid our employees yet, even though we hadn't paid off our bank loans yet, and even though we hadn't considered any expenses beyond the first week, we honestly thought this was all our money. In fact, none of it was ours. All of it—all $6,500—was spoken for already. We just didn't look at it that way.

The next day, Sabin took the pile of cash and deposited it in our business bank account. That was the sum total of our financial planning: make money, deposit money in account. At some level, we understood that we had payments to make, but it never occurred to us to that this would be any more complicated than writing checks to our employees, our suppliers, and our bank. Someone needs to get paid? Here's a check. Loan payment comes in? Here's a check.

That's how children run a lemonade stand. It's not how two reasonably intelligent guys should go about running a business. Remember in a previous chapter how we said we didn't get into this business for money? We can reveal to you now that while those sorts of high-minded ideals are wonderful, they cannot be taken literally. You might not care about money, but your business certainly does. So, in case we have to clarify the point, take an interest in money, if only to know how it works in your business. It's the lifeblood, constantly flowing, providing needed nutrients and oxygen to all parts of your business. Your job, particularly when just starting out, is make sure the money keeps flowing in the right way, to the right parts, in just the right amount. We failed to learn this lesson early on, mostly because neither of us had any interest in finance.

And had we gone on like that, essentially two morons who couldn't be bothered to learn the first thing about finances, then we wouldn't have lasted a year. Cousins Maine Lobster might have ended quietly, slowly succumbing to the inevitable drip, drip, drip of expenses. Or suddenly, as in, one day we look at our bank statement to discover we have no money left. Having been on *Shark Tank*, we've heard stories from previous contestants whose businesses collapsed not long after their episode aired. More often than not, the reason is that they neglected their finances.

They neglected them because they had been lulled to sleep by sales. One of the first things we learned as entrepreneurs is that sales don't equal success. It's a hard idea to wrap your head around. You mean product could be flying off the shelves—or out a truck window—and yet things are going badly? That doesn't make sense. But sales can be an illusion, a very dangerous illusion. If you don't know any better, sales can make you lazy.

Sales give you a false sense of progress. Like us, you might believe that that money in the cash register at the end of the day is yours. It isn't. Most of it belongs to someone else; you are just the middleman. The only dollars that are yours are those left over after everyone else has been paid. It's usually a very small amount. Even then, those leftovers might not be yours for very long. You might need to pump that money—the lifeblood— back into the company's body to buy new equipment, to hire another employee, to add another product. Point is, just because your company is making money doesn't mean you are.

In our case, we were selling $3,000 to $5,000 of product a day in those early weeks. (We quickly learned our first day's sum was a very good day.) We were working our butts off, but doing next to nothing that resembled financial management. In our amateur heads, we didn't need any help because we were *just* a single food truck. We convinced ourselves that our humble goal—just to be happy running a single food truck—would somehow excuse us from the grown-up task of learning how to use a spreadsheet.

Fortunately, Jim's father, Steve, stepped in to save our asses. It wasn't by design. We didn't decide one day that we should bring someone on to help with finances. We *thought* we were already doing that. Steve's involvement was far more coincidental and it couldn't have come soon enough. It happened when both of us were back home, for one reason or another. Being a loving father, Steve had taken an interest in his son and nephew's little venture, but as a businessman, he had his concerns. Those concerns were raised at the dinner table one evening.

The inquisition began innocently enough.

"So, what are your operating expenses?" Steve asked us. We mumbled some round numbers off the tops of our heads. Steve's eyebrow arched ever so slightly.

"And what about your interest and tax expenses?" Oh, right, taxes . . . and interest. Those are important things to consider, we said. That eyebrow moved up higher.

"Tell me, boys, when's the last time you did a P&L?"

To which Sabin blurted out, "What's a P&L?"

That did it. We spent the next several hours taking Steve through Cousins Maine Lobster's financial management routine, which, as you already know, amounted to depositing our sales in a bank account and writing checks. Steve's informal involvement as Cousins Maine Lobster's chief financial officer began that very evening. At first his work started simply, like explaining to us that "P&L" stood for "profit and loss statement." (We're not kidding here; we had to be told that.) Before long Steve was running us through the bare essentials of financial management, shaking his head the entire way. More importantly, he articulated the dire consequences of poor financial management. You could say that early on his consultation was along the lines of "if you teach a man to fish . . ." He was trying to help us understand the basics, so that when we went back to LA, we could start to put our finances in order.

We did, to a point. But we soon learned another important entrepreneurial lesson: if you stink at something, don't do it. It's not worth your time to do something badly. You have to wear many hats in the early days of your business. This is tiring but also a very valuable experience—like earning your MBA in the school of hard knocks. While wearing all these hats— sales, marketing, personnel management, finances—you'll quickly learn which ones you are good at and which ones you suck at. We quickly learned that we both sucked at finances, even after Steve gave us the crash course. We were hopeless.

But we were also very lucky. Seeing the mathematical incompetence in his own flesh and blood, Steve expanded his role from consultant to financial advisor. He didn't let us off the hook entirely, but he took over a lot of the heavy financial lifting, especially in those early days. It should go without saying that there wouldn't have been a *Shark Tank* appearance without Steve all but forcing us to get our finances in order. People to this day tell us how impressed they were with our coolheaded ability to answer the sharks' financial questions. The *only reason* we were able to do that is because of Steve.

In terms of affordable financial advisors, it doesn't get any better than hiring your father. Until he starts to increase his fees, which is exactly what Steve did. Sure, his role in the company had begun to expand, which, had he been anyone other than Jim's dad, would have necessitated a raise, but, come on! He's family!

"Shit doesn't come for free," said Steve, when Jim asked about the increase in charges. Damn it, but he's absolutely right. The reason you do so much when you first start out is because it's cheaper. You also don't really trust anyone to do it for you. So, if you're going to hand over something as consequential as your financial management, then you better be prepared to pay for it. You're not just paying for the job to get done; you're also paying for it to get done by someone you trust.

One last note here before moving on from finances. Perhaps the best thing Steve helped us learn is how to simplify the concept of financial *planning*. It's not just about knowing where the company is today, but where it will be—where you want it to be—in a month, two months, or a year. If you understand your finances, then you can map out your future to a fairly precise degree. For us, we began to project how much lobster meat we needed over a certain period, which allowed us to secure the appropriate funds from the bank to procure the meat (if we didn't have the ready cash), then buy the inventory. Rinse and repeat.

This level of planning requires that you've been in business long enough to know your business at a very intimate level. We weren't operating this way early on, but Steve helped us get there. His contribution was crucial. Buying lobster meat, the price of which can fluctuate greatly, is a hazard of our business. It's what drives so many others out of the business, in fact. When the price of lobster suddenly skyrockets, as it does from time to time, a business owner is faced with only a few terrible options. What usually happens is that the business stops buying the lobster altogether, hanging the Maine supplier out to dry.

We can't do that. There is no circumstance that would make us abandon our supplier or shift to anything other than 100 percent Maine lobster. But for us to do business like that requires a very careful balance of finances and inventory. If we know when the lobster prices usually skyrocket, we can put that into our planning efforts. This has allowed us to weather the storms that constantly rock the industry. It's not always smooth sailing, but we are dead serious when we say that we wouldn't have lasted our first season if Steve didn't smack us upside the head.

"Shit doesn't come free." Ain't that the truth?

# WHEN THE BALL STARTS MOVING

Finances weren't our only problem in those days. In fact, we hardly considered them a problem at all until Steve had to ruin the party. Bigger things were on our minds, like how to juggle a business with our day jobs. This was especially troubling to Jim, who, let's remember, still lived in Boston. He had taken a week off for the launch, but that week was about to end. Yet the truck was doing great business, far better than we had expected. Our inventory was good but we needed more, not to mention that both of us needed to go out on the truck to each location. We were very far from letting go just yet.

So Jim made the decision to extend his time off by another week. But after that, he had exhausted his vacation time. Jim finally had to go home in early May, and it felt like he was leaving his child behind. Sabin could certainly handle the day-to-day operation of the truck. That didn't bother him. What bothered Jim was stopping the momentum. You have to remember that we had no idea if this food truck thing was going to be a success or not. We had chosen to start a business where our presence on the premises wasn't always necessary, because we needed the freedom to continue in our day jobs. Those jobs were a kind of anchor to our old lives. We had a very long line that allowed us to drift, but never become unmoored. The thought of cutting the anchor line was just a little too scary. So, Jim wasn't about to jeopardize his day job more than he had already.

But when we knew that the truck wasn't a failure, we wanted to keep going. We wanted to ride the wave. And, damn, but we had a blast those first few days! We were ready to expand our menu, book more locations, and even start the conversation about getting a second truck. But all that progress seemed to come to a halt when Jim went home. It didn't *all* stop, but we couldn't give our full attention to Cousins Maine Lobster, which was required to keep the ball rolling. That's what hurt Jim the most, stepping on the plane for the five-hour flight home to Boston. He felt like the company was about to enter a stage of limbo from which it might never return.

In hindsight, Jim's fears were a bit unfounded. Not everything stopped when he left. Sabin held down the fort quite well, while Jim used his time on the East Coast to maintain contact with our suppliers and ensure that they were part of Cousins Maine Lobster's growth plans. Jim also helped keep the truck booked Tuesday through Sunday. Meanwhile, Jim maintained a full work schedule at Stryker, his days lasting anywhere from seven to twelve hours. Like Sabin's, Jim's job had him on the road a lot, traveling to hospitals and meeting with surgeons. The schedule afforded Jim the time to work on Cousins Maine Lobster without fear of having to step out of the office several times a day to make calls.

Which isn't to say that never happened. Jim knew that the long hours were beginning to wear on him when, while in the operating room in full scrubs, Jim stepped out to take a phone call, answering with "Cousins Maine Lobster." The call wasn't for Cousins Maine Lobster, and Jim quickly had to catch himself. But as the business in LA continued to heat up, those mistakes became more common. While Jim was able to maintain the rigorous schedule—using every available free hour, which included sleep time, to work on Cousins Maine Lobster—it took its toll, physically and emotionally.

The stress was the worst part. It wasn't in Jim's nature to give anything less than 100 percent to his job. But when you're going full throttle on two jobs—one being three thousand miles away—something has to give. While his bosses never reprimanded or scolded Jim during these trying months, they did ask questions—questions such as why Jim was in Maine (again), when he should have been in Boston. Jim couldn't answer these questions. So, he lied. And those lies started to eat away at Jim's conscience.

Yet all the guilt, stress, and exhaustion clarified one thing in Jim's mind. Cousins Maine Lobster was no hobby. It was a full-fledged business that was on the brink of becoming something big. Jim knew that his fear of managing a company in limbo had been rather naïve. If this was limbo, then imagine what he could do if he gave his full attention to the company. It was time to give the business what it deserved.

Meanwhile, Sabin was dealing with stress of a different sort. He managed a full team of Realtors under the guidance of his bosses and mentors, Rob and Lio. Sabin had also been completely honest with these guys from the very beginning, and was surprised to see how excited Rob and Lio were for him. Every day, when Sabin would come into the Realtor office, Rob and Lio would bombard him with questions about the truck:

"How was the event last night?"

"What are your sales this month?"

"When are you going to get another truck?"

Pretty much everything Sabin learned about starting a business in those early days he learned through hands-on training and from Rob and Lio. They not only offered whatever practical knowledge they could provide—which was a lot—but they also were the company's biggest cheerleaders. This takes a bit of explanation. As we asked earlier, why would Sabin's bosses be so eager to have Sabin succeed at something other than his day job? Because Rob and Lio were self-made businessmen whose greatest thrill was watching someone they respected start something on his own. The way they saw it is that, if Sabin would be better off growing his own business than selling real estate, then why the hell would he sell real estate? They also were very success oriented. The idea of building something for yourself was, in their minds, the ultimate mark of the successful person. They could find another agent, but opportunities like Cousins Maine Lobster don't come around every day.

Their message to Sabin: get after it and don't look back.

It was the sort of motivation we needed. With Jim in Boston, and the fear of being in limbo hanging over all our efforts, we needed someone to keep pushing us. Not that we had trouble finding motivation, but to get motivation from guys like Rob and Lio—guys who knew how to do it because they had done it—that was a different sort. In Sabin's mind, it's like Michael Jordan telling you you're really good at basketball and should devote your life to it. You don't turn down that kind of advice from Michael Jordan. He has no reason to blow smoke up your ass. Neither did Rob and Lio. And their encouragement not only made Sabin's life working two jobs so much easier; they pushed us to grow the company faster than we otherwise would have. (We still balked at buying the second truck, though.)

One story nicely captures the way Rio and Lio encouraged Sabin in those days. Before we had even an idea of the business, Sabin idly mentioned to them how he was thinking about buying a very expensive watch. But, he said, it was too much. Maybe next year, when the truck would be bringing in more money.

"Buy the watch," they said.

"But I can't afford it," Sabin protested.

"You *can* afford it, but you think you shouldn't," they replied. "Buy the watch today and work harder tomorrow to earn it."

In other words, they were showing Sabin how to motivate himself: Don't think that "one day" you'll be able to afford the watch. Buy the damn thing now because you want to, then work your ass off to afford it. It's a somewhat illogical way of looking at success—and certainly something Sabin had never considered. Nor would we advise it in all situations. Buy the watch, but wait on the Ferrari, perhaps. Yet when applied prudently, "buy the watch" is just the sort of motivational philosophy we needed in those early days.

Sabin bought the watch.

But regardless of Rob and Lio's support, Sabin was still working his ass off. To help Sabin with the truck, we made two invaluable hires in those early days: Shauna, who to this day is like the mother hen of Cousins Maine Lobster, and Paul, who eventually became our manager of operations. Be forewarned that it's rare to have the same employees from the start-up phase to the company phase, where we are now. Often the very qualities that you need from your employees when you're just starting out aren't the qualities that are necessary when you're trying to sustain and grow a business. We'll discuss this in greater length in another chapter, but we mention it now because Shauna and Paul were there from the beginning and they helped get us through that critical first year. It's a rare thing and a sign of how lucky we were to find them so early.

Sabin was also learning about the hazards of our chosen industry. We said earlier that we had a lot of sold-out days back then but not all our events were great. We'd usually pack between fifty to eighty pounds of lobster meat on a truck for a given location. But what happens when you sell only twenty pounds, which happened frequently? Well, you can scramble to find another location or, if that fails, eat the cost of inventory. It's one of those built-in dilemmas we had to overcome early on. If, say, you sell a manufactured item, then selling only twenty dollars of it at an event might not be great, but you don't lose the rest of your inventory. But with us, we had to attend only those events where we knew we could sell a certain percentage of our inventory. That took a lot of time to learn, but eventually we developed a kind of sixth sense for it. Lobster isn't always the best accompaniment for every occasion. For example, sometimes the last thing on the mind of a concertgoer is a plate of lobster. So, while we benefited greatly from our novelty status in those early days, we also learned how to say no. It wasn't easy, believe us. But when you might actually lose money selling your product, you learn how to say no pretty effectively.

While we had far different experiences in those first couple months, one thing did unite us: we were both exhausted. It wasn't as if Jim, not being on the truck, was working any less than Sabin. Far from it. Nor was Sabin able to simply coast at his day job because he had supportive, encouraging bosses. He was burning the candle at both ends, too. We noticed, however, that something had changed since the launch. We were working just as hard as before the launch, but the nature of the work had changed. We weren't trying to get the ball rolling anymore; we were trying to keep the ball from going out of control. It was like pushing it in the dark, where the only light is just a few inches in front of you. You try to keep it on the path, but sometimes you don't know where the path is. Sometimes you need to find the path again. But you can't stop the ball; now that it's started, it won't—can't—stop.

That's what it's like running a business. There are no timeouts. There are no halftimes or coffee breaks. It must keep moving. Our job was to keep it moving in the right direction.

## ROB MORAD AND LIONEL SABBAH— 360 REALTY

Much like Jim and Sabin, we've known each other a long time. Since high school, in fact. One of us, Rob, had one of those childhoods that is hard to believe. He came from a successful business family in Iran, but the family was forced to flee during the Revolution of 1979. They had to leave everything behind. After enduring a stint in a Pakistani jail, eventually Rob and his family made it to America, where his father started all over again. Although Lio's experience wasn't quite as harrowing as

Rob's, he, too, is an immigrant, who came from France to this country as a child.

Eleven years ago we became business partners when we started our real estate firm. Sabin was the first agent we hired to run our short-sales division and we immediately noticed his potential. He just had a knack for this line of work: personable, smart, charismatic. Sabin was a natural salesman who actually cared about his customers—a rare thing in real estate, if you can believe it. Even better, he enjoyed his work and did it well. From the beginning, you could say we knew he would be successful no matter where life took him.

So, when Sabin mentioned to us one day that he was considering starting a food truck business with his cousin, we encouraged him. It wasn't just because we knew Sabin would make a great entrepreneur. We also loved his idea—probably more than he did at the time. As you've read, the food truck phenomenon started in Los Angeles, and the street outside our office building was packed every lunch hour with dozens of trucks. To us, this was clearly a hot, young market that hadn't yet reached its zenith.

We also knew that Sabin wouldn't stay with us forever. He was just too good at whatever he did. There's a reason Lio nicknamed him "Forrest Gump," because the guy just didn't fail. Everything he did was successful. That's the type of person who should be doing his own thing, and so we pushed Sabin to embrace this entrepreneurial side of himself. Whenever Sabin was in the office, one of us would be talking with him about the new business. That's the thing about Sabin and Jim: they peppered us with questions about everything.

As successful as Sabin was at real estate, he knew very little about entrepreneurism. But that didn't stop Sabin, nor should it have. We answered his questions but also impressed upon him the importance of just moving forward. If you keep your momentum, you'll figure it out. Especially if you're a hardworking, bright person, you'll soon learn that this stuff isn't rocket science. That doesn't mean it's easy, but you need to be fearless and keep going.

But our pushing did lead to disagreements. When Sabin told us about the opportunity to go on *Shark Tank*, we urged him to jump feet first. Our thinking was that this was a once-in-a-lifetime opportunity. There aren't any guarantees, especially in business. As you know, Sabin and Jim wavered on this opportunity for weeks, driving us and everyone else crazy. Eventually, they did the show, got their dream deal, and their business exploded. As I like to say, the guy's like Forrest Gump.

We distinctly remember helping the cousins prepare for their taping. Lio would help Sabin rehearse his pitch and quizzed him with flashcards. Lio had watched the show and so he knew the questions the sharks would ask. But we also knew what any investor would want to see in a prospective business, so we helped Sabin and Jim understand why they would ask those questions. It's one thing to know the answers; it's another to know why the question is asked. If you know that, then you're far better prepared to answer a question you didn't expect, because you know how an investor's mind works.

Were we sorry to see Sabin leave? Yes, but not as happy as we were that he had found the perfect outlet for his many talents. And we aren't at all surprised that he and Jim have become successes outside of *Shark Tank*. The secret is simple: work hard, prepare, and keep going forward.

# THE GOLDEN AGE

In the years after achieving statehood, Maine entered something of a golden age. Everywhere one looked, Maine industries weren't just thriving, they were dominating the market. Indeed, today's Mainers would look with envy upon their ancestors from the early nineteenth century. Back then, the state's economy wasn't tied solely to the lobster or the tourists. In fact, neither had taken off in any real way. Each would emerge later, when the state economy had all but collapsed, leaving little except for Maine's unrivaled beauty and the tenacious lobster.

Of course, the boom started with the fishing industry. In 1800, Maine's offshore fishing fleet made up just 11 percent of the US fleet, as Colin Woodard notes. By 1860, on the eve of the Civil War, Maine's fleet made up half of the nation's offshore fishing vessels, and Maine fishermen dominated the mackerel, cod, and herring markets. As Woodard writes, "The success of Maine's fishing venture allowed it, in the three decades preceding the Civil War, to achieve a level of national economic importance never seen before or since."[5]

But Maine's economic boom wasn't limited to the sea. Aside from the bounty of fish off the coast, Maine was also blessed with a vast wilderness full of valuable lumber. By 1872, nearly one thousand sawmills and woodworking businesses operated in Maine, whose rivers, mostly the Kennebec and Penobscot, were essentially lumber highways carrying the valuable logs to the ports, from which they would be sent all over the world via Maine's merchant vessels.

Maine is also blessed with an abundance of granite, which led to another industry finding tremendous success in the antebellum era. Just how large did this industry become? Woodard notes:

The U.S. Treasury building and both the New York and Philadelphia post offices were built from [Dix Island] bedrock. Both Boston's Museum of Fine Arts and the great columns of the Cathedral of St. John the Divine in New York were built with Deer Isle granite, while the Ellis Island administration building and the U.S. House of Representatives were constructed with granite shipped from Blue Hill. The New York Stock Exchange, the Library of Congress, the U.S. Naval Academy, the Brooklyn and George Washington bridges in New York, and the interior of the Washington Monument are all built from bits of pieces of the Maine coast.[6]

Finally, in 1805 a Bostonian named Frederick Tudor created an industry nearly from scratch: ice. Before Tudor started shipping Maine ice all over world, humanity's food selection was tied to seasonal harvests and the dried, smoked, or salted meat. But Tudor developed a way to cut, package, and ship ice from Maine rivers so that it would arrive still frozen as far away as Asia and India. Just before the start of the Civil War, Tudor was shipping 130,000 tons of New England ice around the world. Which is why Tudor became known as the "Ice King," and Maine was his kingdom.[7]

And then came war, which drew 73,000 Mainers (the highest proportion of the population of any state in the Union) to far-off battlefields, where more than 18,000 would be killed or wounded. Some would come back heroes, like General Joshua Chamberlain, a professor at Bowdoin College before the war. In 1863, then-Colonel Chamberlain commanded the Twentieth Maine Volunteer Infantry Regiment, which was stationed at the extreme left flank of the Union line during the Battle of Gettysburg. During the second day of the battle, the Confederates under the command of General Robert E. Lee attacked Chamberlain's position at the summit of a hill known as Little

Round Top. Wave after wave of Confederate soldiers advanced up the hill, pushing Chamberlain and his Mainers to the brink of collapse. Then, low on ammunition and facing another assault, Chamberlain ordered his men to fix bayonets and charge down the hill. The brilliant and daring maneuver knocked the Confederates off the hill and saved the Union line. For his heroism, Chamberlain received the Medal of Honor and the Twentieth Maine Regiment guaranteed its place in the annals of US military history.

Heroes on the battlefield, Maine's soldiers returned home to find a state awash in economic devastation. The Civil War had accelerated the technological innovations of the era, pushing Maine's now-outdated industries into collapse. The railroad had opened up vast stretches of the western United States, including the forests of the Great Lakes and Pacific Northwest. The rise of steel destroyed the granite quarries, while the advent of refrigeration made the ice industry obsolete. Fishing was the only industry still on its feet a generation after the end of the Civil War. But, as we'll see, its days were numbered, too.

Writes Woodard: "Virtually every industry on the coast had fallen apart during the late nineteenth century: farming, fishing, shipbuilding, lumbering, and the cutting of granite, limestone and ice. The nation's commerce abandoned the wooden hulls of Maine-built sailing vessels plying the Atlantic seaboard, shifting instead onto steel rails connecting the great eastern cities with the vast resources of the American West. The Maine coast, once at the heart of American commerce, had become an isolated backwater."[8]

Although discovered by tourists, Maine had been largely forgotten by the world of business by the turn of the twentieth century. It seemed to everyone that the state's best days were long behind it.

# LESSON
## KNOW WHO YOU ARE

How a people, state, or an enterprise discovers its identity is anything but a simple process. For Maine, the road led through a period of some of the worst economic devastation ever known in the United States. That period still resonates in nearly every corner of the state; indeed, the trials faced by those Mainers helped to define the Maine people and their character. Those who had to live on despite the loss of their livelihoods only strengthened the spirit of independence and persistence that had marked those early settlers battling the great proprietors of Boston. And their legacy continues in each new generation of Mainers. The inheritance of Maine certainly isn't wealth; it's a fierce determination to live life the Maine way, without excuse or apology.

When we launched Cousins Maine Lobster in April 2012, we thought we knew who we were. We had wanted the product we sell, and the way we sell it, to reflect what we had known as boys growing up in Maine. But through the trials of those first few months, we discovered that our vision had been limited. We weren't quite sure what we were yet—much like Maine itself had to go through its own period of discovery—but we knew what we didn't want to be. Our little truck was more than a food truck because we *wanted* it to be more than that. And that's our lesson from this period.

*Know who you are.* And know that who you are is a result of *what you want to be.* Aim high, even if it sounds absurd to everyone else. Have the vision to build more than a company that sells a product or service. People might laugh. They might say you're taking yourself too seriously. We suppose you could listen, and just be another food truck on the road.

The amount of pressure on a new business can be overwhelming, almost suffocating. When we started out, we had no idea of the power of the forces that would be pulling at us constantly. From booking locations to maintaining inventory to dealing with bad days, we were amazed at how far our original idea for the business would be tested. The temptation of taking the easy route, the shortcut, is everywhere in the early days. You are faced with a constant stream of distractions that, at the time, seem like important matters. The best way to navigate these troubled waters is to *know who you are.* Keep the vision for yourself and your company ever present in your mind. Let it be a beacon, a lighthouse, that guides you.

By the fall of 2012, after just six months in business, we decided that Cousins Maine Lobster would be more than a hobby: it would be more than a food truck, and it would be more than a company. It would be our lives.

# Out of the Tank

Sharks, picture this: it's summertime in Maine. Both locals and tourists alike are in line at Maine's iconic lobster shacks. They're standing alongside the Atlantic Ocean, smelling that salty air. Most importantly, they are eagerly awaiting the chance, the opportunity, to sink their teeth into Maine's signature dish, the lobster roll. Sharks, at Cousins Maine Lobster, we bring the Maine lobster experience to Southern California and we do it via our amazing gourmet lobster shack on wheels. We get our lobsters from shore to door in less than twenty-four hours. So, you know what that means, Barbara? The next time you're hanging with the cousins, you're having the freshest fare possible.

And that's how we introduced Cousins Maine Lobster to roughly 9 million viewers (and Barbara Corcoran) on October 19, 2012. The two of us were back in Maine, watching the episode on a big projection screen in a warehouse with more than a hundred friends, family, and business partners. Although we had entered the Tank asking for $55,000 for a 5 percent stake, we accepted Barbara's counteroffer of 15 percent. Still, we hadn't seen the final cut of the episode, so we were watching it for the first time along with everyone else in America.

We wanted to see how much of our discussion about our e-commerce business the producers had left in the final cut. In the weeks leading up to taping, which had occurred way back in July, we decided that we should use the *Shark Tank* opportunity to boost sales, a sort of insurance plan against missing out on catching a shark. Seems obvious, right? Well, not when your business is a food truck—a *single* food truck. It's a bit hard to boost sales when you have a single truck that can only hold a specific amount of lobster. Our food truck business had a sales ceiling.

Our idea was to raise that ceiling by adding an e-commerce business that shipped overnight fresh lobster, lobster roll kits, and soups like chowder and bisques. That way, we could direct viewers to a sales point other than a food truck that only operated in Los Angeles. By the time of the taping, we only had the bare bones of this e-commerce division in place. But so what? We had three months before the episode aired to finalize the site, buy the inventory, and hire the extra hands to take orders and package the food. Besides, we had just signed a deal with Barbara Corcoran!

By October 19, we had $250,000 of inventory ready to go in an eighteen-wheeler freezer truck. Meanwhile, fifteen packers and eight operators were on standby, ready to take orders all night after the episode aired. Our excitement over the amount of product we would sell was at a fever pitch. We barely noticed that the producers had edited out everything we had said about the e-commerce business. America had heard none of it.

No matter. The booze was flowing that night, and our spirits couldn't be dampened. Surely, at that very moment, thousands of people were visiting our site for the first time, just begging to taste some of our fine Maine lobster for themselves!

The next morning dawned bright—too bright for our bleary eyes and aching heads. Almost immediately the calls from our suppliers started coming in, asking how we did on the e-commerce sales. We quickly checked with our call center to get a round number. "Don't worry about specifics," we said. "Just ballpark it!"

Oh, no.

Back on the phone with the suppliers: "It's, um, lower than we expected."

Suppliers: "How low? A thousand orders? Five hundred?"

"Thirteen," we said.

We had only thirteen orders all night.

Fuck.

## GREEDY CRUSTACEANS

Leaving the "Tank," or studio, is a surreal experience. After your brain, heart, and emotions have been running at full speed, everything suddenly stops. When we emerged into the bright California sunshine, we both looked at each other as if to ask, "What the hell just happened?" In fact, the producers anticipate this and almost immediately after taping, you're hustled to another room, where you meet with a psychiatrist. The reason is because the intensity of the taping, the drama, is very real, even if it's a bit different than what viewers see. The psychiatrist is there to help dazed or rattled contestants regain their composure.

This speaks to the authenticity of the show itself. The actual experience for the contestants is nerve-racking because nothing is scripted. Although sometimes the sharks assume a personality for the cameras, their barbs and critiques can really sting. Imagine if you've spent your entire life savings on your business, only to be told that you've wasted your time. It can be a traumatic experience.

Although we were a bit anxious after our taping, we were also deliriously happy. We had agreed to a deal with Barbara, after entertaining a counteroffer from Robert Herjavec. We got what we wanted: A partnership with Barbara Corcoran. We even addressed her in our opening pitch! And we got her. Everything had worked out just as we had hoped. Yes, we agreed to hand over more equity than we had originally offered, but that was to be expected. If we hadn't been prepared to give up more than 5 percent, then we shouldn't have gone on the show.

That's one of those fine lines we agonized over in the run-up to the taping. Just what do we ask for and offer? Regular viewers of the show know that an outlandish valuation or miniscule equity offer can sink your chances with the sharks before anything else happens. We knew that going in, which is why we spent hours working with Steve to come up with a valuation that we could defend. Let's remember that we had been in business only three months. *Any* valuation, low or high, is suspect with so little sales history behind it. But that's why we were on a television show and not in an investor's office. Our story was good for TV; but most anyone else wouldn't have even bothered to return our phone calls.

But so what? We had been offered this chance to accelerate our growth and we had decided to take it. We just needed to find a valuation number that wouldn't have us laughed out of the Tank—and we almost were. We came up with a valuation of $1.1 million. How did we get there? Fairly simple math and a little bit of guesswork.

First, as previously mentioned, we had around $150,000 in sales over two months. Spread that out over twelve months, and we stood to make $900,000 in sales. Getting there, but still far short. We knew we could add the cost of our truck ($75,000) plus the value on our inventory. We say "value" because our inventory was worth more than the dollars we spent on it. Recall from chapter 2 that our relationship with our supplier is the most valuable business relationship we have. Not just anyone can start buying Maine lobster wholesale the way we do. In fact, Kevin O'Leary ("Mr. Wonderful") asked us directly why he couldn't do the same thing we did.

Jim's answer: "You can start your own truck and hire your own staff. But what you can't do is what you just said, and call up on the phone to Maine. They just don't do business with other guys." That is 100 percent true. But how do you put a value on that? It's certainly worth *something* and must be part of any valuation of the business.

Finally, we included the potential sales from a second truck. Now, we didn't have a second truck when we entered the Tank, but that's what we told the sharks we would do with their investment money. Still, you need to be careful about valuing your company with capital you don't have. Although we factored the sales of a second truck into our final valuation, we were careful not to make it fit too nicely. So, we lowballed the sales of a second truck, included the cost of two trucks, and added the price of our inventory and suppliers. That's roughly how we reached $1.1 million.

And even though we thought we could've valued the business a bit higher, most of the sharks weren't buying it. O'Leary called us "greedy crustaceans." Daymond John didn't really believe what Jim said about our suppliers, and Herjavec responded to Sabin's answer that we would increase our equity offer to 7 or 8 percent with, "You know what? You're a very good actor. You said that with a straight face." This is what the sharks are supposed to do—rip apart your carefully crafted valuation and tell you why your company isn't worth what you think it is.

They do this even if they're interested, because they're bargaining. They want more of your company for less. It's easy to say now that we took these critiques with a grain of salt. We mostly did. But, damn, they make you second-guess your whole life.

Barbara later told us that it was our composure, our coolness under fire, that convinced her we were a good investment. To her, we seemed like more than just food truck guys. We were hungry, and we had come prepared to do real business. We weren't just trying to boost sales for our one truck; we wanted to build something. We weren't exactly sure at that point what we were going to build, but she saw the ambition and the work ethic.

She just wanted more than what we offered. Now, 5 percent is about as low as you can offer. It *almost* says to the sharks that you don't need them at all. That's exactly what we were going for. For starters, we didn't want to hand over a big chunk of a business that was only three months old. But we also wanted to come across as confident, like we knew what we were doing. It's a fine line to walk, not least because we didn't know what we were doing. But confidence, played poorly, can come off as arrogance. No one wants to do business with an arrogant asshole. But greedy? We can handle being greedy—and we loved O'Leary's "greedy crustaceans" line, because if you know anything about the nature of lobsters (and you will, just keep reading), you know that they are some freaking ornery little creatures. They greedily gobble up anything in their path (including lobsters smaller than them) and they protect their homes with a ferocity that's fanatical.

So, yes, hungry and protective—we can live with those qualities.

Regardless, we knew that we would have to accept giving up more than 5 percent, which is another reason why we chose it. Negotiation 101: always start with a number *far* lower than what you'd accept. If we had started with 15 percent, then we better be prepared to accept 25. Start with 25 percent, and it says you'd accept 35.

In any case, everything we said and did when we walked into the tank that afternoon had been carefully planned and scripted. We knew the general questions the sharks were going to ask, even which shark would ask which question. As we said in the introduction, we watched nearly fifty episodes and quizzed each other with note cards. We had our pitch and our business down stone-cold.

We assumed that's how most contestants prepared, but we've since learned that's not the case at all. But usually when a contestant is caught off guard it's because they're not looking for a deal at all. They see the show as a good promotional opportunity and so don't prepare or give their valuation much thought beyond picking a number. So, they get torn apart, which makes for good television, then they go home and watch their web hits skyrocket. But like any shot of adrenaline, the effect wears off. People, especially television viewers, have short memories. That web traffic boost might last twenty-four hours at most, before you're back where you started.

And then you realize you should have tried to get more out of the show.

We wouldn't have gone on *Shark Tank* if we didn't want a deal, specifically a deal with Barbara. So, we came prepared and we came with the one thing that all good players should have: a strategy. We knew our valuation seemed a bit high and our equity offer a bit low. That's exactly what we wanted it to look like—it said we came to play ball. It said we wanted to deal but weren't desperate. We came prepared to defend our offer but also let it be known that we would modify it depending on the counteroffer. We also knew that our ask of $55,000 would start to seem odd the further the negotiations went, assuming they went further. After all, if two trucks are good, then wouldn't three be better?

Herjavec noticed this, and offered $125,000 at one point, just "to get more trucks on the street." It's a fair point, but we weren't ready for that yet. Flooding LA with Cousins Maine Lobster trucks seemed like a good way to overextend ourselves and destroy our novelty status among Southern Californians. Never mind whether there was enough demand for more than two or three trucks, there's something to be said for a product that's hard to get. We didn't want to be everywhere, like a fast-food joint, because we aren't a fast-food joint. Lobster is a delicacy that should be treated as such. Flood the market with high-priced lobster and you'll waste a lot of lobster. We enjoy—and continue to enjoy—a specialness with our product. Precisely because it isn't everywhere, people seek us out. They talk about us. There's a buzz. To be sought is better than being everywhere.

Whether Barbara appreciated this thinking at the time, we don't know. It surely wasn't her intention to keep our business at two trucks. Nor was it ours. But if we were going to expand, we would do it safely and smartly. We had the long game in mind and so did Barbara, who probably understood what kind of business we wanted even before we did.

We understand now, and it's because of Barbara Corcoran that we're at this point. Our intention in entering the tank was to offer the sharks more than a share in a food truck business. We wanted them to see the opportunity to be a part of something special—special because it meant so much to us. That's not for everyone and we weren't looking for any shark. We knew which one was a Mainer at heart and we got her.

## WHAT BARBARA SAW

There are two questions we get asked all the time. The first, "How did you do it?" has resulted in this book. You're reading our answer. The second is, "What's Barbara really like?" We totally get it, people love Barbara. We love Barbara, too, and for the same reasons you do. The Barbara you see on the screen is the Barbara we see in our office in LA or her office in New York or at Jim's parent's house in Maine. She is who she is. Genuine, funny, honest, and supremely confident. But there's the Barbara you see on-screen and there's the Barbara who's the brilliant businesswoman. You don't *see* that. You experience that. You get a sense of that Barbara on the screen, especially when she's analyzing or negotiating—she does this thing with her eyebrow and looks at you squarely, like she's trying to detect the bullshit. But that's not the complete picture. Let's try to fill it in for you.

The deal we "signed" with Barbara on the show wasn't signed until August. This is normal, but our contact with Barbara was fairly limited until then. Even after we signed, our partnership didn't blossom until after the episode aired in October. But during this time, Barbara got to work on fixing the "small" stuff. And we only call it small stuff because that's what we thought it was at the time.

During the show she explained exactly what she considered fixable right way with Cousins Maine Lobster. "I think your truck is terrible," she had said. So, she started to work on the outside design of the truck. But the truck design reflected our overall marketing and branding. It was all bad, according to Barbara. While we thought we were making the most of our Maine story, Barbara showed us just how ordinary our food truck was.

"You're the ones selling your product, not the truck!" she

told us later. This was both a compliment and a criticism. The compliment was that we were very good salespeople. When we were talking about our business in front of a camera, when we were outside the truck mingling with customers, when we sat down with Barbara and her people, we could sell the shit out of our business! The one thing we can do extremely well is tell our story. And people love to hear it. It's a competitive advantage for sure. On that score, we were killing it.

But we can't always be out there selling our business. We need to let other things sell it for us: the truck, our packaging, and marketing materials. These were amateurish, and Barbara saw that immediately. They weren't the best symbols of the brand we were trying to sell. They didn't reflect the Maine of our childhood, they didn't reflect the values we hold dear, and they didn't reflect the two most important parts of the business: us. And we say that in all humility.

This is part of Barbara's genius. She saw Cousins Maine Lobster perhaps better than we saw it. We had started a food truck because we wanted to recapture a moment from our childhood and share it with others. But we didn't extend that vision to our marketing material, specifically the truck, but also to everything else. Customers heard that story about Jim's backyard and our deep connection to Maine when we told them, but we weren't always there to tell them. "You should have your faces all over the truck," she had said during the show. What she meant, as we learned later, is that we need to be with the truck all the time, even when we can't be there at all.

This is just one reason you see our faces plastered on every bit of Cousins Maine Lobster material out there, from our truck to our web site. It's not just because we're showing off our George Clooney/Brad Pitt looks. In fact, the whole marketing campaign around us is a bit uncomfortable (for Jim—Sabin loves it). It's a shift in perspective we hadn't considered in those early days, mostly because we aren't marketing guys. But Barbara saw it immediately and went to work making sure that all of Cousins Maine Lobster told our story, not just the two guys who started it.

After the episode aired, our time with Barbara increased significantly. In the fall of 2012, prior to the airing of *Shark Tank*, we were lucky enough to secure a "home package" from *Shark Tank*. Basically, the *Shark Tank* producers come to your home town and shoot a brief introduction of you and your business, which airs right before you walk into the tank. Being that Barbara was now coming to Maine, we invited her to stay at Sabin's uncle's house in Scarborough and to have dinner at Jim's parents' house in Cape Elizabeth. Today, we wouldn't think twice about sending her an invitation like that, but back then we were still a little star struck. To our surprise, Barbara accepted, and even brought her young daughter. By the way all of us— meaning the members of the Tselikis and Lomac families— reacted, you would have thought that the president of the United States was coming for the weekend. Of course, that's when we met the Barbara that so few people see. The kindness, the humility, the humor—the absolutely wonderful sense of humor. It was no different than having anyone else over for the weekend, except this "anyone else" was Barbara Corcoran, who had given us $55,000.

Of course we talked shop that weekend. We started the groundwork for plans that would come to fruition months (or in some cases, years) later. By visiting the Tselikis's house, meeting our families, seeing the Maine coast, Barbara learned more about us and where we came from, which is what our company is all about. It helped her see the vision behind the company. For our part, we learned just by watching her. In particular, we learned from Barbara that there's no secret to business success; there's just what feels right. You can work the numbers again and again, but in the end, you need to trust your gut. We also learned that not every opportunity is the right opportunity (a lesson experience would reteach us later). And we learned that it's OK to not know what the hell you're doing. We understood this at some level, but assumed that someone like Barbara *always* knows what she's doing. So would we, one day, right?

Wrong.

Follow your gut. Don't chase every opportunity. And, finally, never take no for an answer. At one point during the weekend, over a discussion about expanding the menu, Barbara burst out: "If they can put a man on the moon, we can put lobster mac-'n'-cheese on a food truck!" If it's the right opportunity, the one that makes sense deep in your gut—and, believe us, lobster mac-'n'-cheese makes sense—then find a way. Even when they say it can't be done, find a way.

Our business relationship with Barbara blossomed that weekend. It reached a level we could never had guessed back in the summer, when we agonized over going on the show at all. Our concern—did the show actually work for guys like us?—was answered with an emphatic yes. *Shark Tank* is first and foremost a television show, and everyone who goes on must accept that before anything else. It's also that rare television show that does what it promises viewers. We wouldn't be where we are today without *Shark Tank*. More specifically, *Shark Tank* is how we met Barbara Corcoran.

The show gave us and continues to give us a rare spotlight that so few other entrepreneurs ever get. We got lucky. But we would trade away all that notoriety, all that minor fame, just to keep the one gift the show gave us: Barbara. Without her, we would still be just a couple of guys operating a few food trucks on the side. With Barbara, we run a multimillion-dollar company.

# THE SACRIFICE OF SUCCESS

However, our success hasn't come without cost. If that sounds ungrateful, give us a moment to explain. When we started out as a single food truck rolling around LA as a mobile lobster shack, we never intended to be anything more than that. Back then, it was a labor of love, a way for us to work together selling something that made us happy. But we didn't really consider whether we'd enjoy doing it. It's not like operating a food truck business had been a childhood dream of ours. It's not like either of us had any culinary experience or skills.

But in the process, we discovered that we enjoyed it immensely. We loved going out with the truck and talking with customers. It's like we had stumbled upon a passion we didn't know we had—and that's quite a thrill. It didn't take either of us very long after the first day to realize that this was something we could do for the rest of our lives. It was an unexpected but welcome surprise. Neither of us were strangers to pursuing our passions and interests. Jim had devoted himself to hockey in college, while Sabin studied drama. We knew what it felt like to be engaged in an activity, pastime, or job you love.

This is part of the joy of entrepreneurship. It's one of the few professions where you are tested on a near-daily basis with challenges you *think* you have no skills to conquer. Yet that's when you discover you do have those skills: they've just never been used before or they've been used in a different capacity. Now, talking with customers isn't exactly a challenge. Nor are we strangers to the game of salesmanship. We were essentially both salesmen in our previous careers. So, it didn't shock us that we were good at selling our product or telling our story.

But we were surprised at how much we enjoyed it. It was unexpected. Why was it different than what we had done as a real estate agent and a medical representative? Because this time it was our product, our story. We both feel a tremendous surge of energy and joy when we are out in front of the truck, in our restaurant, sitting with a journalist, or just passing the time with friends talking about what we do and why we do it. We had each discovered a new passion and we felt like the luckiest guys in the world.

This isn't exactly unusual with a new entrepreneur. After all, the reason people start businesses is so that they can do what they love. A baker starts a bakery because she loves to bake, an artist opens an art studio because he loves making art, and two cousins from Maine open a food truck because they love talking about their childhood eating the freshest lobster on earth.

But here's the rub. The moment the baker wants to open another bakery, the day the artist expands his studio into the next-door flat, and the second that the food truck operators put another truck on the road, they must give up what they love. Because at that moment, they cease to be practitioners of their passion and must become managers of it. Put another way, you can either run a company or do what you love. You won't have time for both.

This was made painfully clear to Jim not long after we first opened. You might recall that Jim was in Los Angeles that first week on borrowed time. He had to get back to his job in Boston, but couldn't leave Sabin running things all by himself just yet. What's more, we were both on this incredible high because we had discovered that we absolutely loved this thing.

So, Jim called his father, Steve, to tell him he needed to stay in Los Angeles another week. He told Steve how amazing our first week had been; he told Steve about the lines around the block; he told Steve about the amazing reviews on Yelp. Finally, Jim told his dad how much fun he had being on the truck, being outside the truck, serving up lobster and talking to customers.

And that's when Steve stopped him. He didn't talk Jim out of staying longer. Nor did he talk Jim out of taking Cousins

Maine Lobster as far as we could. But he did say this: "Listen, if you think you're going to make a living by being out in front of the truck every day, you have another thing coming. You can't grow a business if you're standing outside the truck talking with customers. You can't grow the business if you're busy selling lobster all day to Southern Californians."

Steve put it plain to Jim that very day: you can have a food truck or you can run a company, but you can't do both. He was absolutely right.

We rarely go out with our trucks anymore. We still do, but, boy, do we need to fit it in our schedules. And as Barbara taught us soon after we signed our deal, if you're doing one thing, it means you can't do something else. If we're on the truck, then we aren't talking with our suppliers or employees. If we're talking to customers, telling our story, then we aren't on the phone with our new franchisee in San Antonio, Las Vegas, or Atlanta. If we're rolling around Los Angeles having the time of our lives, then we aren't opening a restaurant in West Hollywood. It's a matter of balance. There are times when we need to be on the truck, particularly when we're with a new franchisee. Then there are times we need to be in the office with our staff. We've had to set aside what we *want to do*. These days, we do what we *need to do*.

Of course, Barbara understood this fact of entrepreneurism as well as Steve. It's why she focused immediately on improving our marketing and branding material to tell our story when we aren't around. She knew we wouldn't be around the trucks anymore. She knew we would have to give up our love of being on the truck, talking with the customers, if we wanted Cousins Maine Lobster to achieve its potential.

This is one of the harder lessons for entrepreneurs to learn. To be a successful entrepreneur, you must give up what made you an entrepreneur in the first place. We hope you will discover, as we both did, that the joys of running a company and building a brand are worth the sacrifice. They were for us. But if you just want to be a baker, then be happy with your bakery. If you just want to be an artist, then enjoy your studio. And if you just want to talk to customers and tell them your story, then stay on your truck.

But if you want more, then be prepared to make the sacrifice. Trust us, it's worth it. It's just not for everyone.

## THE RISE OF A BRAND

Lobsters have been synonymous with the Maine coast since the days of the Plymouth Company. Those early settlers encountered the ugly creatures crawling along the shallows as far in as the shoreline back then. As Colin Woodard writes:

> Coastal Mainers had been catching and eating lobsters since Waymouth's day, but nobody had ever tried to make a living from it. Lobsters were tasty, plentiful, and easy to catch. In colonial days, a small boy could bring home enough to feed several families by simply wading along the shore at low tide and gaffing the huge five- to ten-pound beasts hiding among the rocks. Coastal New Englanders ate them in quantity, or fed them to prisoners and indentured servants in place of commercially valuable cod, mackerel, or grain. One group of indentured servants in Massachusetts became so upset with this diet that they took their owners to court, winning a judgment that they would not be served lobster more than three times a week. Lobsters were sometimes taken in great numbers and strewn on the fields as fertilizer. Well into the nineteenth century, fishermen were grinding up piles of lobsters and tossing them overboard in an effort to attract schools of mackerel.[9]

But the lobster wasn't just local to Maine. Up and down the New England coast, from New Brunswick in the north to New York City in the south, some seven hundred miles as the crow flies, lobsters were large and plentiful. Which is why the term "Maine lobster" hadn't been invented yet. In the early eighteenth century, when the lobster industry began, it would be more accurate to call them "New England lobster." Indeed, the first lobster fisheries were set up around Boston and New York, where a sizeable consumer market had developed. Meanwhile, Maine lobstering was almost strictly a local affair. Maine fishermen would catch lobster in between the far more profitable groundfish seasons to feed their families and sell locally.

Elisha M. Oakes isn't a name history remembers, but he is credited with creating Maine's lobster trade. The problem with lobster as a consumer product is that the damn things just don't travel well. You can't smoke them or salt them and they don't last long on ice, particularly as ice was used in those days. But then, some New England merchants developed a new style of shipping vessel that had a large tank in its hold with holes in the side through which seawater could travel. The innovative boat, called a "smack," revolutionized the lobster industry and allowed Oakes to start shipping lobster caught in Harpswell, Maine, to Boston. In just a few years, Oakes had depleted Harpswell's lobster supply and moved his operations to Penobscot Bay. Around the same time, the southern lobster fisheries around Boston and New York also started to dry up. New Englanders had developed a taste for lobster, but the little creatures had abandoned the shallows for the safer waters farther from shore.

Still, New England's lobster industry remained small-scale, particularly compared to the groundfish industry, until some innovative person decided to start canning lobster meat. Forget smacks: now, lobster could be shipped all over the world in easily packaged one-pound cans. The first canneries were set up in Maine, where the supply was most plentiful.

Woodard writes:

> In 1850, these three lobster factories were practically the only canneries of any kind in the entire country. . . . The canneries spread like wildfire and the lobster fisheries followed. By the late 1870s, there were twenty-three from Portland to Eastport, engaging the service of 1,200 lobstermen. Together they churned out two million one-pound cans of lobster in two four-month canning seasons. These were distributed far and wide and introduced the American West and Southwest to lobster meat. Roughly half the production was exported to Europe, particularly England, where well-cooked meat found a ready market.[10]

All of a sudden, lobster—especially Maine lobster—had become a global market. In time, the canneries would die out, as economic troubles and sustainability concerns drove them out of business. But the lobster industry had found its niche on the Maine coast, where the local fishermen were in desperate need of a new revenue stream after the slow but devastating collapse of the groundfish industry.

Nearly three hundred years after the first settlers had arrived on the Maine coast looking for fertile farmland, the inhabitants had finally found their state's true bounty. That lobster became Maine's principal export and source of income for thousands of families and dozens of coastal communities almost by accident doesn't matter. You work with the gifts you are given. Maine was blessed with access to a species whose taste appeals to a great portion of humanity. And thank God for it. Without the lobster, without this brand, Maine's fall into obscurity might have had no bottom.

But once discovered, this new gold mine had to be protected.

Without it, there would be no Maine economy to speak of—a little like how, without Barbara Corcoran, the landscape of Cousins Maine Lobster would be dramatically different.

## THE LESSON
## PLAY THE LONG GAME

The day after our *Shark Tank* episode aired should have been one of the best in our lives, certainly in the life of Cousins Maine Lobster. It turned out to be one of the worst, because we had screwed up. It wasn't the producers' fault that they had left our every mention of the new e-commerce business on the cutting-room floor. Their job isn't to advance our interests, but to produce the best episode they can. We should have foreseen that and not spent a lot of money based on an assumption. But it wasn't just the money. We had promised our suppliers a big day and we didn't deliver. What an embarrassment. When the producers had cut every mention of the e-commerce business from the episode, we not only lost hundreds of thousands of dollars—we could have jeopardized our most valuable business relationship. Or so we thought that day.

But, again, we did have Barbara Corcoran.

Never one to panic, Barbara quickly worked her connections and landed a spot for us on *Good Morning America*'s "Deals and Steals," a kind of lightning-round segment where the hosts interview four or five company owners about their product. This is how, two weeks after *Shark Tank*, we found ourselves in front of the cameras again, only this time our time was limited to about thirty seconds. That's right: we had thirty seconds to sell America on our e-commerce business. That we had just been featured on *Shark Tank* certainly helped, but never has a taping gone so fast for us. The host bit into one of our Lobster Pot

Pies, reacted like they had just tasted the best thing they had ever eaten, then took another bite. That was it. We were on camera, then we were off.

Our hope was that the appearance would stop the bleeding. If we could sell just a few thousand dollars of product, which was still sitting on our eighteen-wheeler freezer truck, then we would save face with our suppliers. We had been humbled by the disaster two weeks earlier and weren't about to get our hopes up again.

The next day, the sales figures came in.

We had sold $250,000 of product in four hours.

Thank you, Barbara.

The entire experience taught us an invaluable lesson that all entrepreneurs should learn early on. Namely, play the long game. Envision your company as a living thing that requires good food, good exercise, and plenty of nutrients and vitamins to grow into something healthy and sustainable. All that takes time and it requires a level of patience that is rare in the young entrepreneur. We get it: you want it fast and you want it now. You get a little bit of money and suddenly you want to expand well beyond what your meager operations can bear. Or, you bet the whole store on a nutty get-rich-quick scheme that leaves you with nothing.

When we decided to go on *Shark Tank*, our intention was to play the long game. We knew we would get a good publicity boost out of it (we still get that boost today), but we wanted something more, something lasting. A publicity boost is like a shot of caffeine in the morning—it gets you going, but it won't sustain you for very long. Publicity is like the sugar rush of the business world. It's a nice treat to have occasionally, but it's not a sustainable strategy. We wanted *Shark Tank* to work for us over the long term, which is why we trained all our efforts on landing the one person we knew could help our little food truck company achieve its potential. We got her.

But then, at almost the same time, we made the mistake of looking for the quick hit. We spent half a million dollars on a gambit that was entirely dependent on what the producers decided to leave in the final cut of the episode. How freaking stupid was that? But we weren't playing the long game. We now know that building the e-commerce business and promoting it on the show wasn't the mistake. The mistake was buying the inventory before we had the sales. The day after our episode aired would have gone much smoother if we hadn't gone for the quick hit of caffeine.

Live and learn.

We managed to minimize the damage from our mistake, thanks to Barbara Corcoran. But our long game had just started. Together with Barbara, we had identified a brand that centered on us, our story, and it was time to see where we could take it. More importantly, we had started to believe that our food truck company was more than food trucks. The food truck was and remains the focus of our brand, but we began to realize it didn't need to be the sole focus.

Our challenge going forward mirrored the lobstering industry's challenge in those early years. We had caught lightning in a bottle. We were the only ones doing what we did, just as New England was the only place to get the American lobster. The temptation to grow beyond your means, to fish the hell out of your supply, is incredibly strong at those moments. The fishermen of Maine, desperate to keep themselves and their families out of poverty, could have easily gone for the quick buck and fished the waters dry. We could have thrown hundreds of thousands of dollars into half a dozen more trucks, and saturated Ssouthern California with mobile lobster shacks.

The lobstermen avoided the temptation and so did we. Our challenge going forward was also very like theirs back then: How to grow the brand we had built in a profitable yet sustainable way? The solution wasn't immediately clear, but then again, it never is.

# PART TWO

# Two Cousins and a Company

# 6

# Finding Your Purpose

Pull up a lobster trap and have a seat. The weather outside is raw and cold, so the boats are lashed down, and we have time to chat. The tale of the great Maine lobster is as old as Maine itself. It is not just our pastime, it is our state treasure. It is to be revered and respected. To be spoken of in hushed tones and wrapped in the lore of weathered lobstermen and battered wharfs. It's a story we have heard a hundred times since our childhoods in Maine. Lobster is a religion and we take it very seriously . . . but with our own spin.

—*Cousins Maine Lobster Brand Book*

There's nothing quite like being out on a lobster boat on a beautiful summer morning. You get to the wharf before sunrise, the call of the gulls beckoning you out to sea. You step on the boat and your senses are overwhelmed with smells: the salt, the diesel, but most of all, the bait—the barrels of rotting herring and red fish heads. The stench should repulse you, yet it's strangely fitting to the surroundings. As you cruise down the Fore River out into Casco Bay, the new sun catches the tree line on the tops of the islands, encasing the whole world in a golden glow. Little Diamond Island is a few points off the starboard bow, Great Diamond Island towering behind. The sea is calm and quiet as the boat glides past Fort Gorges, a Civil War–era stone skeleton, its gun ports and parapets overrun with tall grass. A historic relic with nothing to defend except the peace and serenity of the Maine coast. A gentle spray over the gunwale is the only disturbance on an otherwise perfect day for lobster fishing . . .

But today is not a beautiful day. The morning dawned cold and wet, the precipitation alternating between rain and mist. Just enough to keep your exposed skin in a permanent state of clamminess. The sea rolls with a heavy swell, rocking the boat to a sickening degree while the fish guts spill over the tops of their barrels. You can feel your breakfast roiling in the pit of your stomach and you only hope it stays there. A drenching October gust thrashes the boat as it heaves and sways toward the buoys that bob in the heavy chop. The captain, Jonathan Norton, pulls up alongside the first one of the day, a yellow-and-maroon buoy, the same colors his grandfather used when he fished these waters decades earlier. He catches hold of the line and hauls the buoy into the boat, placing it in a barrel of heated water. He then laces the line around the boat's pot hauler, and starts it up. The hauler buzzes to life, turning, turning, turning, each rotation bringing the first of five traps closer to the surface from twenty fathoms, or 120 feet, below. And while it turns, we wait, wondering what bounty will rise from the ocean floor.

We're out on the bay with our newest franchisees. It's not our first time on a lobster boat but it is theirs. Call it a rite of passage. No one can become a Cousins Maine Lobster franchisee without first getting out on a lobster boat. But we don't stop with the boat. The initiation continues to our lobster supplier and processing plant, which are all within a few minutes of the Portland wharves. The lobster industry is remarkable that way. Everything happens inside a relatively small radius, from the fishing to the processing to the shipping. Maine lobster is a global market, but it all starts here, on the water in a single lobster boat.

We also make sure to show them the cultural side of the industry—by which we mean, yes, we take them drinking. There are a few dives off the tourist path in and around the Portland area that only cater to locals. These aren't just good places to grab a beer; they're also the best spots to talk to the lobstermen and those whose families have been in the industry for generations. Even the two of us are somewhat out of place in these joints—and that's the point. The lobster industry, much like Maine itself, is its own culture. You can't simply adopt it, because it won't adopt you. The reason we make a point of showing our franchisees this slice of Maine that few see is because it's the best way to learn about the people who *are* the lobster industry—and have a little fun in the process.

But right now, the franchisees don't look too happy. We sympathize. We're not all that comfortable either. Lobstering is a relentless profession, because each boat is like its own small business on the water. If the boat doesn't go out, then the captain-owner doesn't get paid. It's like if we were allowed only one food truck and had to be on it all the time. How do you run a business that way?

By going out in weather fair or foul, every day of the season. Being a lobsterman means living in a world that is content to remain stuck in the past, sometime between the turn of the last century and World War II. We'll get to why it's this way in a moment, but know that it's not for the tourists. The communities that dot the Maine coast, and the industry that supports them, take their state's chief export as seriously as Silicon Valley takes its technology. Tourists love to come to the wharves because they want to step back into the past, and the city has responded by beautifying Commercial Street, the main artery running parallel to the water. But Maine isn't Disney. This isn't for show, and the lobstermen and their crews aren't actors. Lobster is how they earn their living, feed their families, build and buy their homes, send their kids to college, and save for retirement.

And, by extension, it's how we do all those things, too. In that way, the lobster industry isn't much different than nearly every other natural resource–driven industry on earth. It's a matter of knowing where your product comes from so that you can appreciate the work of dozens (or hundreds) of people that allows you to make a living. Yet the lobster industry is wholly unique as well. We don't suspect that a burger franchisor has its franchisees visit cattle ranches and slaughterhouses, but perhaps they do. The lobster industry is one of the few in the world that could hold back the corporate onslaught and homogenized industrial processes that dominate the modern economy.

In the movie *City Slickers*, Billy Crystal and his friends play at being cowboys for a week, driving a cattle herd across the plains. The horses are real, the cows are real, even the guides' six-shooters are real; but the whole process is a fantasy. There aren't any cowboys anymore, at least not ones who drive herds of cattle like they used to. If the beef industry still operated that way, beef would be scarce and prices astronomical. The cowboy died out when the world industrialized and cows could be mass produced—and mass slaughtered—on corporate ranches. We might mourn the loss of the fantasy, but we do love our cheap and plentiful burgers and steaks.

Tourists can certainly pay to have a lobster-boat captain take them out for a day. They can live out a fantasy as a lobsterman, then return to their families, share the pictures, and tell the story years later. But this is where the lobster industry stands apart. The lobsterman is back out on the water, doing the same thing the tourist did, the very next day. And the day after. And the day after that. It's a routine that stretches back more than a hundred years, ever since the lobster industry began to regulate itself and time stopped.

We don't bring our franchisees on the water because we want them to play at being Maine lobstermen for a day. We hope they enjoy the experience—some do, some throw up their breakfast over the gunwale—but that's not our purpose. Rather, we're out on Casco Bay on a blustery, wet October morning because we want our franchisees to see where their product comes from; how it's fished out of the water, one trap at a time by one captain operating one boat. We also want them to experience the disappointment of throwing back a perfectly healthy, nice-sized lobster. You can see the anguish on the franchisees' faces when the captain tells them to toss a lobster back into the ocean. They see dollars sinking to the ocean floor and prices back on their truck rising. But it's important for them to understand that this is one of the sustainability measures that Maine takes to protect the lobster industry. It's also important so that when they return to their cities, where food is bought at grocery stores and lobster meat comes packed in neat little boxes, they can remember the captain back on the water, doing the same thing he did yesterday, and the day before that.

We also want them to see the entirety of the supply chain so that they can talk to customers like we talk to customers. We mentioned in a previous chapter that we can't be everywhere, but that we want our customers *to see us everywhere*. Our franchisees are the solution. By learning the lobster industry from the inside, they can then talk as well as we do about what it means to be a purveyor of lobster meat. Our goal is simple but ambitious: to have the most-informed, best-educated franchisees in the business.

And perhaps, when they open that box of Maine lobster as they prepare to load the truck, they will know that they're selling more than food.

They're supporting a way of life.

# FROM SERVANTS TO KINGS

Historians of New England often note that early settlers considered lobster a kind of junk food that was fit only for swine, servants, and prisoners. These claims may be exaggerated. But storms could blow lobsters onto beaches by the hundreds, making them a convenient source of feed or fertilizer for coastal farms, and most scholars agree that lobster was generally considered a low-class dish for human consumption. After their first winter in Plymouth, a group of Pilgrims on an expedition to what is now Boston Harbor gladly helped themselves to fresh lobsters that had been piled on the beach by Native Americans. By the following year, however, the leader of the Pilgrims, William Bradford, reported shame at having to serve lobster in lieu of more respectable fare.

—Trevor Corson, *The Secret Life of Lobsters*[11]

When a resource is as plentiful as lobster was in those early years of the Maine settlements, it's only natural that the wealthy would turn up their noses. Of course, this had nothing to do with taste and everything to do with maintaining and adhering to a strict class consciousness. The poor ate what they ate because it was cheap and abundant; the rich ate what they ate because it was expensive and scarce. How times have changed.

But the change didn't happen overnight. You might recall from the preceding chapter that Maine lobster only developed a market once it was canned and shipped far and wide. We can't imagine eating lobster out of a can, but an industry needs to start somewhere. Because canning was so cheap, canneries by the dozen opened all along the New England coast as far as Nova Scotia. But they were extremely dirty as well as ravenous. The sheer number of lobsters needed to fill a single can prophesied doom for the burgeoning industry. As Colin Woodard notes:

> The process consumed an extraordinary number of lobsters. It took four and a half to six pounds of live lobsters to fill a one-pound can with meat. The bodies were discarded along with the shells, forming great refuse piles behind the cannery shed. . . . But most canneries simply dumped the refuse off the wharf—hundreds of tons annually at each cannery—transforming each harbor and nearby shores into a smelly mess of putrid shellfish.[12]

But no one much minded the smell if lobsters equaled money and jobs, which they did. The number of lobstermen skyrocketed from a "few dozen in the late 1840s to 1,843 in 1880." And it's no wonder. Between 1850 and 1880, the lobster industry, which at one time was mostly just for bait and fertilizer, was making $430,000 a year—a not insignificant industry in those days.[13] As Maine's other industries withered and died, lobster exploded. But there was a downside to the good times. The fisherman noticed that their hauls, which only years earlier pulled in hundreds of lobsters a day, had begun to shrink dramatically. In the 1880s, Swan Island lobsterman saw their daily catch dwindle from 250 lobsters to 75, while North Haven lobstermen noticed that the lobsters started getting smaller. Previously, pulling up a four-pound lobster was par for the course, but the average size during the heyday of the canneries fell to two pounds.[14] The falloff began to affect the canneries themselves, and many began to close due to lack of lobster. But that just made the ones that survived more determined to catch the lobsters that remained.

It didn't take long before a political scuffle broke out between the canneries and the lobstermen, who lobbied the state government to enact conservation measures. In some ways, it's a fight that continues to this very day. The suppliers and consumers of lobster always want more than the fishery can sustain. The lobstermen, fully aware that they can easily fish more, also know that they would be fishing themselves out of a job. Besides, a scarce resource with high demand fetches a better price than one that is easily procured. After some dithering, Maine lawmakers responded and by the 1880s the first conservation measures were put in place. Namely, laws were passed that put a limit on the lobster-fishing season and prohibited the capture of egg-bearing female lobsters as well as small, adolescent lobsters less than nine inches long. A few years later, the minimum size was further restricted to ten and a half inches.

Canneries responded to these measures by moving their operations across the Canadian border to New Brunswick. Once out of the Gulf of Maine, the quality of lobster drops dramatically, but the canneries didn't mind. After all, they weren't fishing the Gulf of Maine for its quality, but rather its quantity. They just needed ton after ton of lobster meat to fill the cans. Despite aggressive lobbying, the Maine government stuck to its guns, and the last cannery fled the state in 1894.[15]

Just as the canneries dwindled and the nascent lobster industry wondered if it could survive without them, Vacationland happened. In the years after the Civil War, tourism to Maine exploded. Tourism itself was a bit of a novelty. The notion that one could take off work to spend leisure time somewhere else was not only new, it went against the Puritan values still held by most New Englanders. But the people traveling to Maine for pleasure weren't exactly from Old Salem. These were the new industrialists and so-called robber barons who had amassed a ton of wealth in the post–Civil War era. Drawn to Maine's beauty and simple, rustic communities, America's new wealthy class found this backwater fishing state just the thing to escape the bustle of the cities. Maine swiftly became, to use a term coined in the twentieth century, Vacationland. And while there, the rich tourists developed a taste for fresh lobster.

It was a perfect storm of events for the lobster industry. Just as the population decline and conservation measures began to make lobster relatively scarce, the rich showed up with wads of cash. Scarce lobster means more expensive lobster and anything expensive to these newcomers was good. It turned lobster into a dish only they could enjoy and so enjoy it they would. The wealthy would arrive for the summer, and stay on vast estates they had bought and developed from native Mainers at rock-bottom prices. Woodard recounts the story of a property speculator who purchased a Bar Harbor lot from a local family for $200, only to sell it a few years later to George Vanderbilt for $200,000.[16]

And as vacationers are wont to do, when they showed up in Maine they wanted to "experience" all of Maine, which included foods that were once the fare of the lower classes. It wasn't just lobster; even clams, which had been sold only for bait, were suddenly a hot commodity. At the end of the summer, when the rich left the resorts and their spacious estates for the city, they took with them a newfound taste for Maine's seafood, sparking a market for live lobster and other New England fish in the great eastern cities, such as Boston, New York, and Baltimore. It stands as one of those curious little twists of history. The canneries had introduced Maine lobster to the world, shipping their tin cans as far as China. But the rich turned up their noses at anything that came out of a can—and we probably shouldn't blame them. Canned lobster meat, even from Maine, doesn't sound all that great. But put a full lobster on a porcelain plate with a bowl of melted butter and a parsley leaf for garnish, and, suddenly, our once-derided crustacean has become a luxury dish. So, while the old canneries died out, lobster, once the food for servants, prisoners, and the poor, had transformed into a dish fit for kings.

As Woodard writes: "The arrival of the summer people would forever alter coastal Maine society, economics, and land ownership patterns. Their effect on the burgeoning lobster fishery was immediate and profoundly invigorating."[17]

## THE DEATH OF AN INDUSTRY

In 1905, Boston's Bay State Fishing Company introduced the first otter trawler in the Gulf of Maine. The 115-foot-long steam-powered vessels could catch one hundred tons of fish through their 80-foot-wide mouths, which were used to scoop up entire schools. Trawlers themselves had been invented by the British, but were mostly derided by New England fisherman, who still relied on the "tub trawling" method—essentially a way to catch a large amount of bottom fish with the traditional line and baited hooks. But with New England bottom fish such as cod, haddock, and halibut suddenly in high demand, and with the New England coast being the world's number one spot for catching large amounts of these fish, it was only a matter of time before the European-style trawlers began to cruise the coastal waters.

Woodard provides an account of the gruesome aftermath of the trawlers' introduction to New England's fisheries. Between 1902 and 1936, he reports, the New England halibut catch fell from 13.5 million pounds a year to 2 million pounds. Also, between 1929 and 1936, haddock catches fell by two-thirds. Even clams, at one time believed to be useful only as bait, saw their numbers dwindle by three-quarters between 1928 and 1930. But the worst was yet to come.

By 1935, fisherman could find no cod or haddock in the upper half of Penobscot Bay, where they had once been prevalent. They continued to fish in the outer bay, first with small boats rigged with little otter trawls, later with larger draggers. By the late forties and early fifties, commercial quantities of cod and haddock could no longer be found in Maine's largest embayment. The story repeated itself up and down the coast and, in every instance, the cod and haddock never returned to their spawning grounds.[18]

In short, New England's groundfish industry was on its deathbed.

By the 1950s, European, Russian, and Japanese "freezer trawler" fleets—so-called because they could store the enormous quantities of caught fish in freezers—had started to fish the waters farther out in the Atlantic, near the Grand Banks, but soon turned their sights on what was left on Georges Bank and the Gulf of Maine. Because of its storage facility, the freezer trawler could fish twenty-four hours a day, seven days a week, or until her two-thousand-ton load was filled.

It was during this time that American households had begun to gobble up cheap, frozen fish caught by these foreign behemoths. It didn't matter if the fish was of a lower quality than what the New England fisherman offered; it was cheap and would keep in the freezer box. This foreign-fish invasion further undercut the New England fishermen, who were already having a hard enough time finding the high-quality catch. And because these fish were caught in international waters where there wasn't any law, there was little the US government, much less the Maine government, could do to help.

And so, the overfishing continued. The trawlers would literally fish a particular species to near extinction, then move on to the next. The other problem with trawlers, other than that they pick up massive quantities of fish with no regard to conservation, is that they also scoop up other marine wildlife. As Woodard notes, "The United Nations later estimated that for every four tons of fish that were landed worldwide, another ton or more of other creatures were discarded as by-catch."[19] There was nothing to stop them and the few voices calling for some measure of conservation were ignored.

Meanwhile, back in Maine, the inshore fisherman bore the brunt of the decades of overfishing. With the cod, haddock, and halibut fisheries gone, they had turned to pollock, herring, and whiting. Different fish, same story. Even though the trawling was happening farther offshore, it captured the same schools of fish that would find their way to Maine—only, they never made it. In 1960, Maine fisherman caught four million pounds of pollock, but only eight hundred thousand pounds in 1970. Herring fell by 80 percent in the same period. In the 1950s and '60s, Mainers would catch fifteen to twenty million pounds of whiting, but only 250,000 pounds in 1977.[20]

Eventually, the world community responded to the foreign trawlers that indiscriminately cruised the oceans by expanding national sovereignty out to two hundred miles at sea. This pushed the trawlers far away from Maine and helped to reduce the damage they did to the fishery and to Maine's economy. But the damage had been done and much of it was irreversible. New England's groundfish industry, once the envy of the world, was in tatters. The more marketable fish—cod, haddock, and halibut—had all but disappeared, taking jobs and entire fishing communities with them. Up and down the New England coast, the ravages of the decline and fall of the groundfish industry could be seen in deserted wharves, closed shops, and displaced families. Many New Englanders, whose families had fished the coastal waters for generations, had to give up the sea and turn toward the factories. It was a painful end for an industry that had once defined an entire region of the United States.

Amid this economic carnage, the lobstermen had watched in dismay as they saw their sister industry fall apart. Many had split their time between catching groundfish and lobster anyway, but there was a limit on the number of lobsterman on the water. Which meant that many of the groundfish captains had to find other work. They wouldn't be back, because the fish weren't coming back. The lobstermen themselves, feeling fortunate that the great foreign trawlers hadn't developed a taste for lobster before they departed, saw in their jobless brethren a warning: greed and shortsightedness had doomed the groundfish industry. Unless they were smarter, the fate of New England's fishermen would be their fate as well.

## LIFE ON THE WATER

"Even your bad days are better than sitting in an office."

Steve Train has never known any other life. Nor did his father. Or his grandfathers. Follow the generations of Steve's family until they fade into the Maine mists and you'll find little else but lobstermen. A father himself, Steve says that children of lobstermen grow up with one overriding ambition, to pursue the family trade. Other kids play with LEGOs and action figures; Steve grew up fashioning forts out of lobster traps. It's no surprise then that his eldest daughter, who's studying marine science at the University of Maine, wants to come home and become a lobsterman—er, lobsterwoman.

"I'm not discouraging it," says Steve. "But I don't want her to think she has to."

But that's the thing: no one *has to* be a lobsterman. Sometimes you wonder why they do it. As we mentioned earlier, a lobsterman is limited to one boat and he or she must be on it to fish. It all starts with the much coveted and highly regulated Maine lobsterman license. There are only about 6,000 licenses available, and the wait list for getting one can last years. Moreover, licenses are managed by individual counties, as opposed to the state government. To get one, you need to be a resident of that county, and must have logged a certain number of hours on a lobster boat. And each county only has a hundred or so licenses to go around. This doesn't even get into the cost of purchasing your own boat, which fetches a price of a couple hundred thousand dollars.

There are clear conservation motivations behind this policy, since it limits the number of boats on the water. But the real conservation measure is that it basically prohibits any corporate takeover of the industry, which is exactly what happened to the groundfish industry. There is simply no way for any company to get a foothold anywhere in Maine lobster, because every lobsterman is in the same boat, so to speak. The flip side is that a lobsterman can't scale his business. He is utterly dependent on what he brings in on his single boat and the price fluctuations of the market. Which isn't to say that lobstermen are destitute, but they live on very thin margins.

The other effect of the one-boat-one-owner policy is that it keeps Maine's coastal communities alive and not wholly dependent on the "summer people," as they call tourists. It's true that Mainers have a love-hate relationship with the vacationers, but it's more love than hate. After all, it's the vacationers who bring the dollars to buy the lobster, stay at the resorts, tour the islands, and give teenagers jobs working on ferry boats, which is what Jim did for a few summers. But Mainers love their independence more, as four hundred years of history have made abundantly clear. It's not in Mainers' nature to rely on the whims of the tourist industry, as many beach communities without any local industry must do. Mainers would rather have a say in the direction of their lives.

Lobster gives them that voice. Lobster is independence, because it means that if all the vacationers never came back—a calamity, to be sure—Mainers would still have that one resource no one else in the world has. Draw this sentiment out across the dozens of thriving fishing towns that dot Maine's coastline and islands and you can appreciate why the one-boat-one-owner policy was put into effect. It allows each community to have its own fishery, its own raison d'être. If an owner could own more than one boat, then what would stop someone from launching a fleet of them from Portland? In no time at all, that fleet would be able to outfish the single-boat guys, who would likely have to find jobs working for the Portland fleet. The result? The lobstermen leave their coastal and island towns for the big city. So, Portland grows, while the tiny communities wither—or barely hang on, waiting desperately for the next wave of vacationers.

Opponents of the law say it's merely an outdated protectionist measure. To which we would reply: yes, it is; but it's also a survivalist one, and very much part of Maine's economic policy. That policy appreciates that Maine's quaint coastal and island communities are rare and highly sought after by tourists. But these communities wouldn't exist without the one-boat-one-owner policy. The policy itself forms the link between Maine's world-renowned resource and its tourism industry. If the link was severed, then the circle would break and Maine would lose one of its primary sources of income, the tourists.

Still, these policies are also in place for conservation reasons. The population, while healthy and strong today, has gone through its own moments of scarcity and concern. As lobster science has improved over the decades, lobstermen have had to contend with fairly restrictive policies regarding their capture. Today, the minimum size of a legal lobster, measured from the eye to the end of the carapace or body shell, is three and a quarter inches. This is to protect the adolescent lobsters, giving them a chance to mature and procreate. Lobster traps are designed with the minimum-size restriction in mind. Each trap has a set of holes that allow smaller lobsters to exit. They don't always make it out, and thus must endure a trip to the surface, followed by a plummet of a hundred feet or so to the bottom again.

But there's also a maximum size of a legal lobster that is set at five inches. Why the maximum? Because large male lobsters are the alphas in any population; they're the ones who have the pick of the females by asserting their physical (and sexual) dominance over their lesser male neighbors. In other words, the lobster population would take a severe hit if all the alpha males were captured. Then there's the restrictions regarding female egg-bearing lobsters. If one is caught, the lobsterman makes a *v*-shaped notch in the tail, alerting the next lobsterman that this is an egg-bearing female who must be released.

What these size restrictions mean in practice is that *every Maine lobster is inspected* before it's captured. It means no indiscriminate trawling—or dragging—of the ocean floor, then dumping whatever is caught in some tank. That lobster on your plate or in your lobster roll was sized and inspected the moment it was retrieved from the trap by the captain himself. Clearly, this isn't the most efficient or economically viable way of doing things. Even if draggers were legal in Maine—they're not—a captain would still have to take time to inspect each lobster he caught.

So, again, why would anyone want to be a lobsterman, given all the uneconomic restrictions and inefficiencies baked into the business? Because it's the life they know and love. Every morning, Steve takes his boat out to do the same job he's done his entire life, since he first stepped foot on a lobster boat when he was eight years old.

"We've had a pretty good run the last ten years on weight," Steve tells us. "But on price it's different. The price has been depressed, because there's been a volume increase down east. So, I'm carrying a lot of debt right now. Also, bait prices have gone through the roof."

For a franchisee, the fluctuations in price can come as quite a shock. We prepare them for this as best we can, but have found that the best lesson is experience. When the price jumps, we all must scramble—the franchisees as well as those of us in the corporate office. With new franchisees, a price jump usually elicits a call to one of us, who must talk down the panicked voice on the other end of the phone. We get it, because we've been there.

When a business says it's going to serve no other lobster but Maine lobster, it's assuming a certain amount of risk. Not only is the price for Maine lobster generally more expensive than its closest competitor, the Canadian lobster, but its fluctuations are also greater. This makes it difficult for a Maine lobster business to plan, not knowing what the price will be in six months. For this reason, a lot of businesses that start out selling Maine lobster bow to economic pressures and opt for its cheaper cousin.

Yet, side by side, there is simply no comparison in taste between Maine and Canadian lobster. A lot of businesses convince themselves that they can simply augment their Maine meat with Canadian to save a little bit. Who but a lobster connoisseur could tell the difference? Well, you'd be surprised. But more important than that, you're lying to your customers. If you want to sell Canadian lobster, go right ahead. But don't you dare call it Maine lobster.

Because you're not just tricking your customers; you're selling out the lobstermen, who makes a living selling the Maine lobster they catch. Charlatans who steal the name but sell a different meat tarnish the brand and make it harder for guys like Steve, and perhaps his daughter one day, too, to make their livings and feed their families.

The lobstermen haven't been immune to the challenges of overfishing. Several times since the nineteenth century, the lobster population has sunk to dangerous levels, causing some scientists to predict the imminent demise of the fishery. But in every instance the lobsters came back, through a combination of science-backed conservation measures and, vitally, the co-operation of the lobstermen. Those first conservation measures mentioned above were on the right track, but a lot of lobstermen simply ignored them. Moreover, the laws created a black market for illegal lobsters that the independent lobsterman was only too happy to sell to.

Until they saw what was happening to the groundfish industry. Around the time of the Great Depression, the lobstermen reversed course and began to police themselves on adhering to the conservation measures, not for any esoteric virtue like conservation and sustainability, but for basic survival. The choice was simple: if you want this life, follow the rules.

Now in his sixties, Steve's answer to why he does it is straightforward: "I'm worn out every night but I can't wait to do it again every morning. This keeps you alive."

## LESSON
## KNOW WHY YOU DO IT

We're starting our day on the lobster boat by walking down a Portland wharf to one of the docks, where we'll wait for Captain Jonathan Norton to take us out. A pickup pulls up next to us and the driver rolls down his window to bid us good morning. Jim exchanges some pleasantries with the driver, one of the wharf employees, and mentions Jonathan's name as well as the name of Jonathan's father, John. The driver smiles and wishes us a good day of fishing before driving on. To the franchisees, what they just witnessed was nothing more than a friendly chat, but to Jim it was a checkpoint.

Every wharf in Maine is privately owned. There aren't gates or guards at the entrances. Anyone can take a gander down the little alley to the docks to check out the boats and the mountains of lobster traps, even if they're not supposed to. But this friendly, inclusive club of lobstering is also very protective. When one of its members sees a group of strangers—obviously tourists, by their clothes—where they shouldn't be, they'll check it out. At the same time, it's a club that is also very welcoming, particularly to those whom it considers friends of the trade. By mentioning Jonathan's and his father's names—John Norton—Jim was signaling that our purpose there was legitimate. All the driver had to do was call up John to know we were vouched for—we were friends of the club. But he didn't. Jim's word was enough for him.

It also helped that Jim knew the driver from childhood. The two had worked together on the ferries that shuttled tourists between the islands and the mainland during the summer. Jim's friendship with the driver alone might have been enough, but combined with Jim's knowledge of the owner of the wharf and his son, the driver knew that Jim and his friends posed no harm. The suspicion turned immediately to trust and respect.

We're not lobstermen. Our franchisees aren't lobstermen. We've never had to make a living hauling up sixty-pound traps, stinking of brine and rotting fish heads. We've done it, as have all our franchisees, but doing it for a day doesn't give one honorary membership. It takes years to become a lobsterman: first as an apprentice, then as a captain-owner, one of the world's few proud holders of a Maine lobsterman license.

When we get on the boat, the *Isla Dawn*, we learn that Jonathan, a thirty-four-year-old family man who's just built a home on Long Island—Maine, not New York—waited seven years for his license. Despite his family connections and his ancestry, he got no special privileges. He had to put in his time just like everyone else.

"Many guys just give up," says Jonathan as he takes us past

his home on Long Island. "I've heard of wait times of ten to fifteen years."

Jonathan isn't exactly happy about that. He feels that the profession needs more young guys like him, but he understands why the process is the way it is. Particularly now that he's an official member, he's as protective of his fellow lobstermen—and of the curious crustacean on which they build their fortunes—as any old-timer.

As is most anyone who spends any significant time with lobstermen. We didn't start out feeling as protective of their interests as we do today. In our early days, we were more concerned with providing customers with as genuine a Maine lobster experience as we could. But we made a choice even before our first truck was on the road to sell no lobster but Maine lobster. This decision brought us into the fold of the Maine lobster industry—this vibrant, sensitive, highly independent group of fishermen whose concern for their resource is nothing short of inspiring. And the more time we spent with these captain-owners, the more we felt pulled by the history of their profession, which, as you've seen, is also the history of our great home state.

And now we're a vital part of that history. We don't say this to be boastful or to assume a level of privilege we know we haven't—and couldn't ever—earn. We say this because our success has provided us with a certain level of responsibility. Our growth helps guys like Steve and Jonathan and also helps the Maine lobster industry as a whole. *Isla Dawn* is more than a typical lobster boat; it's the name of Jonathan's daughter. He gets up every morning hours before dawn to spend twelve hours on a small boat baiting lobster traps with rotting fish heads for her. He wouldn't have it any other way.

"Not too long ago, we were landing about eighty million pounds of lobster," Steve tells us. "Today, we're landing around one hundred and twenty million pounds."

Of course, this surge in business isn't tied to our own, but we have had a small part to play in democratizing lobster, taking it off the porcelain plates of kings and putting it back on the picnic table for servants—or at least the non-wealthy. Every Friday, our suppliers put their entire team to work loading their Cousins Maine Lobster order. We are one of their biggest clients, far larger than the fancy restaurants that used to be the sole purveyors of lobster not so very long ago.

This sense of responsibility for an industry that provides us, our employees, and our franchisees with a living now informs everything we do. It's why we do it. We have been extremely fortunate in becoming part of the great circle of Maine's lobster industry. It's a small part, to be sure, but our sense of accountability is no less for it. Without lobster, Maine wouldn't be what it was when we were kids; it wouldn't be what it is today, which thankfully is almost identical. We want it to be that way tomorrow, and next month, and next year, and ten years down the road. And we will work every day to protect and sustain the Maine we love, because it is darn near perfect the way it is.

Best of all, our support is reciprocated. They also support us, and give us a chance to make a living our chosen way. The respect, the handshakes, the familiarity—these are the things that make this industry special and something we are proud to not only call our own, but also to promote and protect.

For an entrepreneur, knowing why you do it is the true spirit of creation. At first, you build something because you have a great idea or a marketable product. You do it because you want to be your own boss or you want to make more money. You do it because you're tired of your day job and want to wake up every morning with a passion for your work. These are all valid, normal reasons for becoming an entrepreneur, ones which we shared and which still inspire us today. But we've discovered another reason, one we couldn't have predicted, but which has been far more motivational than any selfish desire to build and manage a company.

We have found a purpose in what we do. We do it for guys like Steve and Jonathan. We do it for Maine's coastal and island communities that have withstood economic despair and the demise of one of history's great fisheries. We do it because the families that live on these pristine yet often inhospitable bits of land have been given the gift of a resource that is desired all over the world. But that resource is fragile; it is a gift, a treasure, that can easily be lost, if it is not respected and protected.

That is why we do it. We can only hope that you find your purpose like we found ours.

# 7

# Franchising, in Focus

In October 2015, Cousins Maine Lobster held its first franchisee retreat in Portland. We had booked rooms at the Residence Inn in the heart of downtown, not far from the water, and reserved the conference room. If it wasn't as idyllic as being on a grassy lawn overlooking Penobscot Bay, with picnic tables covered in gorgeous red lobster, well, it was a start. We were thrilled just to have all ten of our franchisees in one place for the very first time.

But most of all, we were thrilled about our keynote speaker, Kat Cole, probably the most accomplished person in Portland that day. And for some reason she had agreed to speak with a collection of first-time business owners and franchisees. Slightly condensed, here's what she said:

"It's kind of funny that Sabin and Jim would invite a Hooters girl to speak to you today. That's right. My second job was as a waitress at Hooters in Jacksonville, Florida, when I was still in high school. I worked because things were tight back home. My mother raised my two sisters and me by herself, and struggled to make ends meet. As the oldest, I tried to help wherever I could, first as a babysitter, then as another source of income.

And that brought me into a Hooters. But I'm here today to tell you that it doesn't matter where you start. Where you start says very little about where you end up.

"So I wore the skimpy uniform, served beer and chicken wings, and helped my mom pay the rent and take care of my siblings. But I also watched and I learned. For whatever you might think about Hooters, it is a phenomenally successful business. It has a specific brand and targets a specific customer. Hooters makes no apologies for this, nor should it. There are more than four hundred Hooters locations and franchises in the world, including forty-four states and twenty-eight other countries.

"By the time I entered college, the first of my family to do so, I still worked for Hooters but I was no longer a waitress. I was nineteen and I had learned the Hooters business model so well that the company had started sending me around the world to open new franchises. I ended up dropping out of college, because my studies interfered with my day job. My mother wasn't too happy with that, but I think I've managed to convince her it was the right decision for me. By twenty-six, I was vice president of training and development. During my tenure at Hooters, I oversaw the opening of nearly three hundred locations worldwide, and watched Hooters become a billion-dollar company.

"Today, I'm the group president of Focus Brands and the COO of Cinnabon. In many ways, I still do what I've always done, going way back to when I was eighteen. I open franchises. Since joining Cinnabon in 2010, we've opened more than two hundred bakeries worldwide. But what I always tell people, particularly new franchisees like you, is that Cinnabon started as one store. Just one, at a mall in Washington State. And that first store was dedicated to doing one thing: making the best damn cinnamon roll in the world.

"Sound familiar? It should, because you're all now part of a company that started as just one food truck that is dedicated to doing one thing: make the best damn lobster roll in the world. And what I'm going to tell you is that you couldn't ask for better franchisors than Jim and Sabin. I've met dozens of franchisors and thousands of franchisees. I know the type of person it takes to build a brand that can be replicated again and again. And rarely have I seen a franchisor with the right combination of respect, hard work, and humility as you have with Jim and Sabin.

"The task before you isn't easy, but you should expect these guys to give you exactly what you need to thrive. But . . . that doesn't absolve you of being an entrepreneur in your own right. By becoming franchisees of Cousins Maine Lobster, you've entered into a formal agreement. The terms of this agreement are spelled out fairly clearly in a bunch of legal language we don't need to recite here.

"But you've also entered into an informal agreement, one that isn't bound by any legal requirements. This informal agreement says that you are responsible for more than just selling lobster rolls. It says you are responsible for building the great brand that is Cousins Maine Lobster with new ideas. Each of you is more than a food truck operator. You must be innovators as well. You must be visionaries. Because the genius of the franchise system is that you are able to work as independent entrepreneurs. By giving you their brand, the cousins have given you your start. But that's all it is.

"Just like I started as a Hooters girl, you have started as food truck operators. You could stay a food truck operator, just as I could have stayed a waitress. Or you can be more than what you started with. How? By building something on your own. By using what the cousins have given you and creating something better. By turning your food trucks into incubators of new ideas.

"This is your responsibility. But I tell you now: it's amazing where you can go when you start to build something on your own. That's my advice to you. You've been given this extraordinary opportunity to join the Cousins Maine Lobster family—for it is a family. What comes next is up to you."

Afterward, Kat stuck around to answer questions from our franchisees, as a kind of group therapy session for everyone. Not that our franchisees were in need of therapy—at least no more than we were at this stage—but when you have the master herself in front of you, you don't waste the opportunity. We could tell that her story, her very presence, had lit a fire under everyone in the room. They just don't get more successful or inspirational than Kat Cole. Which raises an obvious question: Just how did we get her as our keynote speaker?

That's a great question . . .

## THE NEW REALITY

Barbara raised the idea of franchising early in our partnership. But it was just one of several ideas we discussed in those days about how to build the brand. After *Shark Tank*, our immediate concern was whether we could duplicate our success with another truck. This might seem like a fairly simple matter of adding more trucks to the LA fleet, but nothing is ever that simple. We were cautious. The show had thrust us into a kind of minor-celebrity spotlight and our single truck was reaping the rewards. We were selling out wherever we went simply because people had seen us on the show.

Pretty great, right?

Except that we had become a target. A glance through our Yelp reviews in those post–*Shark Tank* days tells a fuller story than the lines at our truck. Previously, we had been lucky to get almost 100 percent positive online reviews. But then *Shark Tank* happened and suddenly those reviews began to slip. Almost without fail, each negative review started in the same way: "*After seeing the cousins on* Shark Tank, *I wanted to see what the hype was all about . . .*" Then BAM! A negative review. It's not that our Yelp reviews went completely south after *Shark Tank*, it's that we found ourselves under a magnifying glass that we hadn't anticipated. Even the good reviews would offer criticisms that we had never heard before. It's as if customers wanted to find something wrong.

A company shouldn't ever take Internet comments too seriously. You're never doing as great or as bad as the commenters say. Moreover, the people who do comment on those sites aren't a fair cross section of your customer base. They make up what statisticians would call an "unscientific" sample size. But they spoke to our new reality. There had been a time when a single customer's bad experience or opinion was just that: just one out of hundreds of otherwise satisfied customers. If the customer came to us directly or complained on a site like Yelp, we did what we could to fix the problem, within reason. Some customer complaints are just unreasonable and you do more harm trying to make them happy.

But now it was as if customers were *looking* for flaws in our business. A customer who isn't 100 percent satisfied at a random food truck doesn't think twice about it. Sure, perhaps there could have been more lobster meat or the price was a tad steep, but they either enjoyed their experience or they didn't. The degree of their (dis)satisfaction was registered by whether they came back. And a lot would come back. But now, they weren't just buying a meal at a random food truck: they were buying a meal at a food truck *featured on* Shark Tank.

The bar had been raised. The customers' senses were heightened. Our room for error had shrunk significantly. In fact, there wasn't any room for error. Because when you're in the public spotlight, people judge you differently than if you're just another food truck. Even if you try to prepare for this, you can't ever be prepared. The sheer number of customers who are visiting your truck just so they can pick it apart is overwhelming. They're going to find something, that's just the way it is. It's like knowing that the *New York Times* food critic is coming to your restaurant on a certain night—except there are hundreds of critics and they are coming *every night.*

What to do? For starters, don't give them a reason to complain. They're going to find something anyway, just don't make it easy on them. We had to up our game. We had to put in place a process to rid the entire service line of human error. Because that's where they get you—when someone screws up. Gone were the days of winging it on the fly; gone were the days of "Fuck it, just eyeball it!" when it came to the right amount of lobster meat; gone were the days of having untrained employees on the truck. Now, everyone on the truck knew their place and what to do. Everyone knew everyone else's job, just in case something went wrong. And with a food truck, something always goes wrong.

The thing is, sometimes those commenters who came just to criticize weren't wrong. We've seen it for ourselves. Heck, everyone has. You hear about a great place, maybe online or from television, and you make a point of going there to try it out. Your expectations are high, and they should be. This venue has received publicity any business would kill for. They know it and you know it. And so, when your experience there is less than what you expect, your displeasure is greater than if you had just found the place on the street. Sure, there's a chance you're being too harsh. But there's also a chance you aren't: perhaps the place didn't live up to the hype because the food just wasn't that good. Or maybe the place with the "million-dollar view" only has a million-dollar view, and nothing else. Maybe the burger joint made a decent patty, but for twenty dollars? For twenty dollars, the burger should have been life changing.

Which is another way to say that we couldn't dismiss all

those commenters. Some made valid points and we got better. It was a bit of a culture change for us, to be sure. After all, we assumed that "winging it" was part of our charm. Being a little rusty, a little rough around the edges—isn't that what people expect when they go to a lobster shack? Perhaps, but how many lobster shacks make it on *Shark Tank*? How many lobster shacks can claim Barbara Corcoran as an investor? But the fair criticisms we took seriously and we tried to make good with the reviewer where we could.

The plain truth is that we had entered a new phase of our company. We had gone on *Shark Tank* because we had wanted to be more than a food truck. Congratulations—we were. Now we couldn't afford to get anything wrong. We had traded our anonymity for national publicity, and the price was that we now had to be perfect, or damn near perfect, because we now attracted a different sort of customer. There are those who want to see the *Shark Tank* contestant and take a selfie. Then there are those who just want to bring you down.

Why? Because they can.

In any case, those early review hits didn't hurt our sales much, but they opened our eyes to the new reality. We were doing better business than ever before, except the ground had shifted. Things were different now. We had to get better. No mistakes.

## NEW TRUCKS, OLD SYSTEMS

Since the day we decided to go on *Shark Tank*, our plan had always been to use the money we got to buy a new truck. Our plan hadn't changed after *Shark Tank*, only now, we were a bit wiser. We now saw that we had a couple problems. First, when the Cousins Maine Lobster truck rolls into the neighborhood, the cousins—at least one of us—better be on it. All over LA people were showing up because they wanted to meet us.

So, despite our busy schedules, we continued to go out with the truck whenever we could. We knew that we had to get through this post–*Shark Tank* patch by being on the truck as much as possible, because almost all of our new customers were there to see us in person. Again, it was the new reality and it wreaked havoc on our schedule, as well as our plans to expand. As Barbara taught us, every moment you're doing something is a moment you're not doing something else. It also complicated our plans to put another truck on the road. The good news is that there are two of us, so even if customers didn't get us both, they usually got one of us.

Regardless, not long after *Shark Tank* we put our second truck on the road. It was an immediate success. Although we had run the numbers and figured that Los Angeles could support two trucks, you're never sure until you try. But it wasn't just whether there was enough demand for two trucks; it was also whether we could replicate the processes and system that had made the first truck a success.

Obviously, our long-term plan was to develop a full-scale standardization of the Cousins Maine Lobster model (whatever that was). We hadn't yet committed to franchising, but expansion of any sort required us to codify our unique way of doing business. For instance, could we hand a new franchisee a how-to kit, complete with a brand-new food truck, and be fairly confident that just following the rules and processes in the kit would lead to success? Or what if we chose instead to pursue a corporate model, where every truck we put on the road was ours? Could we be reasonably sure of success? We weren't sure, but putting another truck on the road forced us to find out.

We mentioned in a previous chapter that as an entrepreneur, you will have to give up the thing you love doing if you want to build a company. A baker who wants to open a lot of bakeries can't stay in the kitchen. He's too busy opening up bakeries and implementing a process where every bakery bearing his name operates as well as the first bakery. In a similar vein, an entrepreneur must also find the discipline for organization. Expansion requires more than customer demand, money, capital, or more employees. It requires, above all, the discipline to combine all those things into something resembling a company structure and logistical plan. You want to take everything that works here and duplicate it there. Easier said than done.

First, you should know what's working here. Why does it only take three minutes from order to service? Have you looked at that? If it's only because one employee on the line is faster than the others, then you need to know that. Can the other employees be as fast as him? What's the average time without this employee?

Knowing the answer to these questions requires the dreaded word: information. Or, more accurately, data. We learned early to be fanatical about collecting data on our processes, from what happened on the truck to what happened back in Maine with our suppliers. We could trace our product; know where shipments were and why they were delayed; keep an eye on a temperature control; and find the bottlenecks and areas for improvement. We'll admit that all of this is exceedingly dull and boring to set up—but once you have a system in place that actually allows you to capture this data, you'll wonder how you ever did without it. It not only enables you to easily find flaws in your current processes, but it also makes it easier (it's never "easy") to transport those processes to another location, or another truck.

———

We had some of these systems in place for one truck; we improved those and added a few others once we got the second truck. But it wasn't a seamless progression. Adding the second truck showed us a lot of the processes and metrics we had simply overlooked with the first one. Part of the problem is that we knew every job in the entire Cousins Maine Lobster hierarchy, such as it was. We could be line cooks, checkout persons, bookers, even drivers. When you can do everything—which all entrepreneurs end up doing early on—then you sometimes forget that not everyone else can. The second truck exposed to us all the jobs, systems, and processes we had taken for granted and never bothered to set down in writing.

It's vitally important to know your business from A to Z. Your early days as a business owner should provide that education, as long as you're doing it right. After all, how can you teach someone else to do something if you haven't done it yourself? We're reminded of that reality show *Undercover Boss*, where CEOs spend a day working at the low-level jobs of their business. The point of the show is that the CEO is supposed to come away with a newfound appreciation and respect for the people who do those jobs. Which is why we'd be terrible on the show. We've *already* done those jobs in our business; we know exactly what our employees go through. But we agree with the show's purpose: we are better business owners because we know these things.

The best way to tackle this phase of your organization overhaul is to deconstruct every process to its barest essentials. What do we mean by that? Look at it like a recipe, which has two elements: ingredients and steps. Every process in your business, from the manufacturing of the product to payroll, must be reduced to ingredients and steps. We found that this is an exercise where it pays to be painfully literal. When we say every ingredient and every step must be listed, we mean *every single one*.

But replication of our system wasn't limited to processes. We also had to deal with our first problem: Who can be the cousins when the cousins aren't there? Put another way, how do we build a company where our presence on the trucks wasn't required for success? Our solution was to give each employee the ability to be able to converse with customers about the company, lobster, and Maine. In short, not only did every new truck need to operate like the first truck, but each employee had to be an extension of us. That was our goal. Which should be the goal of all entrepreneurs: your job during the early expansion period is to replicate yourself. If you're still micromanaging after you've opened a few more locations, then something is wrong with your process. Fix it and stop wasting your time.

This is what we mean by discipline. It's hard to let go when you've been involved in the business's operations from day one. But for the same reason you can't keep baking if you want to own a chain of bakeries, you can't do everything if you want to build a company. Hiring the right people is the first step; but the second, equally important step is to have the discipline to set down your process and practices into a system that can be replicated.

It's the old adage: work smarter, not harder. Just by opening your own company, you must work hard. Both of us benefit from an incredibly strong work ethic. But discipline is different than hard work. Hard work is running around to each of your locations, double- and sometimes triple-checking your employees and your processes, and correcting mistakes. Discipline is setting up a data-capture system that collects information from all of your locations and delivers actionable insight right to your computer screen. A system like that isn't easy to set up, but it's a heck of a lot smarter than the alternative method: you running around like a madman. Don't ever mistake hard work for smart work.

In short, expansion of any sort requires a level of discipline your little company probably never needed. You need to find this discipline if you want to keep the whole shaky edifice from crumbling. Because a lot of the time, failure has nothing to do with your product, customer demand, or money flow. Sometimes it is just a matter of total disorganization. This doesn't necessarily mean that you must do all the organization yourself. Sometimes discipline requires finding the right person or team to organize the company for you. Have the courage to give up a little bit of control to achieve organizational simplicity.

Which brings us to our third truck.

For us, adding a second truck was always part of the plan, but a third? We assumed we'd get there, too, but we weren't in a rush. And that's when we learned something else about expansion: sometimes a business's growth isn't a choice; it's a necessity. We were taught this lesson when going over finances with—who else?—Steve. By this point in our company, we had standardized most of our financial processes, at least to the point that they resembled a real-life business. And while reviewing some numbers one day with Steve, we were looking at some forecasts and noticed they weren't great. We were running a bit short and putting too much on credit, but that's how it goes sometimes.

Or so we thought, until Steve said, "Looks like it's time to get another truck." We sort of looked at him, as if to say, "Are you nuts? We just added a second!" Why did Steve want us to expand at a time when money was tight? That didn't make sense. But Steve's point was that if our two trucks were completely booked, then that meant the market could bear a third. The lesson we got from this is that you shouldn't go slow and steady just because you think that's the smart thing to do. Go slow and steady if that's the *best thing for your business*. But if circumstances point in the opposite direction, have the courage to go fast, too.

And so, only a couple months after putting our second truck on the road, we had a fleet of three. It wasn't long before our trucks were pulling in around $180,000 a month in sales. We stood to make roughly $2 million in sales our second year. We could have left it at that and been considered successful by most definitions of the word. Certainly, any attempt to go beyond that would be a risk.

But we had discovered within ourselves that we weren't content with good enough. If three trucks made that much money in LA, what would a single truck make somewhere else? Say, in Raleigh? Or Dallas? Or Sacramento?

We weren't sure, but it was time to find out.

## "WHAT IS FRANCHISING?"

Do just a little bit of online research about franchising and you're likely to come across some variation of this statistic: "Studies show that franchises have a success rate of 90 percent as compared to just 15 percent for businesses that start from the ground up." You'll even find some sites using a number as high as 95 percent. The funny thing is no one knows where this stat came from, yet franchising brokers and consultants continue to toss it around, luring the naïve into franchising because it's supposed to be easy money.

The idea behind the statistic is that a franchisee doesn't need to do all that much work to be successful; that merely buying into an already successful brand somehow guarantees success, like osmosis or something. This is laughable. We've spent years fine-tuning and improving our franchise kit so that our franchisees have all that they need from us to be successful, but we've learned one undeniable fact about franchising: it all comes down to the franchisee.

Just ask one. Better yet, ask them about the 90 percent success stat, only be prepared to duck. Franchisees have a mean left hook. Or just keep reading. An article in *Entrepreneur*

*Magazine* dug into this pesky little marketing gimmick and found what any franchisee already knows: "The Stat" is crap.

> Bad information is the bread and butter of the Internet, but this particular nugget is especially troubling. Franchising is one of the most heavily regulated industries in the U.S. for a reason—it has suffered from high-profile cases of misrepresentation and fraud. Critics point to The Stat as a willful misrepresentation and an attempt to sucker people into buying franchises. In many ways it really does lure people into franchising, even if a franchisor has never made the claim. The ubiquity of The Stat means that many candidates come into their businesses thinking franchise ownership is practically guaranteed success.[21]

The reporter searches in vain for a more reliable success rate for franchisees only to conclude that success depends on two independent variables: the franchisor and the franchisee. In other words, we're back to where we started. Finding franchise success is no quicker or easier than anything else. We certainly didn't choose a franchising model for our expansion because we thought it would be easy. We chose it because it was the option that made the most sense for the type of business we were at the time, and the type of business we wanted to become.

But let's back up a bit. Our first discussions with Barbara over franchising began soon after *Shark Tank*. They didn't go well. When Barbara asked us about it, Sabin's exact words were, "What is franchising?" Once we got a dictionary, we thought that the franchising model was a good one for us, but that we weren't ready for it. At the time, late 2012, we were just getting ready to launch our second truck. But the thought had been planted and we started to view our new trucks as our first forays into the franchising world. By developing a system that is replicable we were taking our first steps.

There was only one real alternative to the franchising we discussed at the time. We could have chosen to pursue a corporate model, which would mean we owned everything with our name on it. The good part? We owned all the profits. The bad part? It required a lot of capital to get started. It would also require us to employ and manage people from afar. We saw this firsthand with the three trucks we had put on the road in Los Angeles. We had reached that point relatively quickly, but not without a lot of luck along the way. Beyond LA, the corporate model might have made more sense to us after a few years of running three or maybe four trucks ourselves. As it was, we were years away from establishing a corporate presence beyond our LA office.

Besides, pursuing a corporate model would require us to know every market we entered, and for food trucks, that's not an easy analysis. It's one thing to set up a brick-and-mortar in a specific neighborhood—you can readily investigate your competitors, the demographics, etc. But a food truck requires a sense of the community beyond a simple neighborhood. You need to know about food-truck-friendly events, make the right relationships, and find the right people on the ground. It's a different beast altogether.

Franchising offered a faster way to expand without requiring as much upfront capital. Moreover, the franchising model— individual truck owners operating in cities they know far better than we did—seemed like a better fit for a food truck business in general. Sure, we would lose out on most of the profits, but we would also be able to expand smartly, choosing other entrepreneurs like us to promote and protect the brand.

Because, in the end, that was our chief concern. How could we expand the reach of Cousins Maine Lobster without sacrificing any of its meaning? Or, how could we keep the "Cousins" in Cousins Maine Lobster, even though we lived in LA? Our answer was that we needed to find people who cared about it as much as we did. Sure, you can hope to find employees like that, but it's far better to encourage ownership in a brand if you in fact *provide* some level of ownership to them. Franchising does that. It allows each franchisee to know that he or she is working for themselves. They have as much of an interest in promoting and protecting the Cousins Maine Lobster brand as we do.

This mutually beneficial relationship, once we fully understood it, appealed to us greatly because it required people who were just like us to work. In fact, it was during these conversations about franchising that Barbara said to us, "You'll want to find franchisees who are the best average of yourselves." In other words, we're not going to find our clones. But we can find potential franchisees who exhibit *most* of the qualities we like to think contributed to our success. The best average of ourselves. We've been following Barbara's advice ever since.

## FINDING THE FRANCHISEES

Once committed, we set out finding a franchise development group to help us get started. There's this sense that once you've signed a shark from *Shark Tank*, you never need another advisor again. But Barbara has dozens of other investments and interests that keep her busy. She isn't our employee, nor our president. She gives us her time when she's able, and we're thankful for each minute. Still, just because Barbara convinced us franchising was the way to go doesn't mean we knew any more about how to do it.

# CRAIG AND QUINN BETTS—NASHVILLE AND PHOENIX FRANCHISE

There was a point in our early days of operating a food truck when we said to each other, "What have we done?" Neither of us had any food truck experience; Craig was in insurance and Quinn worked at a medical clinic she had opened some years earlier. But we weren't strangers to hard work. Quinn regularly put in twelve-hour days, six days a week, at the clinic. Now we found ourselves putting in eighty hours a week without a single day off. We would come home around nine or ten o'clock at night, having been on the truck all day, completely exhausted. Then wake up early the next day to make the *pico de gallo* and do it all again.

But now, looking back, we wouldn't change a thing.

Our interest in starting a food truck was piqued when we saw a rerun of Jim and Sabin's appearance on *Shark Tank*. It was one of those fortuitous moments that life throws at you. Just when you're thinking about a change, along comes an opportunity that offers exactly that.

At the time, Craig worked for a Fortune 50 company that had moved him all over the country. When Craig landed in Nashville and met Quinn, he had finally found home. But the chances of being uprooted again were better than average.

Watching the cousins explain how they started a food truck got us thinking of doing the same. Our thinking was, "Well, if these guys can do it . . ." But seriously, we immediately saw in Jim and Sabin people with very similar qualities to ours, and with an outlook on life that matched our own. Craig got online right after the show and saw that Cousins Maine Lobster was looking for potential franchisees. We submitted our information online and got a call from the franchise coordinator the next day.

And that's how fast your life can change. Like Jim and Sabin, we didn't quit our day jobs right away. Quinn had collected ten years' worth of patients, whom she couldn't just abandon at the drop of a hat. But she found another practitioner who could take on some of her cases. And just like that we were off.

While those first few weeks were certainly tough, things got better. Each of us had extensive business experience and we put this to good practice opening the truck. At the same time, there was a steep learning curve. But we quickly learned the basics, thanks to Jim and Sabin. We learned how to put in place processes that greatly reduced our prep and serving time, and hired good staff who allowed us to focus our energies on growing the franchise. Today, our expansion plans include adding as many as two more trucks in Nashville in 2017 and opening one in Phoenix, where the operating seasons are reversed.

For now, we have more business than we can handle. We had some anxiety about whether a lobster roll truck would work in a landlocked state that has little experience with Maine lobster outside fancy restaurants. But those fears have died. Tennesseans love their Maine lobster, for the same reason Californians love it and Mainers love it. There's simply nothing like it in the world.

If you had asked us three years ago if we could imagine running a food truck franchise, we would have laughed in your face. But here we are. We're here because Jim and Sabin and the entire Cousins Maine Lobster organization have treated us like family.

Fortunately, Barbara gave us the names of a few franchising groups that handle a lot of these details. It's one of the great benefits of having Barbara as a partner. She can tap her network and give us reputable, successful names, but then it's up to us to find out if we want to go further. In the end we decided to go with one of Barbara's suggestions, a Buffalo-based group named—what else?—the Franchise Development Group.

While FDG helped us put together a document known as a franchise disclosure document, we worked on writing employee manuals, a handbook, and training courses, as well as measuring out recipes to a precision we could never have anticipated in April 2012. On top of this, we were also managing our three corporate trucks and our e-commerce business. Those were some crazy days, to say the least. But the discipline we had shown when putting two more trucks on the road in LA paid off. We had already replicated our system; we had the recipes down, ready to refine slightly for a franchisee.

Indeed, we've discovered that the hardest part of franchising is finding the right people. With a few exceptions, we've been extremely lucky in our franchisees. It took us a while to develop the right vetting process, but eventually we developed three criteria for what we look for:

1. **Hands-on**. We got a lot of requests from investors and investment groups that had deep pockets and wanted to buy their way into a truck. We steered clear from these applicants right away. The last thing our brand needed was another layer of interests between us and the guys in the truck. One of our early franchisees had been invited to set up the truck inside a major theme park. Wow! Things don't get much better than that. There was one catch, though. The truck had to be there at the gate at 7:00 a.m. on the nose. So, what happened? The truck showed up at 7:30 and the theme park refused them.

The franchisee tells us that it wasn't his fault, it was his manager's, whose alarm didn't go off. Sorry, pal. *You* should've been there, not your manager. *You* should've set two alarms, made a pot of coffee, and shown up outside the gate at 6:00 a.m., just in case. We would've. A hands-on owner would've, too. We want the guys (and gals) in the truck to be the interests. The people who put up the money were the ones we wanted running the truck.

2. **Work ethic**. We also stayed away from fast-talking food people. We knew nothing about the food industry or food trucks when we first started. We weren't quite looking for that level of ignorance, but we wanted hard workers over experts. A hard worker is more willing to take direction, particularly early on. They know they don't know anything, which is why they'll approach the business the way you want them to. An expert thinks they know everything already and will fight you tooth and nail every step of the way. No thanks. Take our Nashville franchisee. In July and August, most of the other Nashville food trucks slow down, and some stop service altogether, because the heat is brutal. The conventional, expert wisdom is that no one would stand outside a food truck on a blistering day. Our Nashville guys said, "Well, why not?" Instead of listening to what everyone told them, they went out every day during that scorching July, setting a Cousins Maine Lobster single-truck monthly sales record of $143,000 in sales. Simply said, they outworked everyone.

3. **Fixers**. Finally, we want people who just get things done. This has very little to do with intelligence or experience. It has everything to do with determination; a will to

succeed no matter what. A brief story should explain what we mean. One of our early franchisees was a lawyer, an incredibly smart guy. The problem was that every time the truck broke down, it would take him two to three days to get it fixed. He ended up selling the truck to another franchisee, who would be able to get a broken truck back on the road the next day. The only difference between these two franchisees is that one was determined to succeed no matter what, while the other one wasn't.

## PAUL AND VICKIE SHARKEY— SACRAMENTO FRANCHISE

In the spring of 2014, we heard from a friend that a food truck selling lobster rolls would be in San Dimas, California. We were living in the city of Walnut in Los Angeles County at the time, although Paul, who was born in Massachusetts, often lamented the lack of quality Northeastern fare here on the West Coast. And Paul knew his seafood, having been in the restaurant business earlier in his career.

So, off we went to check out Cousins Maine Lobster for the first time. We got the lobster rolls, of course, and settled in for a pleasant lunch, Vickie chatting with some friends and Paul . . . Well, where was Paul? Vickie looked around and noticed Paul investigating the food truck and writing down the telephone number and email address listed on the side. We had been married long enough to each know when the other was up to something, and Paul was certainly up to something. But he said nothing to Vickie, who soon forgot about it. We both remembered the rolls, however.

"This is the real thing," Paul had said through a mouthful of lobster.

By this point in our careers, we were looking to leave Los Angeles and retire to northern California. The problem was that Paul couldn't stay retired. We had met each other working at the tech company Ecolab, fourteen years earlier. Paul eventually retired but found a job literally the next day. Idleness has never suited either of us. His new job, however, required a lot of travel and eventually we had decided that enough was enough. We needed to leave LA for good and spend our retirement in peace and quiet.

Not long after our first taste of Cousins Maine Lobster, Paul met Vickie as she came home from work. "So, I was thinking . . ." he said, and then proceeded to explain this harebrained idea to open a food truck in Sacramento. "You're going to retire from Ecolab and we're going to sell the house," said Paul. Vickie wasn't only surprised; she was upset. She learned that the day after they ate at Cousins Maine Lobster, Paul had emailed Jim and Sabin to inquire about franchising opportunities. The wheels were already in motion and Paul hadn't said a thing! Vickie didn't talk to Paul for two weeks.

But at the end of that silent treatment we came to an agreement. First, we would ask Jim and Sabin if we could extend our opening till the spring of 2015. Next, Vickie needed to give her boss, who she had worked under for more than a decade, at least a month's notice. Finally, we weren't going to live out of the truck. We were going to retire to Sacramento—and retirement meant finding a home where we could spend the rest of our days. That was almost three years ago. In October 2016, we acquired our second truck, nearly six months ahead of our early projections.

When people ask us why on earth we decided to open a food truck for our retirement, our answer is simple: because we love our customers and we love the brand. Our early days weren't easy by any stretch, but we adapted. Paul drew on his experience in the restaurant business while Vickie found an outlet for her devotion to customer service. More importantly, we learned that serving folks a little slice of Maine was a lot better than sitting on our rocking chairs.

Besides that, we have always known, since the first day Paul emailed them, that Jim and Sabin supported us absolutely. Their warmth, generosity, and values not only make this the best job we've ever had, they make us feel like family. You couldn't ask for anything more when you retire.

But we won't lie. The downside of franchising is that it all depends on the people you choose to protect and promote the brand: the franchisees. Even after you've vetted dozens of applicants, picked the ones you thought were the best, trained them, got them a truck, set up their supply chain—even after all that, they can still be the wrong ones for the job. You just don't know until they get out there. And even after you've decided they aren't the right fit, it's not like you can easily fire them. At the same time, that's the only way to discover what type of person *does* work for your brand. It can be a long, sometimes painful journey, but the rewards of having a team of franchisees who get it—who love what you've built because they're building it for themselves—there's no better feeling.

## GREG AND DEB KELLER—RALEIGH FRANCHISE

A hot food truck scene in the Raleigh, Durham, and Chapel Hill area, the immense value of *Shark Tank* exposure, limited access to succulent Maine lobster in the Triangle area, and a large population of transplants from the Northeast familiar with Maine and its prized crustacean—those were the nuggets that quickly sprang into Greg's head when he caught a snippet of a Cousins Maine Lobster update on *Shark Tank* that Deb had recorded a few weeks before that fateful Saturday in July 2014.

Greg, an executive at a technology company in the area, had often talked to engineers about the food trucks they frequented when going out to lunch. He had heard about the best and most popular ones that had established themselves as favorites in the market, and realized in that instant it was an opportunity that could be lucrative and fulfilling.

Deb had been looking for her next great adventure after raising two children and launching them both off to college, spending immensely rewarding time working as a volunteer for various charities and school activities (she's still heavily involved with Make-A-Wish), and being a deacon at our church for three years. She had been out of the salaried workforce for more than twenty years and was ready to get back into the game, but owning and running a food truck was the farthest thing from her mind when Greg glanced at her and said, "You should do this!" These four words would lead us on a journey that has altered the face of the food truck industry in North Carolina, and have kept Deb and Greg hopping ever since.

It didn't take long for Deb, after rewinding and watching the *Shark Tank* update again, to pull out her laptop and submit our interest on the website. The following Monday CML had reached out, asked for more information, and within a week we had our first call with Jim and Sabin. The next few weeks were a rush of investigation—there were no Cousins food trucks outside of L.A. at that time so decisions had to be made with a lot of faith and speculation—before finally visiting Sabin, Jim, and Shaun in Los Angeles to see their operation in action and to make that very difficult and exciting decision to jump into the food truck industry. It was apparent to Jim and Sabin when we visited that Deb had a unique and untraditional spark that would be the deciding factor in both the cousins' and our decision to bring Cousins Maine Lobster to Raleigh, a decision we have never regretted.

The defining moment in our relationship with Jim and Sabin was when it was apparent we wouldn't have a truck ready for our grand opening, an event that had been planned for months. With a family-first approach, they put one of their L.A. trucks on a flatbed and had it shipped to Raleigh in time for us to open. Those first two days when we launched our business were craziness. We had lines blocks long; Jim helped us avoid near riots when we were forced to shut down the line, but we launched an amazing business.

A wide variety of challenges have presented themselves as we have ramped up the business in North Carolina: the first truck fabricator was a crook; the never-ending quest of finding the right staff; wheels nearly falling off the truck (it's a good thing Deb always answers her Cousins Maine Lobster phone number); constant generator failures, engine rebuilds, and more.

We have been fortunate to have a friend of more than thirty years, Tom Quigley, be a part of our team from very early on and he has been a lifesaver. We now have two trucks in the Raleigh area, a restaurant under construction, and have built our own commissary for food preparation and truck storage. Cousins Maine Lobster has won multiple awards for Best Food Truck in the area, and Raleigh continues to be a top franchise for Jim and Sabin. Deb is recognized as a model for customer service, quality, and attention to detail, and it turns out that she has a knack for hiring and staffing that has allowed us to expand. Not bad for a couple that, four years ago, had no clue about the lobster or food truck business!

# THE OTHER BARBARA

Now, we could lie and say everything we know about franchising we learned ourselves. But you should know by now that we approach nearly every new thing with a breathtaking level of ignorance. And yet we've rarely failed. The secret isn't that we're business geniuses. The secret is that we surround ourselves with business geniuses—and annoy the shit out of them with millions of questions. Barbara Corcoran is one of those geniuses. Kat Cole is another.

Sabin first met Kat while they were filming a pilot for the Food Network in 2014. We had already started the process of franchising but were still very much in the early days. We were a bit overwhelmed, so of course Sabin decided to do a television show. The show wasn't picked up, but introductions were made and pleasantries exchanged. Kat would tell us later that when she told Sabin to call her if he had questions about franchising, she didn't expect he would.

He did. When one of the world's foremost experts on franchising invites you to call anytime, you don't worry about being too forward. You call! Which serves as a good lesson for all budding entrepreneurs out there. There are a lot of opportunities to meet successful businesspeople: seminars, conferences, and talks, for example. It might cost you an arm and a leg to attend these events, but if it gives you a chance to brush shoulders with some of your business idols, then do it. And if you get a chance to talk with these people, don't hesitate to be forward. You might never get another opportunity. The worst that could happen is that they think you're a weirdo stalker and call security. . . . No, the worst that could happen is that they just ignore you, which means nothing happens. Or they give you a card and take your call.

Our next meeting with Kat took place a couple months later in LA, when she came through town on business. Sabin met her for a drink and talked shop. It was during this conversation where Kat, in her words, "laid a bunch of truth on us." That's not an exaggeration. We were very early in the franchising game, just testing the waters, but essentially Kat's message was: "You're going to need a bigger boat."

Put another way, the very characteristics and qualities which had allowed us to get where we were wouldn't be enough to make us successful franchisors. She told us that some of the best business minds she's ever met made lousy franchisors. The problem, in her view, was one of ego. The drive and determination that make one successful in business are not conducive to the franchise world. Can you imagine Steve Jobs being a successful franchisor? Or Meg Whitman? Or Jeff Bezos? These businesspeople are successful because they can mold a business in their likeness by sheer force of will. Nothing escapes their notice; everything is done by their say-so. The results of such an approach speak for themselves.

But that's why franchising is different. Instead of enforcing your will, you must give it up. Instead of leaving nothing to chance, you hand over an appendage of your business to someone else. These sacrifices of a successful franchisor are anathema to most corporate businesspeople. It just goes against everything that they know. In short, Kat told us that franchising requires a level of humility and trust that you just don't see a lot in the business world.

Kat also emphasized the franchisee role as an idea incubator. One of the characteristics of franchising that makes it such a great business model is that the franchisee has enough independence to experiment. While remaining true to the brand, a franchisee can try new marketing ideas, they can invent new recipes, and they can improve the overall functioning of the truck. We encourage all of this. But thanks to Kat, we have in place a process where these great ideas have a way of making it up the chain to us. That way, we can implement the idea across the business, throughout the franchisee network, and improve everyone's bottom line. Kat's emphasis on putting down processes and best practices has proven itself time and again.

But if we could identify the best lesson we learned from Kat, it's this: be open and honest with your franchisees. Just because they have your franchisee kit and a truck doesn't mean they'll never need your guidance ever again. Your franchisees look to you as a mentor, a guide, a guru, and a therapist. It's our job to be available to our franchisees always, ready to answer their questions or even talk them off the ledge. More importantly, we need to be proactive in our communication. We can't just wait for them to call us with questions; if we know that the price of lobster is about to go up, we need to call them and explain why and what they should do about it.

This is what makes the franchisor-franchisee relationship so different from the manager-employee one. In the latter, the manager adheres to a hierarchy, a chain of command, where it's best to keep relationships simple and efficient. A manager expects the employee to do her job and the employee expects the manager to tell them important information. The power structure is very apparent in such a relationship, as it should be.

But you can't treat your franchisees like employees. Kat taught us that we need to treat them like investors and partners, because they've done what employees haven't: given us hundreds of thousands of dollars (sometimes their life savings) on the expectation that our brand sells. We need to honor their commitment, their sacrifice, with complete transparency and respect. Because when a franchisee feels cut off or isolated, they're liable to do something rash that might hurt more than their operations: it might hurt your brand. Bring them into the fold, keep them there, and they'll repay your respect with a dedication and loyalty that you simply cannot buy.

Which isn't to say we never made a mistake with our franchisees. We've made plenty. And we would often call up Kat in the middle of making one and use her shoulder to cry on (metaphorically speaking). Like any good advisor, she didn't coddle or patronize. She gave us the type of tough love we needed to realize our mistake and work to make it right.

In fact, the idea to hold an annual franchisee retreat was a result of Kat's guidance for transparency and respect. After the meeting, we even asked her to take on a more formal role within the company. She agreed. And that's how we got the world's foremost franchise expert (and one of the most successful businesspeople in the world) to be a consultant for Cousins Maine Lobster.

Sometimes we can't believe our own luck. Which is another way of saying: thank you, Kat.

## LESSON
## SURROUND YOURSELF WITH GREATNESS

Barbara likes to say that we have a halo around our heads. What she means is that we've had more than our fair share of good luck with our business. We don't disagree. Besides, when Barbara Corcoran, someone who deals with people like us all day every day, says you're lucky, well, you're lucky. That said, Barbara is being a little tongue-in-cheek, too. She understands as much as we do that our luck is the product of many factors, most of them within our control. Hard work is one of those factors. No one works harder than we do and we aren't too proud to say it. Humility is another factor: we never pretend we know what we're doing when we don't, and that allows us to find the right answers, and learn a lot along the way. We also don't take no for an answer—a lesson Barbara herself taught us. If we want something to happen, we find a way to make it happen. You can call it luck when it happens; we prefer to call it determination.

But if we had to attribute our good luck to anything, it would be the people who surround us. Part of it is an outgrowth of our humility, but we learned early in this game that there are people out there far smarter and better at business than us. Now, we're not too shabby, and we're far better than when we started. We look back on those first few months, before we even launched our first truck, and we're kind of amazed we ever got this thing off the ground. We had almost no help and it showed. Annie, Jim's sister, was the first one to open our eyes to the world beyond our limited vision and experience. We wouldn't have found our suppliers without her. Steve, Jim's father, was the next to come along, and he forced us to confront our own financial management, or lack thereof.

And so, on it went, until we pulled Barbara into our orbit, then Kat. But it doesn't end with family, partners, or advisors. You should also surround yourself with greatness in the people you hire. In this chapter, we've focused on our franchising efforts and you've read the stories of some of our franchisees themselves. We should be very blunt about this: we are only as great as our franchisees. And these guys are pretty freaking great.

When we made the decision to franchise, we understood that a lot would depend on the quality of the franchisees. We just never realized how much. Perhaps we assumed that we would have more control over them than is possible. We simply don't have the bandwidth to micromanage at that level, nor do we want to. But by seeking out potential franchisees who exhibited the qualities we believe contributed most to our success, we discovered magic. Our franchisees impress us nearly every day. Their dedication to their work and to the brand is inspiring. We honestly didn't think we could find a level of dedication equal to our own. We were wrong—and we've never been happier to be so wrong.

That's the lesson we've taken away from franchising; our awareness that we are only as good as the people we surround ourselves with. People like Barbara and Kat, employees like Shaun and Sandy, and franchisees like the owners of our Sacramento, Raleigh, and Nashville operations.

Expansion is part of being an entrepreneur. It's what separates the entrepreneur from the owner of a store or the operator of a single food truck. It's a rite of passage all entrepreneurs must pass through if they want to build a company and a brand. We chose franchising as our principal mode of expansion, but there are a variety of methods available. We're exploring others, as well. But whether you choose to franchise, license, or stay corporate, your success suddenly moves beyond your direct control. You can't be everywhere, doing everything. You can't know everything you need to know. What you *can* do is find those who can be where you can't and know what you don't. And if you're lucky enough to find those who are great, it will lead to greatness in your company, and in yourself.

# 8

# The Immovable Lobster Truck

Cousins Maine Lobster Will Keep
Lobster Mania Alive in West Hollywood

*Lobster rolls are seriously trending*
By Crystal Coser, *Eater LA*

March 18, 2015—The West Hollywood stretch of Santa
Monica Boulevard seems to be the place where restaurant con-
cepts go to die. In this month alone we've seen The Horn and
Gangnam Pocha bite the dust, and now comes word that
Bite Mi Café hasn't fared any better.

The good news is denizens of West Hollywood won't have
to wait long for a new restaurant to take its place. *Toddrickal-
len* reports that ABC's *Shark Tank* favorites Jim Tselikis and
Sabin Lomac will be expanding their lobster truck business
Cousins Maine Lobster into another full-fledged brick and
mortar.

The cousins attempted their first brick and mortar within
[a] Pasadena drinking lounge . . . but quickly closed the place

back in December 2013. Hopefully the new West Hollywood location will survive better, but it's a tough bet considering the history of the neighborhood.

Cousins Maine Lobster will carry on the current lobster roll trend in LA that's been solidified by the recent opening of [another lobster restaurant]. Hopefully the concept sticks around so West Hollywood's restaurant row can finally find some stability.[22]

Yes, our little restaurant is in the same location that once housed a place called Bite Mi Café, a Vietnamese sandwich joint. In any case, there's a lot to unpack in those few paragraphs. But the reason we included this short news clip from an LA culinary website is because of the article's inherent warning: our restaurant wasn't just risky, it was probably going to fail. Read between the lines and you'll see the red flags.

First, our choice of location was basically doomed. Forget the place that was there before us, we couldn't have picked a worse spot to build our immovable lobster shack. It's "where restaurant concepts go to die" apparently, like it's cursed.

Two, our new restaurant would be our *second* attempt. Our first shot at a brick-and-mortar "quickly closed," suggesting to readers that the food truck guys should probably stick with what they know best.

Finally, there's the competition mentioned at the end, which also sells lobster rolls and was about six miles away. There's a hint that we were chasing another restaurant, which had "solidified" the lobster-roll trend, and that perhaps LA wasn't big enough for both of us.

It's a good thing we don't listen to what others say. It's also a good thing we like a challenge, because we got one.

# MANY DIRECTIONS, ONE FOCUS

Of course it wasn't just alternative media writers basically saying we were making a huge mistake. Barbara hated our restaurant idea, too, if for an entirely different reason. Let's go back to summer 2012, right around the time we went on *Shark Tank*. Our goals at the time were fairly small. We wanted to put another truck on the road and we went on the show to get the funding to do that. Simple.

But then we thought about maximizing the *Shark Tank* opportunity. This led us to develop our e-commerce business, which we hoped would get its first big boost after our episode aired. You now know how that went. Then later in the summer we were approached with another opportunity, from the owner of a local lounge. We jumped at that, too, for reasons we'll get to in a moment.

Obviously, we didn't consider these to be mistakes at the time. Only when we look back now, knowing what we know, do we cringe at our impulsiveness. Some might say we were reckless, although that suggests we didn't approach these opportunities in a smart, disciplined way. We did, even if we probably should've passed on them. Rather, we were aimless. We hadn't decided what kind of business we wanted Cousins Maine Lobster to be, so we chased opportunities.

Clearly, from a very early stage in our business, we wanted to go beyond food trucks. Heck, not six months after launch, we were already pursuing two separate ventures, the lounge and the e-commerce business. At the time, we thought these were too-good-to-pass-up opportunities, mostly because we were inexperienced. We couldn't tell a good opportunity from a bad one back then. If we didn't jump on them, we feared, they would disappear.

We had a common ailment that affects a lot of young

entrepreneurs: we were more afraid of *losing out* on opportunities than we were of taking an opportunity that wasn't right for us. It's how amateur investors get themselves in trouble, by chasing crappy investments and throwing good money after bad. This is what happens when exuberance combines with inexperience.

Moreover, we saw ourselves riding the wave—and waves eventually crash. We *had* to pursue these opportunities, because they might not be there a year from now. And what if we weren't as popular? What if lobster prices went through the roof? What if Southern Californians suddenly decided they hate food trucks?! These are the questions that go through your head when you haven't been in business for six months.

Which is why we say that Barbara came along at just the right time, or close enough. From a very early stage in our partnership with her, she emphasized one lesson above all others: not every opportunity is the right opportunity. She saw that we were grasping, particularly with the lounge restaurant, although she wasn't a big fan of the e-commerce business either. She also noticed that we had the right instincts, and certainly enough ambition, but that we suffered from an identity crisis.

We did, and it was this: Where do you go from food trucks? E-commerce, restaurant, franchising—these were all viable options and none was necessarily better than the rest. So, why not do all three, we thought. It's a decision that might seem like overconfidence or arrogance. But it was the opposite of arrogance: it was a *lack* of confidence that drove us into this frenzied state of business development. We wanted to strike while the iron was hot, as they say, because we weren't sure if we'd be around in a year. What if eating lobster from a food truck was just a passing fad, like swing music's comeback in the 1990s? (Remember that? No? Moving on . . . ) We were terrified our luck would run out, and we'd be begging for our old jobs back.

Barbara taught us how to breathe. There are certainly some businesses that depend on the popularity of a concept or trend—

in other words, things outside of the business's control. Lobster isn't one of them. We were purveyors of one of the planet's most delicious delicacies, one that has been selling for more than a hundred years. In 2007, before the economy crashed, lobster landings from the Gulf of Maine totaled about 70 million pounds, certainly down from 2004's historic high of 80 million pounds. By 2013, the industry had rebounded by 60 million pounds to a total of 140 million pounds.[23] No, people weren't suddenly going to stop wanting lobster. We had found a successful niche in a popular market.

But what would happen if the food truck craze dies? We'd need another revenue stream!

This was a more realistic concern, but also very unlikely. One of the ways we were lucky early on is that we were on the leading edge of the food truck insurgency. Although food trucks have been around for decades, the idea of a *gourmet* food truck, as opposed to a corndog vendor, is relatively new. Most industry analysts pinpoint the economic crash of 2008 as the spark that started the fire. With the economy tanking and restaurants taking a huge hit, professional chefs and restauranteurs saw the food truck as an ideal solution. Compared to a brick-and-mortar restaurant, food trucks are cheap to start and operate. And with the limited kitchen, the menu must be simple but also distinctive—food that attracts the restaurantgoers without breaking their wallets.

And then there was the fact that Sabin lived in LA, where the gourmet food truck was basically born. As a March 2012 article in *Smithsonian Magazine* noted:

> At a time in America when finances are shaky, yet even modest big-city restaurant spaces involve multimillion-dollar build-outs, when consumers have wearied of giant chains but still demand food that is novel, inexpensive and fast, food trucks are the new incubators of culinary innovation. The food-truck

phenomenon exploded in cities across the United States last year thanks largely to the success of Kogi, and before that to the mobile fleet of *taqueros* spread out across L.A. Who knew that the cult of tacos al pastor would become a nationwide sensation?

The intersection between food and wheels has driven culture in L.A. since at least the 1930s, when the city was already famous for its drive-ins and roadside hash houses designed to look like coffee pots. Food trucks may be nothing new in the U.S.—every Hawaiian can tell you her favorite plate-lunch wagon, and Portland, Oregon, can seem like a locavore food-truck plantation—but in L.A., where on some afternoons they can be as thick on the freeway as taxicabs are on New York's Sixth Avenue, they define the landscape.[24]

Put simply, the idea for a food truck wasn't divine inspiration. Sabin worked in a city inundated with them. This article, tracing the start of the whole food truck thing to LA, came out one month before the first Cousins Maine Lobster truck hit the road. We didn't invent the food truck craze, nor were we even early pioneers. That credit belongs to those trucks selling upscale Mexican street food and other ethnic dishes, like Kogi BBQ, which sells Korean short-rib tacos. These early trucks exposed Americans to the pleasures of simple yet delicious street fare.

But was it a fad? Had we inadvertently joined a craze long after its heyday?

Between 2007 and 2012, when we jumped in, the industry grew 8.4 percent, a nice bright spot in an economy that was otherwise falling apart. Of course, there was concern that after the economic recovery, food trucks would lose their market. The chefs would go back to the brick-and-mortars, and the customers, now with a little more money in their back pockets, would follow. Except that's not what's happened. Between 2010 and 2015, the industry grew at a rate of 9.3 percent.[25] Turns out that what had been a cheap alternative to a brick-and-mortar during an economic downturn exposed an underlying demand that doesn't seem to be going away anytime soon.

So, no, food trucks aren't a fad.

Which isn't to say that the industry has nothing to worry about. LA distinguished itself early as being a city particularly friendly to food trucks, but not every city is as welcoming. Much like the difficulty ride-sharing services like Uber discover when they attempt to enter a new market, food trucks disrupt the natural order of things. Brick-and-mortar restaurants—and we're talking about big corporations—hate food trucks, because we steal their business with a product that is just as fast as fast food and way more delicious. Some cities have enacted onerous regulations that all but keep food trucks off their streets. For example, Chicago prohibits food trucks from setting up within two hundred feet of a restaurant, which basically explains why you can't find any food trucks in downtown Chicago.

These fights are normal for any nascent, disruptive industry. They confirm that the food truck industry is entering a period of maturity, after a very wild and fun adolescence. Regulatory battles with individual cities will be fought; some will be won, others lost. But the industry isn't going anywhere. If anything, these obstacles are the clearest sign yet that we've established ourselves as a mainstay in American cuisine. The fact remains that some of the best, most exciting, and most creative food in the country is coming out of food trucks. Let's hope it remains that way for a long time to come.

The point is, if we fail, it won't be because the food truck industry suddenly became unpopular. No, if we fail, it will likely be our own damn fault. We're only wasting time worrying about these uncontrollable forces and trends. Barbara taught us that the one thing we can control is our business and that's the only thing we should worry about. We can't make decisions because we're afraid something beyond our control might happen. We should make decisions because it's the right thing to do for our company.

And at that moment, late 2012, we were doing well with our small fleet of food trucks. Barbara's message to us: focus on that! Focus on what you're already doing well, and stop with all the other nonsense. It was time to channel our efforts in a single direction and stick with it. It was time to manage our business with the confidence that comes from knowing what it was and where we wanted it to go. Man, but it was a good whack upside the head.

You're probably wondering at this moment: So why the heck did you start a restaurant then?

Because we're really bad at following Barbara's advice—or our own.

## THE LOUNGE EXPERIMENT

To better understand how we started our second restaurant, we should talk about the first. Now, using the word "restaurant" is giving our first brick-and-mortar too much credit. It wasn't a restaurant in a strict sense of the term. We never owned the location and we didn't have any control of the operation. Basically, the owner of a nightclub lounge in Pasadena approached us with an opportunity to serve our food to his customers. He even allowed us to put our logo over the entrance. It was summer 2012, right after we had filmed our episode of *Shark Tank,* and we were in the mood for new opportunities. Much like the e-commerce business, we thought having a permanent location would be a great way to take advantage of the influx of demand we expected after the episode aired.

What also appealed to us about this particular opportunity was that it seemed to us to be a kind of "pop-up" restaurant. If you're unaware of this trend, a pop-up is a temporary restaurant that usually runs out of a nontraditional location, sometimes a residence, a former storefront, or just a stand on the side of the road. They've become a popular way for younger chefs and restauranteurs to make a name for themselves among a certain group of hard-core foodies.

Of course, the best thing about the pop-up is that it's not supposed to last. The whole marketing strategy behind one is based on word of its existence going viral on social media. If that happens, the pop-up experiences a massive explosion of popularity, operates for a few days, then disappears—leaving its fan base wanting more. That's their appeal. They're here, then they're not. *"Where's the next one going to be?"*

We knew the lounge wasn't a true pop-up, but we believed we could still hope for some similar social media buzz. We envisioned a line of late-night customers, ravenous after a night out and about, hitting up our "pop-up" for some great food and community. Was it the kind of atmosphere we would want to have today? Probably not, although we do make a point of hitting locations with our trucks where we know there will be some late-night revelers. But in these cases, we're not second billing.

In any event, our service at the lounge began in September 2012, one month before our *Shark Tank* episode aired. Almost immediately, we realized that this wasn't the best idea. For starters, there's a problem with any establishment that is trying to be both restaurant and nightclub. Some can pull this off if they clearly delineate when the restaurant ends and the nightclub begins. But we were supposed to be serving our food during the nightclub phase. Customers who came just for the lobster rolls had to pass through bouncers.

In general, you don't want to be carding your customers if all they want to do is eat a lobster roll.

Moreover, a lounge isn't particularly well suited to the type of experience we loved to sell: when you eat our lobster, we want you to visualize and share in the memories of our childhoods growing up on the Maine coast. *That's* what we do best. But how can you do that in a place which primarily caters to partiers who *might* get hungry during their late-night revelry?

Gone was the joy of us talking to our customers about the food, about lobstering, and about Maine. Gone was the sense of community and family which had been our primary motives for starting the business in the first place. In the end, all the lounge provided us was a place to serve our food, and only the food. Whatever else it was, it wasn't Cousins Maine Lobster.

That said, we weren't losing money—but we weren't making money either. The customers appreciated our unique dishes enough to keep buying them, even if they might have wondered what a lobster shack was doing in the middle of a nightclub. And that was the problem. We had no place in a world of fancy drinks and undistinguished club music, where people came to be seen but not engage in the age-old tradition of family and friends. Our place is where they eat off picnic tables, wrangle the kids, and laugh with a mouthful of lobster. We understand this all too well now, but we didn't back then. Remember, we *were* suffering from an identity crisis.

So, although we didn't lose much, we stayed in far too long. Our stubbornness is one trait we share that is both a virtue and a vice. We saw that the lounge wasn't right for us very early on, but stuck it out. We didn't want to admit we had a made a mistake. Moreover, we thought we could turn a mistake into a success if we just gave it some time. But that's one of those tough entrepreneurial lessons that you can only learn by experience. Now that we know a lot of entrepreneurs, we know we aren't the only ones who have tried to make lemonade out of lemons. There seems to be a universal tendency in all young business owners that says if you give a mistake enough time, it will magically become a not-a-mistake.

Part of that is just you protecting your ego. If you close up shop, then you're admitting you made a mistake—and you can't do that! Mistakes are for amateurs! You're a real, bona fide businessman who crosses all the t's and dots all the i's. If you make a mistake, then it means you probably aren't any good at business and you should just get out now.

*Every* entrepreneur has these thoughts. They're as normal as they are wrong. But we have to go through them because we have to make our first mistakes sometime. Making mistakes is how you learn. Mistakes don't mean you've failed. And even if your mistake does lead to failure, that's not always a bad thing. We had to make this mistake with the lounge experiment to learn what we wanted from a restaurant. Almost everything about our experience there showed us what we didn't want. Here are few highlights:

- We didn't want our lobster to be a sideshow, an afterthought.

- We didn't want our location to be anything other than 100 percent devoted to our brand.

- We didn't want our restaurant to take away from the experience that we provide to our food truck customers.

Turn all those things around and you'll see what we *did* want in our next restaurant:

- Our Maine lobster would be the star, the main event.

- Our location would be 100 percent based on our brand of community and family.

- Our restaurant would be part of the experience, from the tables you sit at to the people who serve the food.

When we finally closed the doors on our first restaurant in December 2013, a little more than a year after opening, we put an end to one of the worst mistakes in the history of Cousins Maine Lobster. But we don't regret it. Not for a minute do we regret it, because without that experience, we would never have taken advantage of one of the great opportunities in the history of Cousins Maine Lobster.

## WELCOME TO WEST HOLLYWOOD

Like many moments in our history, the one that led to us opening our own restaurant happened quite by accident. We were familiar with this particular stretch of Santa Monica Boulevard in West Hollywood, especially Sabin, who happened to live nearby. It's a pleasant mix of family-friendly restaurants and more foodie-oriented cafés and bistros. Just what you'd expect to find in a neighborhood that caters to both sets. While the *Eater LA* article makes it sound like no one in their right mind would open a restaurant there, several have done quite well. Like Starbucks.

Seriously, extreme cases excluded, a restaurant's location is only part of what makes it a success or failure. A place in the heart of the action could fail just as easily as one out in the boondocks could succeed. Too often, a great location produces laziness in the restauranteurs, who think they can skimp when it comes to food, service, or experience. That said, if you can snag a great spot *and* run one heck of a restaurant, then you're sitting pretty.

Which is why Sabin, while walking along this stretch one day, suddenly got the idea that we should open our own restaurant. Sabin had found out that a location was available for lease just blocks from his apartment in West Hollywood, and the wheels began to turn. It was December 2014 and we had been out of the brick-and-mortar game for a year, having left the lounge spot in December 2013. In fact, we were knee-deep in starting our franchising business and working fifteen-hour days.

So, of course it's time to open a restaurant.

Now, we likely would have started a restaurant eventually, but the opportunity of landing a prime spot in a neighborhood we knew well certainly expedited matters. We were so excited about the prospect that we put in a bid even before talking to Barbara about it. Not surprisingly, Barbara didn't think it was a great idea, for reasons we explained above. And as the days ticked by with our offer on the table, we started to wonder if it wouldn't be an act of divine mercy to have our offer rejected. We were simply overwhelmed with our franchising efforts.

But then, in January 2015, it was approved. Oh, shit.

So, before we move on, the burning question: Why, after going through the lounge experiment, and now in the middle of franchising, did we suddenly decide to start a restaurant? First, we don't make decisions based off how much work will be required. We're young, healthy, and ambitious. We love this stuff, the whole art of building our business and growing our brand. We don't believe in the idea that we don't have time for something. We'll *always* make time for the right opportunity.

And, frankly, so should all entrepreneurs. If you start a business thinking it will give you the right work-life balance, you're going to be sorely mistaken. There is no "life" in entrepreneurism. There is only work. We were lucky in our early days because we didn't have families—the "life" we gave up was wasting time with our friends, dating, or watching sports. The trade-off we made was spending time working on a business or spending time with friends. It wasn't much of a sacrifice.

But if you do have a family, we can see how starting a business would get in the way of fulfilling your obligations at home. Whether your office is at home or work, you will live there. You will be up late and at your desk early. We only hope you have a supportive partner who will carry the load while you pursue your entrepreneurial dreams. Remember to get them something nice when the frenzy dies down.

In any case, the idea that we couldn't fit a restaurant into our workday was never much of a consideration. The real dilemma was entirely business related. *Could* we open a restaurant? Meaning, could we get all of our ducks in a row to open a place that we would be proud to add to our growing Cousins Maine Lobster family? Let's face it, anyone can open a restaurant, which is why so many fail. But we didn't just want a restaurant; we wanted an extension of our brand that would be a stand-alone success in its own right.

And to be honest, the idea of owning our own restaurant always greatly appealed to us—the type of appeal that goes beyond sound business or financial sense. The reason we passed on it when deciding on our first business in 2012 was because the up-front capital and overhead were just too daunting for a couple of guys who didn't have any restaurant experience other than what Sabin had gleaned working in them growing up. With Jim on the opposite coast, a restaurant was just a bridge too far. But that doesn't mean we gave up the idea altogether.

Quite the opposite. What was our venture at the lounge but us trying to force our restaurant dreams? We could try to rationalize it to you, but what's the point? We suppose it's the same irrational desire some people have to make art, climb a mountain, or visit all fifty states. There's no good *logical* reason to do it; but the desire inside you runs so deep that you know you *must* do it or be left unfulfilled. That's the best way we can answer the question about why we opened a restaurant when we probably shouldn't have: because we wanted to and we could.

That said, we also knew that we shouldn't be the ones leading the project. As previously mentioned, we were already stretched to capacity. But the more practical reason is that neither of us had opened a restaurant before. We had acquired enough business wisdom to know that we shouldn't make this, our first real brick-and-mortar, our trial by fire. Steve's advice, given long ago, came back to us: if you can't do something right or don't want to do it, then hire someone else to do it. We did with our finances; we had no problem doing it with our restaurant.

And that's what we did. Fortunately, one of Sabin's cousins, Aaron, happened to work in the restaurant industry in San Diego. His specialty was opening up new joints. So, we brought him up to LA and hired him as a contractor to oversee the restaurant opening. Looking back, hiring Aaron wasn't just a good decision, it was a sign of our growing business maturity. Learning to hand some tasks over is part of growing a business, but it's extremely difficult for young entrepreneurs. The reason why is because when we're inexperienced in management, we don't trust anyone else to do it.

But as you expand and bring on more people, you learn to let go. You have to, or nothing will get done. So, slowly the fear of giving control to someone else recedes. Two years previous, we probably would've tried to open the place ourselves. But in that winter of 2015, we had to give the project to someone else. Here's what we want, we told him. Get it done.

And Aaron did.

Of course it wasn't without difficulties. Major, headache-inducing difficulties. We gutted most of the interior of the space only to uncover massive problems—which is what usually happens when you gut a place. Our scheduled grand opening in the spring was scrapped for some unspecified date in the summer. The drip, drip, drip was more than the sound of flooding we had discovered: it was our money leaking into the money pit beneath Santa Monica Boulevard. And our location was small—we're talking less than a thousand square feet of eating area that could only seat sixteen people inside.

Gradually, progress was made and we solidified an opening date for July. We were thrilled at what Aaron had been able to accomplish. From the beginning, our designs had a specific image in mind: "A little bit of Maine," is what we called it. Really, we saw the restaurant as an opportunity to do something for our brand that a food truck simply couldn't: create the ambiance of a lobster shack. The food truck has the people, the sense of family and fun, and, of course, the food. But no one mistakes a food truck for a wharf-side shack, no matter how much we want to pretend they do.

But with a permanent space? You better believe we carved up Bite Mi Café to look just like you pulled your dinghy up to the wharf: inside is small and cozy, with no individual tables. It's all communal seating by design. We want you to talk to the stranger gobbling his lobster next to you. Our brick walls are reminiscent of the iconic Maine lighthouses back home, as if at any moment our customers will feel the spray of the surf on their faces. We threw in some cool props, like buoys and a white picket fence outside, to complete the picture. But it's what you experience inside that matters: community, family, and a good dose of the wharf. Trust us, if we wouldn't be written up by the health-code inspector, we would've found a way to make the place *smell* like a wharf. Outside is LA, with its palm trees, traffic, and smog, but inside, it's a little bit of Maine.

Our plan for the opening was to have a soft launch the day before the big one. We invited some local celebrities we knew in town, as well as some of the kids and volunteers from Big Brothers Big Sisters. Remember, the restaurant isn't large, so there's only so much we could do with having a big party. It was more like our way of introducing the restaurant to the neighborhood. There was certainly some buzz—the *Eater LA* article and others helped with that—and folks in the area, of course, knew about *Shark Tank*. Still, we kept things relatively intimate and neighborly. Our mothers were there, doing the things that mothers do, like cleaning up after the patrons. We spent as much time shooing them away as we did conversing with our guests.

In fact, an hour or so before we opened the doors, Sabin wasn't even at the restaurant yet. Jim was down there, putting the finishing touches inside while a line slowly grew outside. The place looked great and Jim couldn't have been happier with what we saw in the staff. Then he peeked outside and nearly fell over. He fumbled for his phone and called Sabin.

"Get down here now!" Jim said in a loud whisper.

"I'm coming," said Sabin impatiently.

"Dude, now! You'll never guess who the first person in line is . . ."

"Who?" asked Sabin.

"Daymond."

## DAYMOND JOHN

My first reaction to Jim and Sabin when they came on the show was that they didn't want a deal. They looked too slick, too polished. But they negotiated hard and ended up with a deal from Barbara. I was impressed and said so. I think that was one of the few times that I openly admitted on-air that I was wrong about the initial impression of an entrepreneur. I usually have a good radar for those who come on the show just for exposure. Others are simply delusional—they're delusional about the value of their company, the value they bring, and the value of a shark. So, when the cousins made their deal with Barbara, I was very happy for them. They came to deal and they got one.

But once a contestant walks back out the door, I

almost never see them again. There are those very few who come back for update episodes, but even then, I rarely bump into them unless, of course, I'm their shark. That said, the sharks talk to each other off the air. We talk about who's good and who's bad; the ones who are really working and the ones with lackluster performance. Since Barbara and I are both native New Yorkers, I see that hilarious and smart woman a good amount. Barbara had a lot of good things to say about the guys and spoke highly of their performance and work ethic. And I would see them every so often when the sharks got together with their entrepreneurs on other shows like *The Chew*. That's how I learned firsthand that they were just great guys all around.

Some of my friends in Los Angeles also knew them, and that's how we became close. I started to take an interest in their growth as businessmen, particularly when they were going through a lot of tough stuff in those early years. I had a feeling they would be all right. At the end of the day, it's how you feel about people, no matter what they might say to you or what other people might say to you about them. I gradually developed a lot of respect for Jim and Sabin. I learned that the cousins reflect Barbara, who is somebody I care deeply for and respect as a businessperson. They're also two amazing gentlemen who go the extra mile for everyone.

The restaurant is a case in point. They were trying to carve their way into LA by opening a brick-and-mortar. I questioned if it was the right thing to do, because their business model of food trucks is great and it's not always good to spread yourself thin. But nearly everything they had tried had worked, so I gave them the benefit of the doubt. When I heard about the opening, I was in LA at the time and the restaurant was down the block from the hotel where I stay. I figured a small gesture such as going down there and supporting them would work wonders for their confidence. It's all about entrepreneurship—they were trying to do something new and I wanted their first day of it to be an exciting one. Besides, I was hungry!

I also wanted to send my support to Barbara, and let her know I was taking an interest in her team. It's a form of mutual respect. She does the same for my entrepreneurs. We like getting to know the entrepreneurs who are worth knowing, because we've been where they are. It's not a large club, but a lot of entrepreneurs just don't put in the work the way the cousins do. So, I wanted to send my support not only as an appreciative colleague of Barbara, but also as a fellow entrepreneur who has been right where they were at that moment—risking a lot on a big idea. And when I saw them, I just wanted to give them a big ole hug.

## LESSON
# NOT EVERY OPPORTUNITY IS THE RIGHT OPPORTUNITY

*Shark Tank* Favorite Cousins Maine Lobster Opens Shop in West Hollywood

By Mike Glazer, *The Wrap*

July 1, 2015—Cousins Maine Lobster, a food truck delivering lobster from Maine to the streets of Los Angeles via overnight UPS, is opening its first brick-and-mortar shop in the heart of West Hollywood.

The company first gained local and national prominence as two likeable, hungry guppy cousins pled their case on ABC's *Shark Tank*, securing a deal back in 2012.

On the eve of the July 2 store opening, select VIPs, friends, and family filled the Santa Monica Boulevard location, neighboring the Starbucks and Trader Joes in "boys' town." They will be serving up lobster rolls ($15), lobster tacos, lobster BLT's, and a *very* dry lobster martini. (It's just lobster chunks in a glass, no booze.) . . .

At the time they closed their deal on the Mark Burnett and Clay Newbill produced *Tank*, they had one food truck in Los Angeles. Now, they have 14 trucks roaming 10 cities and franchisees across the country. The WeHo shop though, is the first brick-and-mortar under the Cousins Maine Lobster name.

Fellow "Shark" Daymond John, who passed on the opportunity to invest three years ago, stopped in on Monday night during a pre-pre opening.[26]

It's always amusing to us what the press finds interesting and what we find interesting. The article didn't end with the Daymond John nugget; it continues for another hundred words or so. The writer slides it in there like it was the most normal thing in the world for another shark to show support for the business ventures of former contestants. It's not.

Daymond's appearance outside the restaurant for the soft launch floored us. We're not kidding: he was *first* in line. That's why Jim yelled at Sabin to get down to the restaurant immediately. Even though we didn't know why Daymond was there, we were going to roll out the red carpet—though, of course, we didn't have a red carpet. We didn't have much of anything.

It turns out we didn't have to worry. Daymond came to our soft launch just to show support. He had heard about the restaurant through Barbara and wanted to see how were doing.

That was about it. Nothing too dramatic or fancy. But to us? It was one of the kindest gestures we had ever been privileged to receive as entrepreneurs. We admire Daymond for the same reason all entrepreneurs and business folk should admire him: he's brilliant. But he's also incredibly warm and supportive, even of those in whom he didn't invest the first time around. That's why he showed up that day. He just wanted to show his support—and probably also get some damn good lobster.

But Daymond's appearance that day told us something else, something he clearly never intended. We had made the right choice. Opening a restaurant, while perhaps not the best thing we could have done while in the middle of franchising, had been the right opportunity. Even if we didn't know it then, we do now. The doubts and debates we had between us and with others, including Barbara, had played havoc with our confidence. Even in the week leading up the grand opening, which you'll read about in the next chapter, we weren't entirely sure we had made the right decision.

Then Daymond showed up and, just like that, we felt all was right in the world. When someone with Daymond's stature stands outside your door like everyone else, patiently waiting for a chance to enjoy the best lobster in West Hollywood, then you've done something right.

Without fear of sentimentality, we can say we love our restaurant. It's cozy, quaint, and the closest we can get in LA to back home. But that's the thing: we can say that it reminds us of our home. Even though we're smack-dab in the middle of Los Angeles, which is about as far away from Maine as one can get, both geographically and symbolically, we had built something that tugged on those childhood memories. In that way, it was an authentic representation of where we came from. And we love our regulars—from Maine transplants to the most California kid in the state; from the blue-collar worker to the celebrities, like Mariah Carey, Doc Rivers, and Dane Cook.

Wherever they come from and whoever they are, they are our customers.

We now know that having a permanent place besides the business office, where our great customers know they can enjoy the Cousins Maine Lobster experience every single day, is one of the greatest joys to be had in business. This, of course, takes nothing away from our food trucks, which will always form the foundation of our company. They are its beating heart. But there's also something to be said for walking into your restaurant whenever the mood strikes you, greeting your customers, hearing about their days, that makes this feel like a bigger accomplishment than the trucks.

There's no formula we can share that lets you know which opportunity is the right one. All we can say is that not every opportunity is right. You'll have to make some bad decisions to learn that for yourself. And you will. We had to make the mistake of rushing the e-commerce business and jumping into a bad situation with the lounge to even begin to understand what the right opportunities are for us. But we also had to learn damn fast. *Shark Tank* launched us into the realm of minor food celebrity, which has its own rewards to be sure. But it's also a status fraught with peril if you're not careful. We were offered dozens of opportunities in those weeks and months after the episode. Crazy, ridiculous ideas from crazy, ridiculous people. But we have to tell you: some sounded pretty damn good at the time. Thank God for Barbara, who has nerves of steel and knows how to say no so that the Ponzi schemers stay away for good.

Of course, you don't need to be on *Shark Tank* to be offered bad opportunities. You don't even need to be all that successful. You just need to be in business, and the opportunities will start to present themselves. How to decide? As we said, you will make mistakes. That's fine. You will learn from them. Mistakes also help you hone your idea of what your business should be, and thus, what the right opportunities are. But you can also help yourself by sticking with your values and your ideals. Remember why you started a business and what you want that business to be, what you want it to say to others, how you want that business to be the best reflection of who you are. If you know the answers to those questions, then you will be able to discern the good opportunities from the bad. Even better, you will be able to say no to the bad ones with the confidence that you are making the right decision for your company, your employees, and your brand.

# The Weight of Success

"It must be great being your own boss!"

"What's it like to set your own hours?"

"I wish I could stop working for the Man!"

These are typical first reactions when people hear you're an entrepreneur. We certainly believed them when we decided to start Cousins Maine Lobster. While we had worked for companies, our old jobs allowed us to operate like independent contractors. We were basically on our own, just as long as we put up the numbers. Which we did. We weren't micromanaged by some overbearing boss and we set our own hours, for the most part.

So, when we went off on our own, free of any entanglements, we thought that our semi-independence would become complete and total autonomy. We were free! And for a good day or two, it certainly felt like it. Then reality hit us. Hard.

What does reality look like? It looks something like this:

At the start of 2015, we were in the process of franchising (and opening a restaurant). We had contracted with a truck manufacturer who would supply our franchisees with a fleet of standardized trucks. We didn't want our franchisees on the hook for acquiring a rather important piece of equipment, and we were very self-conscious of making sure our trucks looked and operated the same, whether on the roads of LA or Raleigh. Going all in with one manufacturer seemed like the best way to get everything we wanted.

Until the trucks failed to arrive on time. In the first months of 2015, we had ten franchisees ready to get to work, but half of them couldn't open because they didn't have trucks. Then we saw with growing panic that though the trucks looked great, they kept breaking after continued use.

We found ourselves in a bit of a quandary. We had franchisees who had given us hundreds of thousands of dollars, because they believed in us and our brand. And our response was to hand them a crappy truck that was, by the way, late? Every day these franchisees had to delay their launches, they were losing money. What could we do except try to get some answers from our vendor?

Except he had gone completely dark on us. As the problems had begun to mount, he had become increasingly hard to contact, and eventually stopped returning our calls altogether. Just like that, we found ourselves in the middle of a nightmare. That's when panic turned to horror.

Be our own bosses? We were entirely at the mercy of some guy who had disappeared. You will never feel as helpless as when there seems no way to correct a decision you made.

Set our own hours? There was a period early in 2015 when we barely slept. We were working all the time, desperately trying to save our franchising dreams.

Working for the Man? We had failed our new franchisees on the one task that we couldn't fail: to deliver new, usable food trucks that proudly carried the Cousins Maine Lobster brand. Never in our professional lives had we felt more under the microscope than we did during these terrible months.

That's the reality of running your own business.

You will never be more accountable for your actions and de-cisions. You will never work harder or longer. And you will never have more responsibilities, which sometimes include man-aging the life savings of your franchisees.

So, still want to be an entrepreneur?

## FEAR IS THE ENEMY

We wrote this to answer a question we get asked a lot: "What's it like to run your own business?" Some people are just curious about the job. They want to know about a day in the life of a business owner, much as they would be curious about the daily routine of their favorite athlete or actor. But there are also those who ask because they want to know if it's something they could do. They have an idea for a business, but they think that running a business is beyond their skills. Put another way, they want to know how we went from operating a food truck to running a business of food trucks. They seem like two totally different jobs—and they are.

Being unable to bridge this mental gap keeps many would-be entrepreneurs on the sidelines. This might seem like a simple misunderstanding, but what we're talking about here is fear. A lot of people are simply afraid of being in charge, of running something on their own. For everyone who's never done it, running a business is a big unknown. You might have a great idea for a new service or product; you might even go so far as to get the service or product into some kind of production. You actually see a lot of entrepreneurs at this stage on *Shark Tank*. They're manufacturing a product or providing a service. They probably have some sales, either online or brick-and-mortar. But that's when they enter the crucible of the show, because the sharks almost never bite on half a business. They want to invest in something that is fully formed, if not fully realized. By this we mean that the business is sustainable on its own, but with tremendous growth potential.

*When* a half business crosses that line into full business depends on a wide variety of factors that are unique to every enterprise. For us, we had a single but profitable food truck with employees, and a sustainable supply chain. Neither of us had quit our day job yet, which is usually a sticking point for the sharks, but we also had very good sales for a three-month-old business. Still, our hesitancy to go all in meant our company was in that gray area of half a business. It would have made perfect sense if all the sharks had passed because we hadn't fully committed yet. You see it all the time.

Yet there are thousands of entrepreneurs who never get beyond the half-a-business phase, and not because some venture capitalist doesn't invest in them. A lot are afraid to give the kind of absolute dedication that is required to turn half a business into a full business. If you've ever run half a business, then you know what we're talking about: you can spend years just getting by, in a perpetual state of limbo, doing just enough business to keep going, but not going anywhere. Why not take the leap? Why not go all in, as we did? Because of fear. For most, it proves insurmountable.

People think that this fear of going all in stems from financial insecurity, family obligations, or health-care concerns—the usual reasons people stick it out with jobs that are less than their ideal. And these considerations certainly come into play. But we also think there's something else going on, something that is actually stronger than the fear of being without something you need. It's the fear of being someone you can't imagine. And it gets back to that question we get asked: *What's it like to run your own business?*

Those with half a business or just an idea for one ask this question all the time because they think the answer will somehow help pull back the curtain on the great unknown. And once they see the little man working the levers of the great and powerful Oz, then they'll see it's no big deal. But, of course, this almost never happens, because knowing how someone else did it doesn't necessarily mean you can do it. There are a lot of books out there, written by some of the greatest business minds in history, that tell you exactly what it's like being a business owner. But knowledge doesn't lead to action. Reading everything there is to read about entrepreneurship won't bridge the great chasm people have in their heads that separates them from business owners.

"*They* can do this, but *I* probably can't."

People only think this way because they can't visualize themselves as business owners. And until you see yourself as a business owner you will never overcome that mental hurdle. Granted, this is easier said than done, but we're also not just making this up. Visualizing yourself as a business owner is just a slight twist on the old business guru's advice to visualize success. And *that* kind of advice is everywhere these days. Just a quick Google search turns up these articles as the top hits, all from respected business journals:

"The Extraordinary Power of Visualizing Success" (*Entrepreneur Magazine*).[27]

"Why Visualizing Success Isn't as Far-Fetched as it Sounds" (*Fast Company*).[28]

"Visualize Your Way to Success (Really!)" (*Inc.* magazine).[29]

You need to make the jump from knowledge to action. You need to see yourself doing all the things you read about in the books, that you have read in this book, and that you hear from other business owners you ask. Start doing it immediately.

And stop telling yourself that the reason you're still in half a business phase is because of financial, health, or family concerns. We're not trying to minimize those concerns at all, but they're not really holding you back. You will never have enough money in half a business phase to feel good about quitting; you either have a way to pay for your health-care expenses or you don't; and your family will either support you or it won't. What we're saying is that those ducks will never be a nice, perfect row for you.

No, what's holding you back is the fear of actually achieving your dream of becoming a business owner. It's a role you haven't been able to comprehend, because it seems so outlandish, so foreign. The potential of success is scary. So, stop thinking of it as a potential and start thinking of it as reality. Not until you turn knowledge into action, and actually start seeing yourself as a business owner, will you ever muster the courage to walk across the bridge and join us here on the other side.

## THE MORE THINGS CHANGE . . .

What you're going to find on our side is that it's actually not all that different. Or, let's put it this way: it's not that different at first. It's the same effect of seeing someone every day for a year versus seeing someone only once a year. In the former, you hardly notice the changes in the person; whether they're skinnier or fatter; balder; happier or sadder. But in the latter, the changes can be dramatic. "Wow, you've lost weight!" (Or the opposite.)

During the first few months of becoming a full-time business owner you won't feel all that different from your previous months as either a half-a-business owner or just someone with an idea. You don't suddenly gain access to the Business Owners' Club. But gradually, as your business grows and matures, change begins to happen, dramatic change. And when you look back one or two years later, you will be astonished at the person you've become. Usually, the transformation is for the better, but not always.

You should anticipate this and plan accordingly. What we mean is that even though you won't notice the changes in yourself, they're happening under the surface. You hope that your best qualities as a business owner come out during this early phase, and they usually do. But your bad qualities come out, too. And whether they're good or bad qualities, the pressures of a running a start-up business will put them in the forefront. That's when relationships begin to strain and friends start to turn on each other.

However you choose to plan for the changes that will happen, you must understand that running your own business can be a traumatic experience. And we don't use the word traumatic lightly. It means that you will undergo extreme mental (and even physical) distress that will leave its mark long after the crisis has passed. There's almost no way to plan for this except to know that it will happen. Neither of us have children yet, but we imagine it's a bit like knowing that one day your child will get into serious trouble. You can't predict what kind, only that it will test your faculties as a parent. And at that moment, everything depends on whether you can handle the crisis properly. Again, it's the old idea of visualizing yourself in that moment: how will you respond? Will you be the leader that running a business has made you? Will you control your emotions and strive to see the path forward?

But simply handling the crisis well won't always diminish the trauma it has inflicted on you. You will live with the scars. Returning to the child analogy, if your child got into trouble because of a lie they told, then it would be very hard for you to trust that child again. Everything they say will be suspect. You might have helped the child get out of danger, but that loss of trust is the scar that remains. In this way, you are changed for better and worse. Better, because perhaps your distrust will save your child from another crisis down the road; worse, because the world has become just a little darker.

Which is why it helps to remember the best things about yourself. Not only that, but also those activities or moments that bring out those qualities. You will begin to cherish those things much more than you did in your earlier life. They will be like little life rafts in the great ocean of business ownership. We identified our own rafts early on and still cling to them to this day, perhaps more tightly than we did when we were younger and dumber. One of those you've already read about, the recuperative powers of family. We each still find love and joy in our families and retreat to our little fortress on the Maine coast as much as possible.

Another is more banal but no less restorative. To this day, in Jim's office, we have our old *NHL '94* video game. The cartridge is always in the console (we play no other games), and the controllers—the ones that have known our hands since they were small and clumsy—are ready to be picked up. You might remember that it was while playing this game in Sabin's apartment in LA in 2011 that we started the conversation that eventually became Cousins Maine Lobster. There's a reason for that. Our business is nothing if not a reflection of the things we love most in the world: family, our values, and simpler times. Playing against each other immediately returns us to those very things, if only for the duration of the game.

Perhaps we've just had a huge argument with each other. Time to play. Perhaps we just heard that a long-term, valued employee was caught stealing. Time to play. Perhaps we are told that the price of lobster is closing in at an all-time high. Definitely time to play.

By playing, we are able to block out these distractions and return to our center. We're able to rediscover the reasons we started down this road in the first place, which is sometimes the only thing that will keep you from quitting. And, lastly, it's just a way two friends can relax during the workday. We even make it interesting by playing a best-of-seven series with some money stakes. And if the loser gets swept, he needs to pony up $500. As far as we can remember, this has only happened once—but the loser doesn't want to admit it in print. Not only does this make the contests more fun, it all but forces the business distractions from our heads. There's money at stake! During these moments, we aren't business owners; we're just two cousins having some fun. It's good to be just that every once in a while.

So, yes, we fight, we argue, we have good days, we have terrible days. Sometimes one of us is having a great day, while the other one's day is in the toilet. That's just how it goes. But those little things add up and if you don't have a way of bringing yourself back to your center, then they will become huge things down the road. Because the fact of business ownership is that you will change. The goal is to do all you can to make it so that the more things change, the more you stay the same.

## A PARTNERSHIP . . . OR A MARRIAGE?

One thing we get asked all the time is, "What's it like working with your family?" Our response is usually immediate: "Great! Wonderful! Wouldn't have it any other way!" And these are accurate reflections of our true feelings. We wouldn't be here without each other. Put another way, we would never have decided to go into this business if we hadn't decided to do it together. Family first was our motivation from day one and will remain our motivation for the rest of our lives.

That said, if you're someone who's on the verge of starting a business and you have the potential to go into it with a family member, there's a very practical question: should you? Is it better to run a family business, or should you instead run one by yourself, or with non-family partners?

Our answer is going to be nuanced, so bear with us. Before we officially started Cousins Maine Lobster, we decided to take a personality test. We were family and we were friends, but that says very little about whether we would make good business partners. You might love your sister, but would you want to work with her every day? If your answer is an immediate no, well, that's probably the only test you need. But if you think the answer is yes, then you should make sure you're certain. That's why we took those personality tests. We wanted to know if our personalities would be compatible in a business relationship. Our tests suggested that they would be, and so we forged ahead.

And what we've since discovered is that we make an excellent team. We each bring to the table complementary characteristics that shore up whatever weaknesses we might have individually. So, for example, Sabin would say that Jim is the hardest worker he's ever met, while Jim would say that Sabin's tenacity in the face of adversity or setbacks is second to none. We still have our disagreements, but these are surface arguments. They aren't, to use the marital law term, irreconcilable differences. Each of us is stronger with the other than we would be on our own.

Our shared blood also makes our business bond stronger. Again, look at it like a marriage: if two people decided to enter into a relationship, but forgo marriage and all the legal entanglements that come with it, then the bonds that hold you together are tenuous. In other words, it would be quite easy to walk out on each other. But you can't just walk out of a marriage, not without triggering a whole host of legal and financial procedures. That might seem like a hassle to some, but it actually is a boon. Why? Because those potential entanglements make us work just a little bit harder to keep the relationship strong, to overcome disagreements, and to remember why we work better together than apart. Besides, if we ever break up, we'll still have to see each other over Christmas and that would just be awkward.

We hasten to add that our experience doesn't mean we believe going into a family business is right for everyone. We only took this step after we felt that our family bond would strengthen, not detract from, our business bond. It might be different in your case. In fact, if you learn that you and your family member(s) wouldn't make very good business partners, then *don't go into business with them*. We each have a lot of friends and family we love dearly and with whom we spend a lot of time. But we probably wouldn't work well with most of them.

It's the same for you.

You might think going into business with your spouse, or family member, or best friend would be easy, fun even. But the characteristics that make for a good marriage or friendship don't always make for a happy business relationship. In the same vein, your perfect business partner might be someone you don't have much of a friendship with at all. Now, this is unlikely, since people aren't in the habit of starting a business with someone they don't like, but it certainly happens. You don't need to be friends to have a good working, creative, and collaborative relationship with someone. Our point is that you can't assume how well you'll work with someone based on your normal relationship with them.

## THE FIRST HIRE, THE FIRST FIRE

Managing human beings isn't the easiest thing to do. We sometimes envy those who run one-man businesses that never require dealing with the complexities of another person, much less a large group of people. But this is part of business ownership—it's a *major* part of business ownership. You are nothing without your employees. That's the easy part to understand. The more difficult part to understand is that you can't be dragged down by bad employees. You always want to give them a break, a second chance, a shot at redemption. You'll quickly learn that doesn't work. Yet, unless you're an egotistical monster who has no ability to sympathize with others, firing employees for professional or personal reasons will be one of the toughest things you will do as a business owner.

The good news (or perhaps bad news) is that it gets easier. We'll explain.

Early in our business, before we ever had the thought of franchising, we concluded that we had to fire one of the first people we ever hired. We need not get into the reason why the relationship stopped working, but it had begun to take a toll on each of us. We had never fired anyone before, and we certainly didn't want to fire someone who had helped launch our company. Perhaps, we told ourselves, his faults could be overcome by his dedication to the company, his willingness to take a chance on us before we proved successful.

But those kinds of justifications almost always prolong the problem. We knew what we had to do; we just weren't quite ready—or experienced enough—to do it yet.

For a variety of reasons, the task of firing fell to Sabin. He worried himself sick about it, so much so, in fact, that Barbara had to intervene. She didn't minimize the pain we felt over firing this person, but she gently pushed us to understand why it had to be done. In other words, she made us face facts: this is part of running a business. Keeping bad people on your payroll doesn't help your company, no matter how much you may like them personally. So, when the fateful moment came, Sabin was able to go through with it and move on. What we did had been done in the best interests of the business—and *that's* how a business owner must think.

There's no mincing words here: to be a business owner is to

understand that the business comes before everything else. We know this sounds harsh. Isn't family more important? Isn't your health or the health of your employees more important? Those things are extremely important and you must take responsibility for them. You must care for your family and care for yourself. You must allow your employees to take care of these matters when they arise. But none of that changes the fact that the business is the first responsibility of a business owner.

We can also look at it in a more positive light. For example, say an employee of ours had to take extended leave to care for a sick relative. As a productive, hardworking employee, this person is extremely valuable to our business. We're not going to let her go simply because she needs some time off. Doing so would be worse for our business than waiting for her to return after the emergency has passed. Getting rid of your best employees because they have personal concerns isn't an effective way to run a business. It's the same if the employee is sick. We want that employee back and will do everything in our power to have that employee back, even if it means they need an extended period to recuperate.

One of the first things you learn as an entrepreneur is the difficulty of finding good people. It's so difficult, in fact, that we'd rather hang on to mediocre employees than go out and find new ones. Hiring is a frustrating, time-consuming process. We don't want to fire anyone, and it's not because we're just a couple of swell guys. It's because we don't want to deal with the hassle of replacing them. At least we know what we're getting with our mediocre employee compared to someone new and entirely unknown. For we've learned that you *never* know how someone will perform based on what they've done. The only metric that matters is what they've done *for you*.

However, sometimes you can't avoid it. Sometimes you must fire an employee because they have ceased to be a positive force for the company. As an entrepreneur, you will be disappointed by some of your people. When this happens, there are two ways of handling it: you can give the employee another chance, or you can fire them. In our early days, we chose the first option often—and it bit us hard. This goes back to the trauma we mentioned earlier. Trying to be Mr. Nice Guy doesn't work; it just doesn't. We have the scars to prove it. It takes a lot for an employee to disappoint us, but when it happens, we cut the cord swiftly.

The reason for this is fairly simple: the vast majority of firing cases involve personal, as opposed to performance, reasons. What we mean is that the employee wasn't the kind of person we wanted at Cousins Maine Lobster. We don't know this right away, obviously. It's more a pattern of behavior that builds to a breaking point. And as we've become more experienced with this sort of thing, our breaking point has fallen dramatically. We simply don't put up with disrespect or a personality that is a distraction.

There is a case to be made that an underperforming employee should be allowed to improve. The caveat is that this usually means the employee simply isn't the right fit for the job. So, unless you're willing to transfer the employee into another position, letting them go is usually the best option. But we don't tolerate bad habits, bad behavior, or a bad attitude. Again, we don't *want* to be this strict, but we have scars from giving that type of employee too many chances.

Particularly in the food-service industry, our capacity for tolerating bad performance is razor thin. It's just the way this business works. A case in point is a manager we had hired to help open the restaurant. This wasn't Aaron, Sabin's cousin, whom we had asked to come up from San Diego to help us with the restaurant. Rather, this was someone whom we hired to help with the details inside the restaurant, from stocking the kitchen to hiring servers and receptionists. Yet as we got closer to our opening, we noticed with growing distress that this manager had failed in most of these basic responsibilities. Unfortunately, it wasn't simply a case of the manager being a bad fit; it was negligence. We had no choice but to fire him immediately—and right before our opening. But when you're in the food industry, you rarely have the luxury of time. Things happen quickly and we couldn't afford to give the manager another chance.

Sometimes, it's just a matter of fish or cut bait. Even though you might lose someone in an important position, you will be better off. Yes, sometimes this means that everyone else needs to do more work and take more responsibility, but as a team, you get better. These moments also solidify your core by forcing everyone to lean on each other. That's how the best teams are forged, though adversity. In the end, despite the difficulties, you and your company will be better off than if you had kept the bad employee.

We know this is a lot of gloomy stuff. It certainly isn't what makes running a business such a fulfilling job. We hate to fire anyone, and not only because it means someone is now unemployed. It means we had failed to find the right person for the job. That means we're back at the drawing board, searching for a diamond. It's a simple fact of business that you rarely find that diamond—but when you do, boy, *that* is what makes this a fulfilling job.

From the family members who have worked with us since day one to our employees at the corporate office to our franchisees spread around the country, we are in daily awe of the team we've built. It didn't come about without a lot of painful lessons in the art of managing people, but you learn, and, as a business owner, you can't afford to forget. The joy is in finding that employee whose passion for the business and the brand rivals your own. They love not just the work, but the people they work with.

You don't find this type of team overnight. Like most everything else about running a business, it takes a long period of trial and error before you know the type of person you want.

But you'll get there. Now, when we interview an applicant, we can tell fairly quickly whether that person will be a good fit. We usually already know whether the person can do the job; that's what a resume is for. This is also why we fire so few people for performance-related reasons. The bigger, harder issue to figure out is whether that person *fits* with the type of culture you've built. We're going to talk about culture more in a later chapter, but we can say now that culture is something that takes time. When you're just starting out, you don't know what type of person would work well in your company. Or, put another way, you *think* you know—but you soon discover that you're wrong.

You need to stick with it. At the beginning, if you're like us, you're going to want to be everyone's best friend. But as you grow into your role as a business owner, your focus shifts away from personal relationships. You don't need more friends. You need strong employees, because that's what the business needs. The ultimate change that happens to every successful business owner is when they can distinguish between the needs of the business and their personal needs. One belongs in the office; the other stays outside.

## MATURING INTO A PROFESSIONAL

We also soon learned that the edge we had acquired in dealing with employees extended to other parts of the business as well. Whether it was the lounge restaurant experiment or the truck vendor, we've made plenty of mistakes in our time. It doesn't matter if those people let us down in some way. *We* made the decisions and we had to take ownership of our mistakes if we hoped to move forward. It's the same reason why we faulted our franchisee for his manager's mistake of showing up late—and thus, losing an amazing opportunity. The franchisee believed it was his employee's mistake. But that's not business-owner thinking. It was his mistake for not taking the opportunity seriously enough to be there in person. And it was *our* mistake in bringing that franchisee on board.

Because at the end of the day, our employees' mistakes and the mistakes or failings of those with whom we do business fall on our shoulders. An employee moves on to the next job; a business partner finds another. We're left with the aftermath of the mistake, wondering how we don't make the same one in the future. And as our company has grown, we've had to accept that the consequences of our mistakes have grown, too. Making a bad choice with a lounge owner when we were in business less than six months is forgivable, but mostly because we didn't lose that much. But the mistake with the truck vendor? We're still paying for that one years later.

Unsurprisingly, this influences your character. Those scars make you harder, less trusting. The fact that we've been burned by otherwise decent people hawking bad ideas stings terribly. *Why* didn't we see it was a bad opportunity? Because we were young and we were more trusting. Our vetting process was not as evolved as it is today. That's not a fault; the fault is if you don't learn from it. The fault is if you cling to the idea that everyone with a smile and firm handshake has your best interests at heart. It's not a pleasant experience knowing that there are people out there who want to take advantage of your good nature. But that's part of being a business owner. You see a dark side of humanity. Or, at least, you better.

On the outside, we like to think that we're the same guys we were when it was just the two of us on a truck slinging lobster rolls. We still wear the same clothes, we still talk the same, we still have the same friends, we're still a couple of mama's boys who love our families, and we still love what we do. Yet internally, and especially when we're in our business-owner mode, we've had to evolve into something harder than the two aw-shucks kids we were on *Shark Tank*.

One side of this edge is simple caution. We're far more skeptical when approached with new opportunities, particularly from people we don't know. We also don't pursue new ideas as haphazardly as we did in our early days. Admittedly, that was part of the fun in those days. We just did (almost) every crazy idea that popped in our heads. This reckless abandon got us into some thorny predicaments, but we also believe it was a big reason we became so successful so quickly.

But the other side is what we hinted at above. We're more mature today. This isn't just a matter of being distrustful; it's knowing that a mistake can lead to severe consequences. We're very much aware that we're responsible for dozens of employees and franchisees. A long time has passed since it was just the two of us counting money on the floor of Sabin's apartment. The more successful you become, the more responsibilities you acquire. And those responsibilities include people who have bills, and rents, and families. They have dreams, too. They have given us their time and talents. The coldhearted businessperson's response is to say that we've given them a job and salary. Fair trade, right?

Nah. By giving us their time and talents, our employees and franchisees have also given us their ambitions, hopes, and dreams. We don't just repay that with a regular salary; we do our best to reward their time with smart business decisions that justify their decision to join us—and stay loyal. So, we don't take chances that aren't carefully considered. We don't play games with shady actors who have a sweet deal to offer us. We've learned from experience that those golden apples are best left untasted. The potential consequences are just too severe.

And part of this maturity shows itself in our newfound ability to keep our mouths shut. We used to blab endlessly. We talked about what we were doing and what we wanted to do with everyone who cared to listen. We just liked to talk about our business, because it was exciting to us. But loose lips can get you in trouble. We've since learned it's best to keep things a bit closer to the vest. Unfortunately, this includes what we say with family and friends. The fact is that success brings competitors and copycats. The competitors we can handle; that's part of being in business. It's the copycats who drive us nuts, because they don't create anything new. And being creative, being original—these are the essence of business success. We didn't appreciate that in our early days; we do now.

Our relatively swift success means we've had to learn and adapt much faster than is normal for business owners. At the same time, we've never grown comfortable in what we were doing. We haven't had much time to grow complacent or arrogant. And this has allowed us to keep our humility, which is one of those qualities we hope to never lose. Our ability to laugh at ourselves, to ask questions, to remember where we came from—these are the very things that have made us successful business owners.

We like to think that we've had to mature, because we need to protect the best thing we have.

## LESSON
## KNOW WHAT BRINGS YOU BACK TO YOUR CENTER

We wish we could tell you that the experience with our truck vendor turned out all right in the end. The ending certainly could've been worse, but it wasn't good. We eventually worked things out with the franchisees, who now use their own truck vendors. Besides the money, our determination to use one vendor to supply all our franchisees with standardized trucks became a casualty of the ordeal.

For example, our Raleigh franchisee, Greg Keller, was one of those who lost tens of thousands of dollars on a truck that ended up breaking all the time. He was rightly upset with us. We talked on the phone and Sabin assured him that we would make it right. So, we sent him one of our LA trucks to get the franchise up and running. He used that truck for the next six to seven months, until another one could be built for him. It was the right thing to do, but it also meant that we lost money—that truck wasn't on the road in LA during the busy summer months.

Throughout the entire mess, there were many opportunities for us to completely lose our heads. And while we certainly lost our tempers, we didn't have the luxury of losing control. We had a business to run. Our customers don't care that we've been screwed over by some crook. Our employees probably cared that we'd lost a bunch of money, but they still need their paychecks. And our franchisees certainly cared that they were still waiting on trucks that might never arrive, but they expected us to live up to our end of the contract.

Those were long days, to be sure. And perhaps it was during those days that we became true business owners. We were tested like never before. We were also forced to confront the consequences of our mistakes. It was harder than training for Division I hockey and harder than not having a dad around growing up. But because of these trials from our youth, we found we could handle this.

We know we emerged from the crisis stronger, more educated, and better prepared. Our faults had been rubbed in our faces, but we also had rediscovered our virtues. We saw more clearly what made us a great team and what made Cousins Maine Lobster a great company. And we learned to cling to those virtues a little bit tighter than before.

As should you. Being a business owner means confronting tough truths about yourself and the people with whom you work. But it also means appreciating the things that made you successful in the first place. For us, it's our families, our friendship, and our home. Those are the things that bring us back to our centers. And the higher we climb, the closer to our centers we want to be.

# PART THREE

# Two Cousins and a Brand

# 10

# Built to Last

In early 2015, we traveled to the opening of our Dallas truck. We met the customers as they waited in line, introducing ourselves and asking how they heard about Cousins Maine Lobster. We talked with one customer in line who couldn't say enough about how much he loved our food.

"But the truck just opened," said Jim. "Have you been to LA?"

"Oh, no," he said. "I live in Orlando, and I go to your truck all the time there. I even have your app on my phone."

"Wonderful," replied Jim, who started to walk away.

"And I've eaten at your Atlanta and Houston trucks," the man continued.

Jim stopped cold. "You mean you've been to thirty percent of our entire business?" he asked.

"Well, of course," the man said. "I travel for work a lot, all over the South, and whenever I'm in a city where there's a Cousins Maine Lobster truck, I make a point of checking it out. You've never disappointed."

During the opening of our Raleigh, North Carolina, franchise, we visited the truck on location at a food truck rodeo featuring over fifty trucks. It's a massive event in our industry but the organizers have a strict 11:00 a.m. to 6:00 p.m. service window. Our line was enormous, with hundreds of people waiting hours to put in their order. When the clock started inching toward six o'clock, we noticed that there were still about forty or fifty people in line. Even though we sped up our process as fast as we could, we knew we couldn't get to them all. Then, promptly at 6:00 p.m., an organizer came by the truck and ordered us to halt operation. The people in line overheard him and immediately started to boo. Loudly. Over the rising tumult, we pleaded with the organizer to allow us to stay open until we could serve everyone left in line. Either Jim's charm or the prospect of a riot convinced the organizer to let us keep serving. At which point, Jim climbed on top of the truck and announced the good news. The crowd erupted in applause and wild cheering. It was the closest Jim knew he'd ever get to the feeling of scoring a goal in a Stanley Cup play-off.

———

In the fall of 2016, Jim was walking out of our restaurant in West Hollywood when he saw a mother and her son eating on the patio. Jim noticed that the woman was frantically typing away on her phone, but decided to introduce himself anyway.

The woman looked up and smiled broadly. "Oh, why, hello. I was just sending you an email."

"Oh, shit," thought Jim. In the food industry, emails from customers are almost never a good thing. To the woman he said, "Well, how can I help you? Is there anything we could've done better?"

The woman laughed. "Not at all," she said. "You see, we're

from Texas and I've been to almost all of your trucks back home. But my son goes to school here in LA, and this is my first time visiting him. He told me when I got off the plane, 'Mom, the first thing we're going to do is eat at Cousins Maine Lobster.' And so, here we are. I was just writing to tell you that the experience and food is just as good as back home."

Jim was floored. Los Angeles has plenty of "first things to do" for out-of-town guests. There are the beaches, the Walk of Fame, the Hollywood sign, Rodeo Drive, and Grauman's Chinese Theater, to name just the most obvious. But Cousins Maine Lobster? Apparently, that's on the list now, too.

## IT'S NOT AN ACCIDENT

We relate these stories not to brag. We know we have good food. Rather, these stories symbolize for us how the Cousins Maine Lobster culture has grown far beyond anything we could have anticipated when we started. Now, some of our popularity can be tied to simple good fortune. We had the luck of appearing on a very popular show and we'd estimate that a good chunk of our popularity comes from people who just want to see us in person—by which we mean, eat our food. But more is going on here, too, because our *lasting* popularity and success is no accident. The relationship we have with our customers is something we intended and have consciously fostered. We worked to get to the point where we're more than just one of several lunch choices.

The best way to illustrate what we mean is to use the most mundane of examples. If you walk into any Disney park in the world, you know what to expect. There are twelve Disney parks and resorts in four countries and *every single one* provides the same experience. Yes, the Disney park in Paris has its own distinctive features compared to its counterparts in Tokyo or Orlando, but these are surface differences. Disney has built a global empire by selling a unique experience. Its value is that customers know exactly what to expect when they walk into any of its parks, regardless of where they are.

It goes without saying that this type of experience doesn't just happen. Disney has worked for decades to discover, promote, and fine-tune its brand. From the way the characters interact with the children to the placement of the rides, every inch of a Disney park is a carefully coordinated experience. A lot of people are paid a lot of money to make sure this happens in every Disney park on the planet. Moreover, they can explain to anyone who asks exactly why the experience is the way it is. They'll throw stats and a bunch of numbers at you that reveal that nothing at a Disney park, resort, or restaurant is left to chance. It's all by design.

This is the true genius of Disney. People come back again and again and again. They've been on the rides dozens of times, and they have every intention of going on them a dozen more. The Disney experience is designed to make you want to come back. It's not just about attracting customers; it's about building loyal customers. *Shark Tank* certainly gave us a boost, but it didn't build a devoted following for us. It gave us a lot of first-time customers curious about these guys they saw on TV. But once that curiosity is satisfied, what would make them come back? The experience. It works for Disney and it works for us.

But enough of Disney. Say you're a bakery owner who's looking to open your second shop in a different part of the city. You think that your quirkiness is part of your appeal and want to make sure your second shop has the same feel. You pride yourself on confections that are creative and new, that push the envelope of what people have come to expect from a bakery. Do you just let the manager of your second store do what she wants? "Go hog-wild!" you say. "Our culture is that we have no culture!"

This is a recipe for disaster. Because what you're building isn't a second bakery that simply caters to a different geographic area; you're building a *separate* bakery that might have your name on the sign, but will otherwise bear little resemblance to the bakery that has made you a successful entrepreneur. Besides, despite your protestations, "no culture" is still a culture; it's still part of your appeal and brand. It's the reason you've built a large-enough customer base to think that opening a second shop is a good idea. There are a lot of bakeries in any given city, some that cater to more pedestrian customers, others that sell baked goods with a twist. The reason your bakery is successful is because you've built something unique, something that appeals to a section of the bakery market that wasn't being satisfied by the other options. The next step isn't to find out if a wholly different bakery, though still under your name, will be successful somewhere else. Your next step is to find out if *your* bakery can be successful somewhere else.

When we started selling lobsters from a food truck we were just one of many food trucks cruising around Los Angeles. As you read in a previous chapter, we didn't invent the food truck craze. That market was already alive and quite vibrant before our Cousins Maine Lobster truck rolled onto the scene. We were successful because we offered something unique and different than what our competition offered. Yes, people came to us for the outstanding lobster rolls and because they had seen us on *Shark Tank*, but they came back because they enjoyed the overall experience we provided. We learned this by talking to our customers to find out exactly why they kept coming back. This told us that our next step wasn't to open another food truck that sold something completely different. Our next step was to replicate what had already proved successful to reach a larger market.

Even if you design the shop yourself, using the same quirkiness that you brought to your original store, and standardize the menu and recipes, you can't leave the rest to chance. From the top down, from the feel of the napkins to the manager and employees you hire to run it, everything in your second bakery must be chosen based on a plan and an eye to your brand. Our first steps toward building a culture around our brand were small. Details like having all-black trucks because black symbolized strength and sleekness, something that would stand out, were early decisions that moved us along this path toward identifying our culture. What does black have to do with Maine or lobster? Absolutely nothing, but it was a conscious choice that helped define our brand in a way that allows a Cousins Maine Lobster truck to stand apart.

"But I don't want the same feel!" you might protest. "I want my bakeries to be unique." We hear you, and we'll get to the importance of creativity and innovation in your other locations in a moment. But recognize that your most important task when you decide to expand is replication. We're talking replication of success. You already have something that works; now do it again. Just putting your name on any bakery won't allow it to become successful. You must prove that you've identified a model that stands out. Focusing on the ingredients and processes of that model should occupy your focus, rather than starting from scratch. It was hard enough to create one successful shop; don't make your life harder by trying to create something entirely new.

This process also forces you to find your story. If you recall way back in chapter 1 we talked about the importance of your story and the need for passion. We talked about how story and passion combine to produce something unique, something valuable and worth buying. We were lucky in that our business has a personal connection; our story was there from the beginning. But even though that's where the story started, it's not where we ended.

For the same reason Cousins Maine Lobster is no longer just food trucks, our story has moved beyond Jim's backyard to encompass an idea far larger than the inspiration that started it all. But none of it happened by accident. Our conscious efforts to build a brand that mattered to us has led to this enlargement of our story. It started by picking the right color for our trucks and making sure we had the right kind of split roll. It moved into making ourselves the face(s) of Cousins Maine Lobster. From there, it's branched out in a dozen different directions, from our West Hollywood restaurant to our e-commerce business. Everything had to have the same feel, the same look, the same experience. They were all different endeavors but they were still Cousins Maine Lobster. Now our story and our brand are entwined. They've grown together.

As will yours, if you try to identify your culture early. What are the values you hold dear? How do you try to run your business? What do you look for in an employee? What do you want your customers to see, hear, and feel when they walk into your shop or buy your service? You won't know the answers to all these questions right away, but they are all tied to your story, and everything about your business must be dedicated to telling that story. If you look at all those tiny decisions in *that* way, then they suddenly don't look so tiny. They are all part of the experience of your brand.

The stories we related at the beginning of this book reveal more than our success and popularity. We're extremely happy to have both, but we don't need to brag about them. Rather, what those stories reveal to us is that our efforts to build a brand that tells our story and provides customers with our experience have paid off. Those stories are the result of our dedication to protecting and promoting our brand across all our platforms. Those stories tell us that what we are doing is working.

Think of a sprinter winning a gold medal in the hundred-meter dash. All the spectators see are nine seconds of an incredibly gifted athlete doing what he does best. That's why they're in the stadium; those nine seconds are what they paid for. What they don't see is all the work this incredibly gifted sprinter put in that allowed him to run those hundred meters as fast as he could. Genetics—luck—gave him his start, but everyone on the blocks has good genes. Genetics didn't give him the victory. Years of hard work and dedication to his craft, fine-tuning his God-given talents, allowed him to run those hundred meters hundredths of a second faster than the next guy. So, when he crosses the finish line first, his gold medal means more to him than a trophy for finishing first; the gold medal validates those years of hard work that only he and his coach see. Winning feels great; but what's greater is the sense that all your hard work has paid off.

Those stories are our gold medals. They are the validation of our years of effort in creating a brand that brings people a little bit of happiness. We don't expect our customers to understand this, just as you shouldn't. All customers care about is the end product and the experience—those nine seconds that go by in a blur. They cheer and tell you how wonderful you are, because they enjoyed the result. Celebrate that, but that's not why your heart is full. Your heart is full because you know what went into giving them that little bit of joy.

Now, let's talk about how we did it.

# FINDING YOUR BRAND

If you've read this far then you know we have a personal connection to the sandwich chain Amato's. There are only a few in the country, and all are packed into New England. We love these sandwiches and they have a very special place in our story as entrepreneurs. There was even a moment before we decided on lobster rolls where we considered selling sandwiches just like the ones we loved from Amato's. But we had no story with that type of food. It wasn't authentic *to us*.

But lobster was different. Not only did we have that connection, but we saw an opening in the market. This presented us with two primary objectives early on, before we ever put a truck on the road. One: provide the best lobster rolls on the West Coast; and two: serve those rolls with a little bit of Maine on the side. These goals were not mutually exclusive; they depended on each other to be successful. If we opted for second-rate meat, the cheaper kind that isn't as good as Maine lobster, then we wouldn't have only failed in our first goal, but we also would have failed in the second. You can make a pretty decent lobster roll without using Maine lobster, but it's not the best, and, crucially, it's not what we ate as kids in Jim's backyard. Similarly, we could have focused all our attention on making the lobster roll the greatest in the world, but if we skimped on customer service then we would have missed the "Maine on the side" part. For us, Maine is all about family values, a strong work ethic, and a connection to the community. We try to impart these qualities to our customers through a quality of service we believe is second to none in the food truck industry. We don't simply want our customers to enjoy their food; we want them to have fun eating it. We want them laughing, smiling, and chasing their kids around with mouthfuls of succulent lobster.

Now, it's true that delicious food is its own experience. Rarely will you find someone enjoying an amazing meal who isn't also having a good time. That's why using the best lobster meat in the world also helps fulfill our second goal. But as we mentioned earlier, we quickly found a passion for "working the room," as they say. In our case, working the room meant getting out of the truck and talking to our customers. We didn't necessarily realize we were fulfilling our second goal at the time; we were just having fun. Slowly, however, we saw that milling about outside the truck, meeting our customers, was *part of our experience.* We were selling that just as much as we were selling lobster rolls or lobster mac-'n'-cheese. Barbara helped us realize this when she urged us to plaster our mugs all over our marketing materials, including the website and on the side of the truck. But by then we had realized the power of our contribution to the Cousins Maine Lobster experience. Just like any good chef will come out of the kitchen to greet his patrons, customers like meeting the folks behind the experience they're enjoying. Suffice it to say, it has become an integral part of our brand.

The point is that any successful brand must have something more than the quality of its product or service. A bakery might serve the best damn rolls in the city, but if the overall experience for the customer is otherwise terrible—slow service, rude employees, messy eating area—it's a good bet that the rolls won't save the business. Likewise, a bakery might serve mediocre rolls but its unique spin on the average bakery could turn it into a neighborhood hot spot. We happen to think we serve the best lobster roll in the world, but we don't leave it there. We also make sure that our customer service—whether at our trucks, our restaurant, or online—is second to none in the business. We're able to satisfy our second goal of "Maine on the side" through our customer service. Your task as an entrepreneur looking to expand is to find your own "Maine on the side" feature that augments your principal service or product and becomes part of the overall experience of your brand.

How do you find this unique feature, or set of features, that helps your business become a brand? It's usually a combination of your business's story, your personality, and the type of customers you want to attract or are attracting. Talk to your customers. Ask them what they like about your business. Likely, it's not only about your outstanding product. Are they the customers you thought you'd attract or are you surprised that a certain type of person enjoys what you're doing? Also, be conscious of how you work, and what kind of processes and systems you use. Do you like dealing with customers or would you rather the product speak for itself? Not everyone should be in the front of the house, after all. Finally, know your product beyond what you put on your shelves. By this we mean, what sort of industry you are in and what that industry means for you. Our understanding of what it meant to be in the Maine lobster business has radically transformed how we see our company. Moreover, it's helped redefine our purpose. Our brand isn't isolated; it's part of a larger Maine lobster culture that we told you about in a previous chapter. We're honored to be part of this culture and we want everything we do to be in service of it.

This journey toward finding your brand isn't a one-and-done proposition. We're still working on it today. You must work to find it and then, once it's found, you must work toward incorporating it into your business. And we're not just talking about the side of the business the customer sees; we're talking about all levels and channels of your business. At its best, a company's culture is noticeable by anyone who comes into contact with it, from customers to suppliers and partners to your employees.

What does this look like in practice? For us, exceptional customer service doesn't begin at the truck. It starts much earlier in our processes. It starts with us and our principal, core group of employees. From there, it branches out to the truck workers and our franchisees and their employees. If they see that the person above them goes the extra mile to solve a problem, then they will learn that that's how things are done at Cousins Maine Lobster. Therefore, when we talk about the experience, when we talk about the brand, what we're talking about is your company culture. It should be the same, from the interactions we have with each other to the interactions our truck employees have with the customers. We don't have a division between what happens at the office and what happens on the truck or at the restaurant or among our franchisees. It's the same—or, we want it to be the same. We work tirelessly for it to be the same. And so should you.

Because in the end your brand isn't just what the customer sees. It's something that imbues your entire organization, whether it's just you at a keyboard or a corporation with dozens, even hundreds, of employees.

## CULTURE STARTS AT THE TOP

A company's culture starts with the people in charge. Harry Truman's "the buck stops here" line is a cliché but it's also undeniably true. However our customers perceive Cousins Maine Lobster, we're responsible. However our employees or franchisees perceive Cousins Maine Lobster, it's on us. However our suppliers and other business partners perceive Cousins Maine Lobster, it's a reflection of the way we've led (or have failed to lead) our company. If service is slow or otherwise inadequate at our restaurant, a customer has every right to complain directly to us. If our supplier has a bad experience working with one of our employees, we take the fall. Now, this doesn't mean we let those directly responsible for the mistake off the hook. But when it comes to making things right with those who interact with our company, the buck stops with us.

This isn't just good business practice; we operate this way because it's how we expect our employees and franchisees to operate. If they see us taking responsibility, then they know that passing the blame won't go far with us. Moreover, it's a practice that gets things done. Everyone screws up; God knows we've committed our fair share of mistakes. But we've never had the luxury of pushing the blame onto someone else. That's part of being a business manager. There's no one above us to blame. This is just as true now as when we first started out. When it was just us and our handful of employees on a truck, if something went wrong, we had to find a way to fix it—fast. It's this sense of accountability that we want throughout the Cousins Maine Lobster enterprise.

Easier said than done, of course. Which is why a company's culture ultimately comes down to the people you hire. You can plaster your walls with your company's ethics; you can fly out speakers to rally your troops; you can have them read all the great business books in the world—and none of it matters if you have the wrong people. Yet this is one of the hardest tasks facing any business owner. You can't be everywhere at once, yet you also can't expect everyone to perform as you would perform. This isn't their company; it's your company. So, the dilemma is, how do you find the right people who are the closest representation of you? That's the goal of any employment strategy. If you want your company to operate in a certain way, if you want your business culture to imbue the entire enterprise, then you need to find the people who work like you, think like you, and believe in the same things you do.

It's never an easy road. Especially at the beginning, you're going to hire the wrong people. But you must go through this difficult phase if only to find out what you don't want in an employee. Meanwhile, you'll make up for those hiring mistakes by continuing to do most of the work yourself or relying on the few good hires to pick up the slack. This is partly why growing a business can be so hard. It's a bit like taking one step forward, two steps back. Just know that every business has been in that situation before. We were. And that's when things start to happen. Slowly, you gather a core group of dedicated, committed employees whose loyalty and sense of ownership in the business matches your own. At the same time, you begin to acquire a sense for the right type of employee, and rarely does it have anything to do with resumes. We certainly look at resumes, but in our experience, resumes tell you very little about a person's work ethic, their values, or their creativity. You can't discern all these qualities in just one interview, but we're continually surprised how right our initial gut reaction to someone usually is. We can't teach this; you can only learn it through experience.

## SHAUN HIGGINS—DIRECTOR OF FRANCHISE OPERATIONS

It was April 2012 when I received a call from my old college roommate, Sabin. I could barely hear him over the noise in the background, but managed to decipher a bit of it. "Dude, we have eighty people in line!" "This is going to be something special." And finally, "If this thing takes off, would you come out here?"

Yes, it was the very first day of Cousins Maine Lobster, and I had never heard my friend so excited before. Two weeks earlier, he had called to tell me that he and Jim were about to launch a food truck business. I wished him well but didn't think much of it. While it was clear they were taking it seriously, I got the sense that Sabin saw it more as a side gig—something he could do with Jim. And I definitely didn't think he would ask me to get involved in any way. What the heck did I know about food trucks?

At the time, I was working for the Long Island Rough Riders professional soccer team in New York. I had started with the Rough Riders a few years earlier as a player, then went into coaching. I went back to the squad when they asked me to help develop their youth soccer program as the director of soccer operations. I loved my job, but when Sabin called again two years later to ask if I would help them get their franchise business off the ground, I didn't hesitate. I said yes, even though I didn't know a thing about franchising.

Which isn't to say that my experience with the Rough Riders was irrelevant. The idea behind the youth soccer program was that we were going to expand the Rough Riders brand beyond the team itself—indoor centers, camps, clinics, and training teams—and into an organization where soccer was more than a game, it's a culture. Franchising isn't much different: you're essentially expanding your brand by entrusting others to be your brand ambassadors. We want our franchisees to experiment and push the envelope with new ideas on the menu and service, but we also strive for consistency of experience.

When I joined Jim and Sabin in Los Angeles, our shared belief in replicating a culture of excellence formed the foundation of our franchising work. The road ahead wasn't going to be easy, but it was made tremendously easier on me knowing that the cousins shared my vision. For us, it all started with a superior product and exceptional customer service. Presentation was the key, from the wax paper that lined the paper "boats" to the amount of meat in each roll. Nothing could be left to chance.

But we also wanted to encourage creativity. Every start-up has the same challenge: How do you keep the energy and innovation going but also codify and regulate your processes? It's a tough needle to thread, but it starts with hiring the right person to operate the franchise—someone who will find joy in serving others and want to experiment with new ideas. Our franchisees can use approval forms when they have a new idea, and we make sure to look at every one.

Back at the home office in LA, we take a similar approach in the way we hire and manage employees. We want applicants to appreciate that we're still a small company and that everyone has to wear a lot of hats. The phrase "that's not my job" is anathema to our culture. If one of our employees sees a problem or has an idea, we want them to take care of it. A simple email doesn't suffice. As members of the Cousins Maine Lobster family we expect our employees to feel a sense of pride and ownership.

As for me, Jim and Sabin might be the founders, but this is my company. I feel a profound sense of responsibility every day I go to work, which is why I rarely take a day off. Some might see that as a burden, but for me it's a privilege to have a job in which I take an incredible amount of joy.

That said, we can identify the qualities we want in our employees. It's no coincidence that these are the same qualities that make up the Cousins Maine Lobster culture. As we said above, your employees *are your culture.* You can't have a culture of accountability with an employee who blames everyone else for his mistakes. You can't have a culture of creativity if an employee doesn't ever contribute ideas. You can't have a culture of family with an employee who lies, cheats, or steals. So, the following qualities are what we believe constitute the Cousins Maine Lobster culture.


## FAMILY VALUES

Admittedly, "family values" is an amorphous term. It can mean different things to different people. But for us, family values consist of a devotion to those around you, a spirit of community whose abiding rule is that what happens to one of us happens to all of us. It means when someone in our family needs support, we step up and help the best we can. It means we share in their achievements, just as much as we support them in their failures. "Failure" isn't a bad word with us, because everyone fails. If one of our employees has failed honestly, after putting their full effort into it, then we let them know that we'd rather have them try and fail, then never try at all.

Above all, a family should trust each other. Early on in our business, we looked to a lot of real family members to help us with certain tasks, such as asking Jim's father, Steve, to handle the finances. This was more than a matter of convenience. When you're in those early days, trust is a huge consideration. Young businesses are very fragile, and small mistakes can doom a promising future. We gravitated toward family members because we knew we could trust them. We knew that they weren't going to flee at the first possible moment, because they helped us out of love.

When we started to ramp up our hiring, we thought we wanted the same thing from our new employees—a dedication to us and the company. But we discovered that the reality is something different. Just because you treat an employee or franchisee like a family member doesn't automatically lead them to return the affection. After all, they're employees; their first concern is earning money. We don't blame anyone for wanting to receive an honest wage for honest work. We once worked for companies ourselves. But we discovered that there's a difference between treating someone as if they were family and hiring someone who understands what it's like to be part of your family. In the former, you're assuming that someone will treat you like you treat them. But this is a fallacy with employees. Perhaps they don't want to be a part of a company "family." Perhaps they just want to put in their eight hours and leave. That's fine, but it's not what we look for anymore. Instead, we hire applicants who *want to be part of a family*; who understand that the trust we provide should be returned. We want employees who work best under these conditions, who in fact seek out this type of working environment.

Because what we've found is that *these* employees, when we treat them as family, don't just return the favor to us; they treat our customers, our suppliers, and our businesses the way we would treat them. They know that Cousins Maine Lobster is more than just the people who work directly for the company or one of the franchises; it's the entire network of businesses, organizations, and people who contribute to what we do. They're part of the extended family, you could say. And this is how our commitment to family values contributes to our culture. Our suppliers enjoy working with us, and not just because we give them a lot of business (although that doesn't hurt). They feel a sense of kinship with our operations just as much as we feel the same with theirs. And it's the employee who gets that relationship and who wants to be a part of it who we value at Cousins Maine Lobster.

## LOYALTY

It's another cliché to say that loyalty is earned, not given. As we just said, it's not enough to call someone part of your family and expect that they'll return the favor. We must show them what loyalty means: they must see that loyalty is a two-way street. One of the ways we do that at Cousins Maine Lobster is by giving our employees a tremendous amount of responsibility. Because we're still a small company, this isn't surprising. But by giving them responsibility, we're also saying that we're investing in them—and we want our investments to mature. Put another way, we look for employees who want to rise within an organization. We stay away from applicants who only see the job as a waypoint to something better. You will never get loyalty from that type of employee, because they always have one foot out the door. They might be tremendous performers, but they will skip to the next best thing at the first opportunity. We're not looking for journeymen; we're looking for a family member, someone who will stick with us through the good times and bad. Why would they do that? Because we're giving them a chance to rise; we're offering our loyalty and treating them as members of the Cousins Maine Lobster family.

This is where our gut reaction to an applicant during an interview comes into play. We can usually tell in that first meeting if someone is just looking for the next best job or if they want to grow within an organization. Resumes also help in this regard, although we're careful not to judge too harshly an applicant who seems to have jumped around a lot. We'd rather let them explain those multiple moves over a short period than immediately conclude they're journeymen. We admire ambition, because it usually means that the applicant has a strong competitive edge (more on that later), but we don't want selfish employees—those only out for themselves. Those employees won't ever give you their loyalty, because their only purpose is to climb the ladder. More power to them, but they're not welcome at Cousins Maine Lobster.

Again, this idea of loyalty among all of us at the company seeps into the culture, especially in our customer service. As those "gold medal" stories help illustrate, we have loyal customers. Hard to believe that a food truck could attract groupies, but there you are. And we love every single one of them. Because they give us their loyalty, we return the favor. We listen to them when they talk to us; we make things right where and when we can; and we give those who have shown an extraordinary interest in our brand privileges that the onetime customer doesn't get. This isn't all that much different than how a lot of big-name brands use loyalty cards or points to reward their returning customers. It's the same idea, although we like to think our particular take on it is more personal. Which is why employees who appreciate the gift of loyalty are the best brand ambassadors. They love talking to our loyal fans just as much as we do, and they feel a sense of responsibility as well. After all, loyalty is a two-way street.

## CREATIVITY

Akin to the idea that we don't punish honest failure is the idea that we want our employees and franchisees to take ownership. This means more than simply taking ownership over their particular job, although that is vitally important as well. Rather, we want them to feel like Cousins Maine Lobster is their company as much as it is ours. It's another one of those "easier said than done" qualities. *Of course* a company would want its employees to work like it's their company, because no one works harder than the founder or owner. But at the end of the day, it's not their company. They work for a paycheck. Just telling them they should take ownership will be about as effective as telling them they need to work every weekend but get paid the same. People don't work like that.

Which is why you need to give them a reason to feel ownership. For us, this means giving them a voice in the company itself. We want our employees to come up with their own ideas and run with them. We're definitely a top-down company, in that the two of us set the tone and direction for the company, but we also know that some of the best things we've ever done didn't come from us. They were ideas that came from employees and franchisees. We make a point of embracing and adopting the good ideas, but also are conscious not to discourage an employee with a bad idea. We want ideas. We're hungry for them all the time. The worst possible future we could imagine for Cousins Maine Lobster is one where nothing has changed. Ideas lead to change, and, frankly, we're way too busy with other matters to come up with all the ideas ourselves.

But there's another side to creativity that goes beyond simply finding something new to do. Particularly in the food industry, our service moves at a lightning rate. Something will always go wrong. Which is why we need employees who can think on their feet and solve the problem without passing it up the chain of command. The idea that something "isn't my job" doesn't exist at our company. If something goes wrong and you're the closest person to the problem, it has become your job. A creative person thrives in these stressful situations. They quickly find a solution and fix the problem. Even if the solution doesn't work, we'd rather have an employee try *something* than whine to us that they didn't know what to do. We can't tolerate whiners. It might sound extreme but we'd rather have an employee lie to us about something they did wrong than be a whiner. At least we can understand why they lied; but we can't work with someone who doesn't have the energy or creativity to find a solution.

Creativity works with our culture of customer service because our loyal customers know that when something goes wrong, we get it fixed. And even if we can't fix it right then, we'll follow up with them later. One of the greatest surprises for us being in the food industry is the way customers respond to genuine effort. It's like they don't expect it when a food truck or a restaurant goes the extra mile, or provides just a little bit of extra attention to one customer.

## SUCCESS

We've said it before and we'll say it again: we love to win. We're very competitive people in all aspects of our lives and our company is no different. Even though we started as just a single food truck, we had every intention of growing if possible. We're simply not the type of people who can be content with coasting. We want to face the next challenge, and revel in the joy of overcoming it. We can say that in our company's short history we have achieved the goals we set for ourselves. We have no intention of stopping now.

How do we find employees with the same competitive drive as our own? Ambition plays a part. We want people who want to better their careers and improve themselves. But ambition is a double-edged sword, as we hinted at above. We don't want someone only out for themselves, even if they are a phenomenal performer, because we can't expect their loyalty. So, while we look for ambition, we also want that competitive spirit, which is slightly different. Let's use a sports analogy. An *ambitious* athlete wants to be the best in the league in his particular position. Winning or losing is important insofar as they have a chance to shine and buff up their stats. A *competitive* athlete, however, wants to win at all costs, even if that means sitting on the bench or letting someone else take the glory. One athlete plays for himself, the other for a team. A team is nothing if it doesn't win. That's why it exists in the first place.

We feel the same way about our company team. We're here to win, we're here to be the best at what we do, we're here to crush the competition. If we weren't, then why the hell did we start a company? Yes, a company can have a higher purpose than being successful, but it's nothing if it's not successful. An unsuccessful company can't fulfill any of its larger goals and ambitions; it's just trying to keep its head above water. So, our drive to win has a purpose: success doesn't just mean we're the best Maine lobster purveyor out there. Success means we can provide for our employees. Success means our employees can grow as professionals and share in our victories. Success means we can support an industry which has given so much to us. Success allows us to give something back.

How does this apply to our culture? It might seem simple at first. We want to succeed because that's what companies should try to do. This is true, and perhaps that's how we saw it at first. But our competitive drive has matured, you can say. Today, we want to succeed because we believe in what we do. We don't just want to be the best; we know we are the best. We want our employees to know that when they come to work at Cousins Maine Lobster they are working for the best. It's this feeling of pride, of wanting to expand on what's come before, that we want to share with our employees. We don't want employees who think that this is just another company. We want them to appreciate, as we do, that this is a company that means something for so many; that it deserves loyalty, respect, and their total dedication. Because we're not just another sports team that wins for winning's sake. Working for Cousins Maine Lobster is a chance for our employees to turn their competitive drive, their will to succeed, toward preserving and promoting something that matters.

## SANDY GUILLEN—DIRECTOR OF OPERATIONS

In 2014, I accompanied a friend to a job interview at the Los Angeles office of Cousins Maine Lobster. At the time, I was the cashier manager at a different food truck company, but also had a lot of other responsibilities, like doing payroll. You could say I knew my way around a food truck. Perhaps my friend mentioned this to Sabin, with whom she was interviewing, because he poked his head out of the office and asked me to come in. After talking for ten minutes about my work, Sabin offered me a job.

I was a bit stunned. I was on the verge of looking for a new job, but not that very day! Sabin noticed my hesitation and said, "Think about it. I'll match whatever they're paying you." I didn't have to think about it for too long. I had had a good talk with Sabin and liked what he said about the direction of the company. By this point, Cousins Main Lobster had four trucks in LA and a restaurant on the way. They were expanding rapidly and the excitement was evident in the office. I accepted.

Sabin didn't have a particular job for me in mind, but I started out doing what I knew best: managing the trucks. I learned everything I possibly could, from repairs to staff management. I must have done well, because the next job they offered me was one I had no experience in whatsoever. The manager the cousins had hired for the new West Hollywood restaurant hadn't worked out; the cousins fired him and were left with a bustling restaurant and no one to run it. They needed a replacement fast and offered me the position.

I accepted, but it wasn't easy. It was my first time managing a restaurant and it was the cousins' first time opening one on their own. My plan was simply to take everything I knew about running a food truck, from training to customer service, and just plug it into the restaurant. That seemed to work, or at least work well enough that we stayed in business those first few months. In some ways, it was actually easier than a food truck, because this one stood still. Equipment can certainly break in a restaurant, but it usually doesn't cripple you like it can on a food truck.

That said, we had some tough times. I got through them because I had the trust of the cousins, which pushed me to do better. Perhaps I had done my work too well, because they assumed I would always find a way! That feeling of trust—of mutual respect—is something I had never felt at a job before. It made me work harder and smarter not just to get a paycheck; I did it because I didn't want to let the cousins down. Besides, I could look at how the cousins had fostered my career growth—from cashier manager to restaurant manager in less than a year—and know I had joined the right team.

You don't need to work at Cousins Maine Lobster long to see that they truly value their employees as family. It's part of our brand, but it's also part of our culture; it's just the way they treat employees and expect employees to treat others. It's infectious. When someone values like you like a family member, you want to spread that feeling to others. Because you know it makes you a better employee, you want everyone else you work with to feel it, too.

The cousins are also bosses who want every employee to feel a sense of ownership. Sometimes that comes in the form of just expecting an employee to solve a problem. If you're aware of a problem, but must be told to fix it, then this isn't the company for you. But by treating this company as your own, you feel a tremendous sense of pride when it does well.

This sort of management style also forces an employee to keep learning. No one handed me a manual on how to run a restaurant. I had to learn. But when you learn something for yourself, it makes whatever you're doing that much more meaningful. It becomes a part of you in a way that being given a list of responsibilities just doesn't. It's not a job; it's a passion, a pursuit. Since I joined Cousins Maine Lobster, I've been learning constantly and it's the reason why I feel so strongly about what Cousins Maine Lobster means to me.

So, am I happy Sabin offered me that job? Yes, I'm very happy.

# LESSON
## BUILD A SUSTAINABLE CULTURE

Time now for a bit of honesty: building a company culture through a set of ideals and employees who believe in those ideals is terribly difficult. We can't say we're where we want to be, yet. And perhaps we never will be. In many ways, we're still a young, small business that has only just begun to embrace the culture that has grown around it. You'll probably find, as we did, that your company's culture begins organically, without much conscious thought put into it. If you're like us, you'll start with a set of principles and ethics that you hope guide your actions and those of your employees. Those principles will be tested early and often, as the temptation to ignore them grows. As hard as it is to build a culture that means something to you, that's how easy it will be to set your principles aside because it's convenient.

What makes it harder is that this temptation to set aside your principles will occur whether you're successful or struggling. A successful company can become too prideful, too focused on winning at all costs. On the other hand, a struggling company will do anything to survive another year, another month, another week. Either way, those who run these companies will likely find themselves at a point where they've forgotten why they started their company at all. But building a culture that you can be proud of is more than simply good business; it's what sustains you during those difficult moments. When you're right in the shit, the mere knowledge that you've built something that goes beyond the product you sell will help sustain you. It's at those moments when the people you hired, the people who share your principles and vision, shine. They rise to the occasion because you've given them more than a paycheck every two weeks; you've given them a purpose in their professional lives.

We know because we've seen it. Our employees, the ones who have provided their own words here and others who have gone unmentioned, embody our ideals. Cousins Maine Lobster is no longer just about the cousins. This company that was born out of a late-night revelry between two long-lost cousins and friends has come to matter to more people than we ever could have imagined. We recall one example in particular. During a Halloween festival, the point-of-sale system on one of our trucks broke. This is the absolute worst time for something like that to break. The event was huge and the lines were enormous. Yet without any urging from us, Sandy spent the next two hours on the phone with the vendor trying to find a solution. Even when the representative on the other end said that it couldn't be fixed that day, Sandy didn't accept it. She didn't accept defeat, you could say. Her dedication to fixing the problem paid off and she got the system back online.

Now, why did Sandy do that? Because we gave her a paycheck? Hardly. Sandy was going to get paid the same regardless of whether it got fixed. The problem wasn't trivial. We were looking at a $15,000 loss. Yet, we would have accepted it if Sandy couldn't solve it. But she tried to solve it anyway. We had customers waiting to enjoy our food and Sandy wasn't about to let them down. None of those customers even knew what was going on, but that didn't matter. Now *that's* culture.

A company's culture is more than what customers see when they encounter your brand. It's more than the atmosphere in the office or among employees. Culture is what sustains a company *even when we're not there.* The company will go on without us because the culture we have built is sustainable. That's our lesson to you. You don't create a culture because it's fun; believe us, it's not fun. You don't create a culture because you want everything to look right or feel the same way. You create a culture because it takes on a life of its own; because employees know what to do before you tell them; because it means that even in the worst of times, everyone, from the founders to the line cooks, is on the same team. And it's a team worth fighting for.

# 11

# The Joy of Giving Back

The longest night of Sabin's life was the one he spent in a Worcester, Massachusetts, jail cell. He was a teenager and not even old enough to drive, but there he was, surrounded by the type of people you would find in jail late at night. Between the bouts of fear, one thought kept running through Sabin's mind: How had it come to this?

Of course, a criminologist studying Sabin's childhood up to that point would have probably said the lad was right where he was supposed to be. Sabin had the textbook background of a delinquent: raised by a single mom, little money, but also resourceful and bright. It's a mistake to think all aberrant teenagers aren't smart. It's the smart ones who figure out how to get ahead on the street; the dumb ones just follow along. From an early age, Sabin had the hustler's knack for making the best of a bad situation. Had he not found himself in a jail cell, he would have been known as precocious and charismatic.

It's not that Sabin was any sort of street tough or hard-core criminal. In fact, other than getting busted for scalping concert tickets in Worcester that night and resisting arrest, the worst crimes he had committed were graffiti, fighting, and truancy.

Yet sitting there in that cell, Sabin saw a possible future, one where he spent his days in and out of jail as he worked dead-end jobs. But there was also another side to Sabin that was hardworking and sweet. Which is what made young Sabin a bit of a contradiction. He was the jock who was friends with the dropouts and the druggies. He was a varsity athlete who made the honor roll, but also fought, did drugs, was habitually suspended from school, and had several run-ins with the police. He had over thirty jobs before heading to college and was just one of those kids who could have gone in either direction.

And Sabin was well aware of his dichotomous personality. He knew he had the abilities and talents to break away from the dark path he was on, but also felt a strange compulsion to break bad anyway. Why not? He had all the excuses. But thoughts of his mother, the one who had sacrificed everything to raise him as well as she could, had always kept Sabin from going over the edge. He danced on it, but couldn't make himself jump. Thank God for a mother's ability to inspire a guilty conscience . . .

Like many who had stared into the abyss, Sabin decided to change his ways that night in jail. And just like many who had made such vows, Sabin wouldn't wholly keep to it. But sometimes the willingness to change is enough. Not long after Sabin was released, he got a phone call from a guy named Stephen. Sabin had been expecting his call, ever since his mother told him she had signed him up for Big Brothers Big Sisters of America, a nonprofit organization whose goal is to help all children reach their potential through professionally supported, one-to-one relationships with volunteer mentors. Sabin had been on the waiting list for two years.

Like a typical teenager, Sabin was leery of this older guy who wanted to be his "brother," which sounded more to him like an authority figure. He answered the phone entirely prepared to tune out everything Stephen was about to say. Except Stephen didn't sound like any other authority figure Sabin had heard. He sounded like, well, just another guy. It helped that Stephen wasn't that much older than Sabin at the time, just twenty-two. It also helped that Stephen was a guy's guy, who loved sports, beer, pizza, and most of the things Sabin liked.

That phone call was the beginning of a friendship that continues to this day, more than twenty years later. Sabin's behavior didn't change overnight. He was still a teenage boy who got into trouble, but he eventually grew out of it. By the time he left for Hofstra, Sabin could look back at his night in a Worcester jail as the turning point. He had decided to change his ways—and then Stephen came along and made him stick to it. Sabin was the best man in Stephen's wedding, Stephen named his son after Sabin, and to the day, the two are closer than ever.

## STEPHEN LACOVARA—BIG BROTHERS BIG SISTERS OF AMERICA

You could say my life was changed by a newspaper advertisement. In 1996, I was twenty-one and stationed in Portland, Maine, serving in the Coast Guard. After having served aboard a Coast Guard cutter, out of Governors Island, New York, where it felt like your time was not your own, going to shore duty where I had three days on, three days off, left me with some extra time on my hands. Even with working a second job to save for college, helping coach soccer at a local high school, and leading a fairly active nightlife, fate would intervene when I came across an ad in a free local newspaper while doing my laundry.

The ad was for Big Brothers Big Sisters of America. I was immediately intrigued. I had always volunteered for community and social work when I was a kid, and this seemed like a great way to spend my days ashore and perhaps help a troubled youngster. I called up the local office, put my name in the hat, and then waited for them to call.

It's probably good I didn't know what I was getting into, really. Maybe I wouldn't have done it, although I want to think that I still would've. I know now what it means to be a Big Brother. You assume a heavy responsibility, probably more than a twenty-one-year-old should be expected to shoulder. But when the call came and the woman on the other end asked if a teenager named Sabin Lomac could call me, I had no reason to say no. I was excited, in fact.

As you know, we hit it off immediately. We didn't come from the same background, but that didn't matter as much as our shared interests. We both enjoyed sports and were very social. I could tell that Sabin was mature for his age, but that he needed a male role model in his life. Being close in age, I could still remember what it felt like when an adult talked down to you. It sucked. So, I made sure to talk to Sabin like an equal. Or like a friend.

But it was a friendship Sabin made me earn. I still vividly remember his mother calling me in tears after Sabin had been arrested for spray-painting some graffiti. I spoke to him not long after and tried to set him straight. What to say? Well, I told him about my childhood growing up in Woodbridge, New Jersey. It wasn't the mean streets by any means, but there was still some racial tension. I said that there are people I grew up with who made things worse by doing bad things, like graffiti. I told him that he was only making things worse by making his town look like shit, and that I didn't hang out with people who did shitty things. Apparently, it was the right thing to say, because Sabin never did it again.

Fortunately, those moments were few and far between. Sabin was a good, smart, sociable kid, who sometimes gravitated toward the wrong crowd. One friend in particular I could tell was bad news just by the way Sabin talked about him. I was straight with him: I told him that if he continued to hang around this guy, he would end up dead or in jail. Of course, the kid ended up in jail, but Sabin had severed ties long before that.

It was these aha moments that I think were the most valuable to Sabin. I would give him bits of wisdom that I knew went in one ear and out the other, but would leave behind some lasting impression. The idea is that weeks, months, years later, Sabin would experience something and go, "Oh, so that's what Stephen was talking about." An aha moment.

I would say that my role as Sabin's Big Brother ended a long time ago, but that's not really true. I consider him a real brother, and just like any brothers, we still talk and see each other regularly. After high school, he would call me up from time to time to thank me for helping him out. Eventually, I told him to stop, because he helped me as much as I helped him. As I said, it's a big responsibility having a kid look up to you, respect you, and listen to you, especially when you're not more than a kid yourself. You learn a lot about yourself and what really matters. I truly believe I learned more from Sabin than he did from me.

Although I will say that I couldn't help but smile when Sabin called me a few years ago, after he became a Big Brother himself. "What made you do this?" he asked me, the exasperation evident in his voice. It's not an easy gig, but it is the most rewarding thing I've ever done outside being a husband and a father. After all, there's a reason my son's middle name is Sabin.

## SOMETHING THAT MATTERS

It was sometime around the fall of 2014 that Jim was up late one night reading Blake Mycoskie's *Start Something That Matters*. Mycoskie is the founder of TOMS, whose unique business-charity model gives a pair of shoes to children in poor countries for every pair it sells. Mycoskie's book chronicles the evolution of the company as well as the founder's adherence to "conscious capitalism," which he describes as "creating a successful business that also connects supporters to something that matters to them and that has great impact in the world." It was a concept that struck a chord with Jim.

Since he was a teenager playing hockey with dreams of going pro, Jim had fantasized about giving back to his friends and family. He imagined how good it would feel to give tickets to his games to those who meant the most in his life and those who had contributed most to his success. It wasn't philanthropy really; Jim's young mind hadn't considered giving tickets to strangers who were less fortunate. But it was this idea of giving back that had always appealed to him. If he ever went pro, Jim understood at a very deep level that he wouldn't have done it on his own. From his parents, who sacrificed for his education and hockey dreams, to the coaches who saw a gifted kid and spent their off-hours honing those skills, Jim had a long list of people he wanted to recognize.

Of course, Jim never had a chance to make good on those childhood dreams. After college, he moved into sales, which, while lucrative, didn't give Jim the platform to give much of anything. So, he tucked his charity dreams away, thinking that they probably had died with his hockey ones. Then everything changed. He was running a business that had the great fortune of being featured on *Shark Tank*. He and Sabin had grown the business into a successful nationwide company, with franchises popping up all over the place. It was at this moment, sitting there one night reading Mycoskie's book, that the dream he had forgotten was remembered.

Unlike Mycoskie, we didn't start Cousins Maine Lobster with philanthropy in mind. Perhaps in our wildest dreams we thought that it was a possibility, but only after we had achieved a measure of success neither of us dared to dream about. Even with the small measure of success and notoriety we had achieved by the fall of 2014, we were far from the threshold where philanthropy entered the picture. Only large, multinational corporations with billions in sales could afford philanthropy, right? We were small fry. To even think about it seemed to be more about our own ego than whether we had the means and resources to give back. No, we weren't ready for philanthropy. What a crazy idea!

But Mycoskie also writes this: "When you have a memorable story about who you are and what your mission is, your success no longer depends on how experienced you are or how many degrees you have or who you know. A good story transcends boundaries, breaks barriers, and opens doors. It is a key not only to starting a business but also to clarifying your own personal identity and choices."

What Mycoskie says is that philanthropy isn't something you tack on *after* you're successful. It's one of the key ingredients that makes you successful. Philanthropy, charity, giving back . . . these should be as much a part of your story as the lobster industry is for ours. They should be as embedded in your company's culture as Jim's backyard is in ours. Too often, entrepreneurs look at philanthropy the way we did: "It's something *I'll get to.*" When? When you have a million dollars in sales? "Eh, not yet." How about ten million dollars? "Well . . ." OK, you give me a number. "Um . . ." This doesn't mean we don't get all the costs, rainy-day funds, and investments that chew up a company's sales figures. Believe us, as guys whose sanities rise and fall with lobster prices, *we get it*. And because we get it, we know the million-and-one excuses that convince you that the day for philanthropy hasn't arrived yet. But, of course, the day will never arrive, as long as you think like that. It's always just a little farther over the rainbow.

In any event, that night, reading Mycoskie's book, Jim felt his earlier passion for giving back return. He took to heart Mycoskie's words about how success isn't a reflection of how much money you make in sales. It doesn't matter how many zeros are on the end of your bank statement. It's about whether giving back is incorporated into your story. So, why shouldn't charity be part of Cousins Maine Lobster's story?

They certainly had a platform and an audience. For as small as the company still was, *Shark Tank* had given us a measure of notoriety that was far above our station. We had done everything we could with that notoriety to build a successful, growing business, but perhaps that wasn't the best way to use it. Perhaps it would be better to give thanks for the luck we had early in our business by giving something back.

## THE RIGHT WAY TO GIVE BACK

The next day, Jim called Sabin and his father to discuss Cousins for a Cause. The name had come to mind almost immediately the night before, once Jim had started to think about using the company for philanthropy. Both Sabin and Steve loved the idea, but then we had to answer the most basic question: How would we give back?

Surprisingly, Big Brother Big Sisters of America didn't immediately come to mind. One of Jim's first ideas was to hold a contest of sorts for some underserved constituency, probably children, and give the winning applicant a gift certificate or something, much like the Make-A-Wish Foundation. Jim further proposed filming the awarding of each certificate to promote the cause and build awareness. We kicked the idea around a bit, but got hung up on what we would be giving out. Certificates for lobster rolls? A scholarship? Money?

The discussions seemed to go on endlessly. First days, then weeks, then months went by and we still found ourselves no nearer a solution than the day Jim had proposed the idea. We kept getting hung up on how we could incorporate philanthropy into our business—in short, what made sense for a lobster-truck company? Apparently, not much, because we couldn't find an easy answer that was both practical and possible. And it wasn't just what we would give back, it was how. It turns out philanthropy can be a complicated process for beginners, and we were still two guys trying to run a business. So, the idea languished.

But much like other answers that had escaped us at first, the solution was staring us in the face. Eventually, Sabin suggested that we should get more focused. What he meant was that instead of spending time trying to come up with a creative idea about what to give away, we should instead pick something we would want to support. Our earlier idea of helping children stood out, at which point Sabin mentioned his continuing involvement with Big Brothers Big Sisters. By then, Sabin was a Big Brother himself to a boy named Lawrence, and had been associated with the organization for nearly twenty years.

It was the perfect idea. Instead of trying to compete with other philanthropy organizations, we would support one we both believed in. It solved the problem of what we would give and how we would give it. It also greatly simplified the task of setting up a philanthropic foundation, since Big Brothers Big Sisters is a massive operation that has a presence in every state. Finally, like everything else we tried to do with our company, it was genuine. Big Brothers Big Sisters was part of Sabin's story, which made it part of Cousins Maine Lobster's story.

The only problem is that Jim wasn't a Big Brother and had never been a Little Brother. So, while Sabin went to work on setting up Cousins for a Cause, Jim contacted Big Brothers Big Sisters and put his name in the ring. In short time, he was matched with a boy named Jake, who remains Jim's Little Brother to this day.

As our foundation took shape and began to grow, our enthusiasm for the cause we had adopted as our own also expanded. Or, we should say, it became more focused. You must understand that the bond between a Big Brother and a Little Brother only works if there's some measure of respect and friendship. As Sabin had feared when he first spoke to Stephen, a Big Brother or Big Sister can't come off as an authority figure, as a dad or a mom or, worse, a teacher. Most of the kids in the program have rebelled against authority figures their whole lives. If you come at them with a bunch of rules and to-dos you will instantly lose their attention. "You're just like all the rest," is what they'll think. And who can blame them? For a troubled kid who has lacked any meaningful mentor in his or her life, meeting with an authority figure is the same thing as being punished. They've done something wrong *again*.

But, of course, Stephen hadn't been like that at all. He was in the Coast Guard at the time, but he didn't throw a bunch of "bootstrap" nonsense at Sabin. In fact, he didn't do much at all except talk about what he liked and listen to what Sabin liked. And, wouldn't you know it, they liked a lot of the same things. There's a reason it's called Big Brothers Big Sisters, because a sibling is more a friend than a parent can ever be. And that's really what these kids needed—a friend who knew a thing or two about life. That's what connected with Sabin. He finally met someone who didn't throw a bunch of rules at him, but also called him out on his bullshit. It was just what Sabin had needed at the time, and he never forgot it.

## DAYMOND JOHN

In October 2016, I was acknowledged by Big Brothers Big Sisters of America as the Walt Disney Man of the Year. The organization had a fund-raising gala at the Beverly Hills Hotel, where I ran into Sabin. That's how I found out that Sabin was tightly connected to the charity. I knew nothing about his involvement until then, which is very much like Sabin. He doesn't brag about those things. And I get that. When you're committed to mentoring young people, giving a little something back, there's no reason to broadcast it to the world. It's clichéd, but you do it for the kids. Our backgrounds are very different in many ways, but also similar; there's a reason we're passionate about giving other kids some guidance. We've also been extremely fortunate in life, and I've always believed, as does Sabin, that that gives you a responsibility to share some of it with others. Now I know that Sabin has given his heart and soul to Big Brothers Big Sisters for quite some time and was named the 2016 National Big Brother of the Year. More than anything else, that's why I respect Sabin and Jim— who's also taken on the responsibility of being a Big Brother—as much as I do.

The larger point is that there's an unspoken age restriction when it comes to the organization. We don't mean that Big Brothers Big Sisters won't accept you if you're above a certain age, or that a kid will only bond with someone under thirty. It's more of an attitude, a way of approaching a kid that shows you still remember what it was like being a kid. It just so happens that younger people get this better than the older generations. It struck us that, as we started down this road, it would be better if we spoke directly to those younger people—the very ones who should be Big Brothers and Big Sisters. We didn't simply want to help the organization with fund-raising—although that is the chief purpose of Cousins for a Cause—we wanted to be ambassadors for the organization and encourage others around our age to become involved as well.

Which is why we try as much as possible to be out in front talking about Big Brothers Big Sisters. We go to their conferences, we discuss them in interviews, and we spend time talking to others about why they should join the organization. We don't do this because we're trying to promote Cousins for a Cause; we do it because we think that everyone has a chance to give back—and they should.

## LESSON
## REDISCOVER YOUR PASSION

In January 2016, we had the opportunity to go on ABC's *The Chew,* a daytime talk show featuring celebrity chefs. Before we were set to tape, we asked the producers if we could promote Cousins for a Cause and Big Brothers Big Sisters of America. Not only did the producers accept, they centered the whole show around it. Boy, but were Lawrence and Jake excited to be on television!

"Hopefully, I'll be a Big Brother one day and change somebody's life as Sabin has changed my life and his Big Brother has changed his," Lawrence said to the cameras.

"Jim's my best friend," said Jake.

Pardon us, there's some dust in our eyes . . .

We mentioned earlier that part of being an entrepreneur is giving up the very thing you love to do. If you're a baker with dreams of a chain of bakeries, you won't be a baker anymore.

We loved going out with the food truck, but we simply can't anymore. Your passion turns to your business, even as your heart stays fixed on the thing you love to do.

But that's why it's so important to include philanthropy in your company's story. It turns what is otherwise a very serious moneymaking enterprise into something more. It imbues your entire organization with passion and with a purpose. You no longer bake delicious cakes to make money: you bake delicious cakes to give back to someone in need. We now see Cousins Maine Lobster as a purpose-driven company, a company that matters, because we created something that matters. So, while we can't go out on the trucks as much as we would like—just as you won't be able to do only what you love if you're successful—we have held on to that passion. We go to work every day knowing that part of what we do helps someone less fortunate.

Our challenge to you is to replace that passion that you can no longer enjoy with philanthropy. Find a cause that means something to you, that's a part of your story, and weave it into the story of your company. Turn your company into something that matters. And don't wait! Don't fall into the trap of saying you'll get around to philanthropy when the time's right. You know when it's the right time? Now. Do it now.

There aren't words to express the happiness Cousins for a Cause—and being Big Brothers to Jake and Lawrence—has given us. We sometimes think we do it more for us than for them, because it's just that damn awesome. And as an entrepreneur, it's a joy you can have, too. We hope you find it, just as we did. Trust us when we say that it will be the greatest part of being an entrepreneur.

# 12

# The Life of an Entrepreneur

The life of a lobster is not a life of leisure. It's tough down there on the ocean floor of the Gulf of Maine, where survival hangs by a thread even for the largest lobster. Size certainly matters, because the rules of Darwinian evolution are ruthless. The little guys (and gals) don't just have to worry about the predators, humans included; they also have to worry about their larger brethren, who could just as easily rip off an appendage as kill and eat them outright. But even the four-to-five-pounders, once so numerous in the early days of the Maine settlement, must be careful. There's always a larger fish waiting to pounce on an unwary crustacean who's grown fat and happy in his little underwater kingdom.

As we find elsewhere in the animal world, lobsters live by a strict hierarchy. Males must fight for even the tiniest piece of property, a place to call their own. Once established as the neighborhood's alpha male, the champion lords over his domain as mercilessly as any warlord. The smaller males slink away, destined to live wandering lives, crawling from rock to rock, until they're found by the food chain. If they're really lucky, they might even mate once in their lives. Female lobsters aren't just picky; they're also quite efficient. As Trevor Corson writes, "After copulating once, an older female can produce and fertilize two entire batches of eggs without bothering to molt or mate a second time. . . . veteran ladies need a man around only once every four or five years, but they still produce eggs more often and in vastly greater quantities than their smaller counterparts."[30] Good luck, guys.

But the warlord? The warlord lets the females find him. They all but line up outside the entry to his castle, perhaps an abandoned and rotting lobster trap, awaiting their turn. Not a bad life, right? But even the strongest, most alpha of alpha males must abide by the rules of his own biology. In this case, this means that a large male lobster is just as vulnerable to the elements and predators during molting as any of the lesser males.

Writes Corson: "The lobster's shell gives the animal all of its rigidity. Under the shell, the lobster is little more than a jelly-soft flesh and floppy organs. The problem with this arrangement is that the lobster is constantly growing, while the shell is fixed in size. To get bigger a lobster must literally burst its seams, escape its old shell, and expose its vulnerable inner self to the hungry world while it constructs a new shell large enough to allow its body to expand."[31]

Lobsters have no choice in this life. The clear majority of lobsters live lives that are, in the words of Thomas Hobbes, "solitary, poor, nasty, brutish, and short." Now, Hobbes was referring to human beings during a particular moment in history, but his words can just as easily apply to lobsters . . . or entrepreneurs. As entrepreneurs, we've chosen this life. We've chosen to live in a Darwinian world not unlike the one inhabited by the lobster. A lobster can't call on his stronger pal to protect him, and neither can you. Nor can a lobster simply allow another to enter his domain, steal his food, and take his mates. He must fight, and so must you, even if you're smaller. A lobster must expand, exposing the fragile body underneath his hard exterior, if he wants to survive. That hard shell you've built around your venture won't protect you forever, because you will outgrow it. Periods of expansion can be some of the most difficult for any business, precisely because you haven't yet formed the shell. But knowing when, how, and where to expand will greatly increase your survival chances.

Survival is a daily concern for lobsters, as it is for us. Despite our success and our (minor) celebrity, we wake up each day concerned that another lobster is out there, just waiting to gobble us up and take over everything we've built. At the same time, we also wake up each day more determined than the day before to avoid the carelessness and stupidity that dooms otherwise healthy businesses every day. We're aware that our own actions and decisions are a far greater threat than anything that might be out there lurking and waiting to take a bite. Some might think that that's the difference between an entrepreneur and a lobster, but dumb lobsters don't reach old age. And neither do dumb, lazy entrepreneurs.

Before you close this book, we want to leave you with some final lessons. But one stands out that we'll state right here: just choosing to be an entrepreneur isn't enough. No less than the lobster, an entrepreneur is thrust into a cold, harsh environment where mere survival is about the best one can hope to achieve. For many entrepreneurs, survival is enough. Survival means you're living your life on your terms. Survival means you eat what you catch and aren't dependent on someone else for subsistence. Survival means you fight for your little corner of the ocean and fend off intruders.

But for the rest of us, survival isn't enough. We want to thrive in this dangerous world. We don't just want a corner, we want a kingdom. More so than any other profession, being an entrepreneur allows you to build a kingdom. It's not without its sacrifices, but then, nothing worth having ever is. It's also not without its dangers, but you didn't think this would be easy, did you? There's a reason so few choose to live in this world. Of those, few survive. And of those, fewer thrive. But if you've understood what we've said and have a little bit of luck, then you'll find those of us on the other side are the happiest people in the world. We want you to join us, but some final matters remain.

## YOU'RE ENTITLED TO NOTHING

Some business books claim anyone can be an entrepreneur. This isn't one of them. We've lived in the real world and have met a lot of different types of people. Most of them are hardworking, decent people, but that doesn't make them entrepreneurs. Yet we would never discourage anyone from taking on the challenge of entrepreneurism, particularly if we don't know them. So, take what we're about to say with that in mind.

The very idea of this book sprung from conversations we would have with customers who asked us how we did it. Not everyone who asked us wanted to be an entrepreneur. There's a natural curiosity out there about business creation—heck, any creative endeavor—regardless of whether one wants to do it himself. We hope those readers without entrepreneurial dreams have gotten something out of this book, because we wrote it to answer their questions. But we also wrote it to help answer the other question we sometimes get asked, usually right after "How did you do it?" The question is "Do you think I can do it?"

By charting the course of our business, as well as the lessons we've learned along the way, we've tried to show that none of our success was inevitable. Any lingering belief that we are where we are solely because of *Shark Tank* should be smashed by now. We are thankful every day for the opportunity to succeed *Shark Tank* afforded us, but that's all it was: an opportunity. The list of companies who signed deals on the show only to fail anyway is longer than the list of those who are still around years after their episodes aired. That's not *Shank Tank*'s fault. The show does exactly what it claims to do: the deal signed with a venture capitalist is real and the support and mentorship the sharks provide is real. But a deal isn't a golden ticket. Signing with a shark doesn't entitle you to any more success than the company that didn't sign.

You would think this would be a fairly obvious point, but not everyone gets it. We've encountered former contestants from the show who signed with a shark only to be left bitter and resentful of what happened afterward. They *did* expect the golden ticket. They *did* feel entitled to more than support and mentorship from their sharks. We can only guess, but they probably feel this way because they saw *Shark Tank* as an end unto itself. Not only did they get on the show, but they signed a deal! This proves they're great entrepreneurs!

It proves nothing except that a shark saw potential in either them or their business. Which, when you think about it, is about as far away from success as you can get. Potential doesn't pay for a damn thing. If all it took to succeed was potential, then the ranks of millionaire and billionaire business owners would be as long as the phone book. Just because you have a good idea, make a few sales, or convince someone to give you money doesn't mean you're a success. Unfortunately, not everyone understands this, and it's not just former *Shark Tank* contestants.

We've also encountered people who have the same sense of entitlement simply from becoming an entrepreneur. They assume that merely putting themselves in the game means that certain things must happen. After all, they took huge risks and the universe rewards those who take risks. Let's be clear here: the universe doesn't give a damn about your risk. It doesn't care how super terrific your idea is. It doesn't care how much of your savings you've dumped into this idea. It doesn't care how many late nights you've spent working on it. And it doesn't care how depressed you've become when no one else sees the brilliance of your idea.

So say it with us: the universe doesn't care. You're entitled to nothing.

But there are some people—we've met them, you probably know a few yourself—that simply won't get that. This doesn't make them bad workers. Nor does it prove their idea is awful. But they won't approach being an entrepreneur the same way we've approached it or perhaps you approach it. This type of person *expects* things to happen, when a real entrepreneur *makes* things happen. We felt great after signing our deal with Barbara, but we never expected Barbara to turn us into millionaires. We didn't see the deal with Barbara as being an end unto itself; it was only the beginning. Put another way, the hard work we had already put into the business—the late nights, the long days, the stress—these things were only just starting. It would get harder. We knew that. You should know that. If you don't know that, then don't be an entrepreneur.

The point is that not everyone can do what we do. We won't pretend otherwise to try to sell books. There are a lot of bad personality traits that can doom any would-be entrepreneur's dream, but in our experience a sense of entitlement is the deadliest. It simply strips you of your edge, your killer instinct. And from it flows all sorts of other bad traits: lack of confidence, laziness, apathy, and resentment. As we said, we will never discourage anyone from starting their own business. But that's far different from saying that everyone should.

## PEOPLE DON'T CHANGE

In chapter 9 we mentioned that it's better to cut bait when it comes to bad employees. Indeed, our tolerance for a bad employee is paper-thin these days. Problems with performance are one thing; an otherwise hardworking, ethical person can be trained to do his or her job better. But a lazy, duplicitous worker, even one who does their job extremely well, is an unsolvable problem. Why? Because we've come to learn that people don't change—and it's not our job to try to change them.

Of course, this has application with regard to your employees, but it doesn't stop there. Your employees aren't the only people you'll be dealing with during your business day. You deal with customers, suppliers, investors, and, most especially, yourself. We've learned that it's far more important to know these people *as people*—their strengths, flaws, and demeanor—than as anything else. But whatever else these people do for you they will do it as the person they are. A supplier doesn't leave his character at home when he goes to work. A potential business partner might play some hardball when it comes to the deal you're putting together, but if he's a decent person, he will treat you decently. And then there's you—whatever defects of character you woke up in the morning with will be the same defects that you go to sleep with at night.

Put simply, don't try to change the bad apples. Not only will they upset you in their determined effort to stay exactly as they are, but you will be exhausted from the experience and your business will suffer. This isn't an easy lesson to learn. It took us years to finally get it, because we didn't want to get it. You won't either. You will want to assume the best of everyone, because that's what normal, decent people do in their everyday life. You will want to give people multiple chances. You will want to learn why they act the way they do. You will offer your help to them. And you will go home after every effort thoroughly disappointed in their inability to change.

Remember, you're not their therapist. They aren't paying you to make them better people. Nor are you paying them on the hope that one day they might become better people. Your relationship with them is based almost entirely on what they can do for your company. Now, from that hard-nosed relationship true friendships can flourish, but that's just the icing. Nice to have, but don't expect it. When you start out, you're going to want to be friends with nearly everyone. It's natural. We felt the same way. But you'll learn that not everyone needs to be your friend to help your business. They just can't be assholes.

And this goes for you, too. The process of becoming an entrepreneur is the process of finding out who you are. It's a plunge into a deep, dark pool of your own psyche and it can be a revelatory experience. A lot of it is good, don't get us wrong. We started Cousins Maine Lobster assuming certain things about ourselves—mostly good things. Our journey has confirmed some of those assumptions, proven others woefully off, and revealed aspects of our own characters we never knew about. Not all those unknown aspects are good, by the way. For example, we didn't expect that we'd come so naturally to accepting this very lesson, that people don't change. But we haven't only accepted it; we can be quite unforgiving of those who break our trust.

At the same, we also discovered that our philanthropic side is as big as our business side. As you saw in the last chapter, we don't just give a little bit here and there to our favorite charities. We've become proud ambassadors of Big Brothers Big Sisters of America. It's one of those characteristics that probably would have laid dormant had we not become entrepreneurs.

But this isn't so much about the good as about the bad stuff you'll discover about yourself. To be an entrepreneur is to wear multiple hats, particularly in those early days. You end up doing everything because you must. It's no surprise that you'll find you're good at some stuff, really good at other stuff, and just flat-out awful at everything else. In time, you learn to focus on what you're good at and leave the awful stuff to people who are much better at it than you.

But what happens if you find you're bad at a lot of stuff?

This doesn't necessarily mean the end of your business, just so long as you have the humility and clarity to see your faults. Plug your weaknesses with good people where you can and keep struggling. But, of course, there's a difference between being bad at, say, finances and just being lazy. The former is a problem, to be sure, but one that has a solution. But if you're lazy, if you simply can't find the motivation to work at the level your business requires, then you must be honest with yourself about that. It's very likely that you're simply not cut out to be an entrepreneur.

Now, perhaps you can find it within you to fix these fundamental flaws. We firmly believe that people don't change, not even us, but there are exceptions to the rule. There are people walking the earth right now who rid themselves of the demons holding them back. If an employee or partner came to us with promises to change, we would wish him well. But he wouldn't be part of the Cousins Maine Lobster family anymore. If he or she is going to change, then they're going to do it on their time. And you should have the courage not to waste other people's time struggling to build a business that you're unfit to build. Because no matter what type of business you want to start, you can't do it alone. You will bring others in, and these people will look to you for leadership. You owe it to them to be honest with yourself.

We say this because we know there's a misconception out there about what it means to run your own business. We mentioned it in chapter 9, but it bears repeating: you will never work harder than when you're your own boss. There are no shortcuts to being an entrepreneur. As Jerry Maguire tells Rod Tidwell, "It is an up-at-dawn, pride-swallowing siege that I will never fully tell you about." OK, it's not that bad . . . but you have to live it to know it. That doesn't stop us from scaring you straight about the work ahead. It will demand your full focus and complete devotion. Work-life balance is the biggest joke among entrepreneurs. There is no life. Yes, things get better, but only by degree, not by kind. Unless you have the constitution and fortitude to take on the monumental task before you, don't.

Recently, Sabin was talking to a friend who was lamenting the state of the economy and how hard it is out there for working folks. Then the friend said, "But you wouldn't know what that's about. You're doing fine." *Doing fine.* It's not the first time that phrase or something like it has passed someone's lips in front of us. The idea that because we're "doing fine" we don't know what it's like to work hard is about the biggest bunch of bullshit we've ever heard. Yes, we are indeed doing fine, but just because we're making money doesn't mean we're sitting by the pool drinking piña coladas while our grunts carry the load of the business.

Also, don't confuse what we're talking about with personal faults. You can be an excellent employee, even a member of the C-suite, and be a lousy entrepreneur. It's not for everyone. You won't know until you try, of course.

## ALL IT TAKES IS ALL THAT YOU GOT

This one should go without saying, but we're including it here, at the bitter end, because it is the unofficial motto of Cousins Maine Lobster. The saying, "All it takes is all that you got," comes from one of Jim's hockey coaches, but it has guided him—and now us—during this entrepreneurial journey. We just said that you can be an excellent employee but that that doesn't mean you'll be a good entrepreneur. We said that in the context of discovering uncomfortable truths about yourself—truths that inhibit your ability to run a start-up business well. But not every bad entrepreneur has these flaws. Many are very hardworking, motivated, brilliant people. But even then, some are unwilling or incapable of giving all that they have to the business.

We stress that this isn't a fault, in the negative sense of the word. A mother might be a brilliant entrepreneur but her responsibility to her family keeps her from giving all that she has. A father might have the greatest idea for the next, best mousetrap, and have investors banging down his door, but he needs to care for his disabled child. You get the point. Through no fault of their own, certainly nothing that we can criticize, these people can't do what needs to be done to make their businesses thrive. We imagine it's a terrible feeling, knowing that you could have done it, but had other priorities to attend to.

But the thing is that a business is a harsh mistress. She demands your entire life. Not just Mondays through Fridays, nine to five. It's seven days a week, often eighteen hours a day, for 365 days a year. There aren't any breaks, vacations, or kids' soccer games for the entrepreneur, particularly in those early days. There is only the business.

This is often too much for some people. *And it should be.* Being a family person, a volunteer, a coach for your kid's basketball team on the weekends—this is what life is about. It's not a flaw of character to put these matters above your work. Unless you want to be an entrepreneur. Then, those are all secondary considerations. You will make it home for family dinners *if you have time.* You will volunteer to work at the local soup kitchen *if you have time.* You will help coach your child's basketball squad *if you have time.* But you won't have time. If you can accept that—more important, if your family and other obligations can accept that—then join us.

People often ask us what the secret is to our success. Here it is: no one will work harder than us. That's it. Every other lesson we've taught you in this book comes down to that: we will not be outworked. This ethic comes out not only in our day-to-day managing of the company. It haunts us at night, as well. Sabin likes to say that he wishes he knew now what he'll know in a year. It's that feeling—What am I missing? What don't I know?

What should I be doing?—that made us ask a million questions, that made us prepare for *Shark Tank* as much as we did, that continues to drive us every morning when we wake up.

As it should drive you. Be driven. Be fearless. And give it all that you have.

# NOTES

1 Colin Woodard, *The Lobster Coast: Rebels, Rusticators, and the Struggle for a Forgotten Frontier* (New York: Viking, 2004), 76–80.

2 Ibid., 113–114

3 Ibid., 107.

4 Ibid., 152.

5 Ibid., 162–163.

6 Ibid., 165.

7 Ibid., 165.

8 Ibid., 193.

9 Ibid., 170–171.

10 Ibid., 177–179.

11 Trevor Corson, *The Secret Life of Lobsters: How Fishermen and Scientists Are Unraveling the Mysteries of Our Favorite Crustacean* (New York: HarperCollins, 2004), 25–26.

12 Woodard, *The Lobster Coast*, 179.

13 Ibid., 186–187.

14 Ibid., 188.

15 Ibid., 189.

16 Ibid., 184.

17 Ibid., 180.

18 Ibid., 206.

19 Ibid., 211.

20 Ibid., 212.

21 Jason Daley, "What Is the Real Survival Rate of Franchised Businesses?" *Entrepreneur* (August 2013): www.entrepreneur.com /article/227394.

22 Crystal Coser, "Cousins Maine Lobster Will Keep Lobster Mania

Alive in West Hollywood," *Eater Los Angeles*, March 18, 2015, http://la.eater.com/2015/3/18/8252723/cousins-maine-lobster -lobster-roll-food-truck-west-hollywood.

23 "American Lobster," Atlantic States Marine Fisheries Commission, www.asmfc.org/species/american-lobster.

24 Jonathan Gold, "How American Became a Food Truck Nation," *Smithsonian Magazine* (March 2012): www.smithsonianmag.com /travel/how-america-became-a-food-truck-nation-99979799/.

25 Richard Maize, "Are Food Trucks a Good First Commercial Real Estate Investment?" *The Huffington Post*, August 31, 2016, www .huffingtonpost.com/richard-maize/are-food-trucks-a-good-fi_b _11779140.html.

26 Mikey Glazer, " 'Shark Tank' Favorite 'Cousins Maine Lobster' Opens Shop in West Hollywood," *The Wrap*, July 1, 2015, www .thewrap.com/shark-tank-favorite-cousins-maine-lobster-opens -shop-in-west-hollywood/.

27 Matt Mayberry, "The Extraordinary Power of Visualizing Success," *Entrepreneur Magazine,* January 30, 2015, www.entrepreneur.com /article/242373.

28 Laura Vanderkam, "Why Visualizing Success Isn't as Farfetched as It Sounds," *Fast Company*, January 8, 2015, www.fastcompany .com/3040487/why-visualizing-success-its-as-far-fetched-as-it.

29 Marla Tabaka, "Visualize Your Way to Success (Really!)" *Inc.*, October 4 ,2012, www.inc.com/marla-tabaka/visualization-can -help-you-succeed.html.

30 Corson, *The Secret Life of Lobsters*, 121.

31 Ibid., 35.